This is a collection of portraits of twelve outstanding women who lived and worked in Cambridge during the century before women were admitted fully to membership of the University.

The subjects include Jane Harrison, distinguished scholar of Greek religion, Mrs Sidgwick, founder of Newnham College, Eileen Power, medieval historian, Nora Chadwick, scholar of Norse and Celtic, Honor Fell, cell biologist and driving force behind the Strangeways Laboratory, Frances Cornford, poet, and Rosalind Franklin, whose work on DNA was essential to the Watson–Crick model. All were outstanding personalities as well as distinguished scholars, and the 'twelve portraits' give a vivid account of their lives and work. The book does not, however, fly a feminist banner or seek feminist scapegoats.

CAMBRIDGE WOMEN

TWELVE PORTRAITS

CAMBRIDGE
WOMEN
TWELVE
PORTRAITS

EDITED BY

EDWARD SHILS

AND

CARMEN BLACKER

CAMBRIDGE
UNIVERSITY PRESS

Published by the Press Syndicate of the University of Cambridge
The Pitt Building, Trumpington Street, Cambridge CB2 1RP
30 West 20th Street, New York, NY 10011–4211, USA
10 Stamford Road, Oakleigh, Melbourne 3166, Australia

© Cambridge University Press 1996

First published 1996

Printed in Great Britain at the University Press, Cambridge

A catalogue record for this book is available from the British Library

Library of Congress cataloguing in publication data

Cambridge women: twelve portraits / edited by
Edward Shils and Carmen Blacker.
p.   cm.
ISBN 0 521 48287 8 (hc) – ISBN 0 521 48344 1 (pbk.)
1. Cambridge (England) – Biography. 2. Women intellectuals –
England – Cambridge – Biography. 3. Women scholars – England –
Cambridge – Biography. I. Shils, Edward Albert, 1911–95.
II. Blacker, Carmen.
DA690.C2C2 1996
920.72'09426'59 – dc20   95–18992   CIP

ISBN 0 521 48287 9 hardback
ISBN 0 521 48344 1 paperback

CONTENTS

vii

Contents

ILLUSTRATIONS

PREFACE

Here are portraits of twelve remarkable women. All of them lived and worked in Cambridge during the century after women's education became established there in the early 1870s. All of them did their best work in the days before women were formally allowed to take the degrees which their examination results had deserved. The fact that they were not acknowledged as members of the University in no way dampened their passion for knowledge, their intellectual distinction and their powers of original and creative thinking.

Cambridge was in fact the last university in the British Isles to admit women to full membership. It took one world war to persuade Oxford to give degrees to women in 1921. It took two world wars to persuade Cambridge to do likewise, for it was not until 1947 that the proposal to admit women to the same degrees as men was passed without a division or a murmur of dissent.

Before 1947 two brave attempts were made to secure recognition for the academic attainments of the women students of Girton and Newnham Colleges. These two colleges, founded in the early 1870s, had within a decade, thanks to the courageous efforts of Professor Henry Sidgwick, Mrs Eleanor Sidgwick, Miss Emily Davies and a few other far-sighted pioneers, put up their first buildings in the Cambridge area. Permission was granted to the modest numbers of their students to attend lectures, heavily chaperoned, and to sit for the same examinations, assessed on the same standards, as were set for men undergraduates.

They were, however, in no way recognised as members of the University. They were not awarded degrees, nor could they be given any kind of University office. Stringent rules hemmed in their social lives.

The first attempt, to secure the modest recognition of mere 'titles of degrees', was made in May 1897. 'Titular degrees' meant no more than degrees in name, with no substance or reality behind the name, and no membership of the University. But even so unambitious a measure in 1897 roused extraordinary passions on both sides. In the camp hostile to women it was alleged that women were dowdy swotters, firmly in the middle second class, but at the same time silly and frivolous, and likely to undermine the education of men.

It was a long time, *The Times* noted shortly before the vote took place, since the Universities had been 'agitated by a controversy so acute and bitter as that now raging in Cambridge over the question of degrees for women'. For weeks beforehand a committee, composed of MPs, QCs, FRSs, archdeacons and earls, had worked tirelessly to mobilise support against the women. A special train was engaged to carry non-resident MAs from King's Cross to Cambridge to register their votes against the women's cause. Free lunches were offered in colleges for those ready to vote non-placet.

Among the undergraduates even fiercer hostility was fomented against degrees for women. They plastered Cambridge with posters in huge red letters proclaiming 'Down with Women's Degrees' and 'Beware the Thin End of the Wedge'. They organised a debate in the Union on the motion 'That this meeting strongly condemns the recommendations of the Women's Degrees Syndicate'. It was carried by a huge majority.

On 21 May the special train arrived crowded to capacity with non-resident MAs, mostly clergymen. When voting started in the Senate House, a huge crowd of yelling undergraduates gathered in the street outside the railings, while a hideous dummy of a woman in 'rational dress' dangled from the window of the shop which is now the University Press Bookshop. As the voting got under way, the crowd began to pelt the MAs on the Senate House lawn with eggs, dirty flour and lighted fireworks. When the result of the vote was announced, that the women had lost by more than a thousand votes, there was a rush of furiously cheering undergraduates to Newnham. Had not Mrs Sidgwick had the presence of mind to close the iron gates, considerable damage might have been inflicted on college property.

The next attempt to secure the admission of women to degrees, and to membership of the University, was not made until 1920. Already Oxford had chosen to open its doors. But in Cambridge the arguments adduced against admitting women were much the same as in 1897. It was the 'thin end of the wedge'. Women were out for power, not for education or intellectual training. They meant to rule, not to rest content with mere equality. They were boring swotters, always first into the lecture halls, closely followed by 'gangs of Indians'. But at the same time they were frivolous and addicted to dancing, and would exert feminine wiles to lure examiners into giving them unfair advantages over men. They would contribute more to the general good by darning stockings, or helping 'at home' in a valetudinarian father's vicarage, than in discussing the binomial theorem.

Again, as in 1897, the undergraduates outdid their seniors in their ferocious hostility to 'the women'. And when, as twenty-three years before, 'the women' were defeated, they again made a furious rush to Newnham. This time they managed to smash the iron gates, though no further damage inside the College was perpetrated, and no attacks on persons. A fund was later set up to pay for the damage.

Though still denied full membership of the University,

and still debarred from taking the degrees they had earned in their examinations, women were at last, in 1922, admitted to the 'titles of degrees'. They were not allowed to wear gowns, let alone go before the Vice-Chancellor to receive his Latin blessing of admission to a degree. Their lives were still compassed about by a body of rules of fatuous prudery. But in listening to lectures, though always on the lecturer's sufferance, in writing essays, in expanding their intellectual vision through contact with dedicated teachers, their opportunities were apparently hardly less rich and promising than were those of full members of the University.

Soon after the Second World War, when the issue was again presented for a vote, the grace was passed without a single dissentient voice. 'A slight tremor' in the waiting crowd was the sole reaction that one witness observed. The issue which on two previous occasions had been rejected with yells, cheers and near rioting, was now passed without a murmur. The Queen (Queen Elizabeth the Queen Mother) was the first woman to receive a degree from Cambridge, *honoris causa*, in 1948.

The twelve women in this book were all working against such a background. Their dedication to learning, their intellectual integrity, their refusal to waste precious opportunities in political lobbying, seem today all the more remarkable. They rose above the inveterate stereotype of the bluestocking, which clung to them with the limpet-like obstinacy of a folk-tale motif.

Eleanor Sidgwick was one of the founders of Newnham College, a mathematician of distinction in her own right, and second in the line of Principals whose administrative skills have guided the growth and development of the College. Helen Fowler describes her unique personality, powerful, yet remote, and her 'working partnership' with her husband, Professor Henry Sidgwick, in the inception both of the new college for women, and of the Society for Psychical Research, which was bold enough to try to study scientifically those intrusive phenomena in life which elude scientific explanation.

Jane Harrison's work on Greek ritual and religion helped to initiate a new era in classical studies in England. Hugh Lloyd-Jones, in a notable study which we believe will set a number of recent misconceptions to rights, fully endorses Gilbert Murray's remark that nobody can write about Greek religion, even today, without being influenced by her work.

Mary Paley Marshall was an early exponent of economics, whose literary style remained nevertheless so unpolluted by jargon that her short book of reminiscences, *What I Remember*, gives us a fascinating glimpse of Cambridge in the early part of the century. We asked Professor Sir Austin Robinson to write about her. 'You won't get anything better than what Keynes did in 1944, and certainly not from me,' he replied. We offer therefore what seems one of Keynes's most sparkling *Essays in Biography*.

Helen Cam's work as a medieval historian, on the Hundred Rolls of Cambridgeshire and Suffolk, on Assize Rolls and monastic cartularies, on the survey of the city of Cambridge which appears in the *Victoria County History*, kept her an honoured figure in Girton for twenty-seven years. As Janet Sondheimer describes in her portrait of this austere, dedicated and kindly scholar, she was the first woman to be appointed to a University Lectureship in History, and the first woman to earn the distinction of a 'title' to a Litt.D. degree in 1937. The hollow titular degree was substantiated in 1947 to the reality of a scarlet gown.

Marjory Stephenson's work on bacterial biochemistry earned her the distinction of being one of the first two women to be elected Fellows of the Royal Society in 1945. Joan Mason shows how, before 1929, a woman could be debarred from being a Fellow of such a body because she was not a 'legal person'. And how, despite the Sex Disqualification (Removal) Act of 1919, and despite her work on enzymes and bacterial metabolism which would have earned her earlier election had she been a man, it was only in 1945 that a sympathetic lobby of FRSs procured her election, with Kathleen Lonsdale.

Frances Cornford is the only one of our dozen women with no formal affiliation with either University or college. But Helen Fowler shows us in a vivid portrait that she was always an important honorary member, at the centre of a network of influential minds, how her poetry grew from Cambridge soil and how for many it still expresses the essence of the Cambridge scene.

Eileen Power is still remembered outside the circle of medieval historians for her *Medieval People* and her *Medieval English Nunneries*. Maxine Berg reveals her as one of the first women scholars to break out of the older mould of single-mindedly dedicated dons into a newer generation which took for granted a wider perspective in university life. With what have been called her 'graceful and penetrating studies', she helped to build a tradition of social and economic history hitherto lacking in the historian's purview.

Nora Chadwick is vividly recalled, and her notable scholarship in Anglo-Saxon, Norse and Celtic assessed, by Hilda Davidson, for many years her pupil and friend. A remarkable and inspiring personality, she refused to confine herself to these exacting disciplines, and in another 'working partnership' with her husband, Professor Hector Chadwick, broadened her scope so far as to write a substantial part of the monumental work in three volumes, *The Growth of Literature*. I recall her telling me that while she was absorbed in writing this great work she did not go out for a meal for twenty-five years.

Enid Welsford, whose diminutive figure and fiery energy are still recalled by many with affection and nostalgia, is here brought to life again by Elsie Duncan-Jones, who again, as pupil and friend, knew her intimately for many years. Her notable studies of *The Fool* and *The Court Masque* are landmarks in the early years of 'English' studies in Cambridge. (The Tripos in English was not fully completed, it should be remembered, until 1926.) Her brilliant teaching, in which she excitingly conveyed to her pupils the literary issues of the day in sessions which occasionally continued until midnight, made her the kind of character round whom anecdotes, and later legends, cling and evolve.

Audrey Richards was one of Malinowski's first pupils, and went to Rhodesia in 1930 to put his principles of anthropology into practice in her studies of the Bemba tribe. The first anthropologists had scarcely moved from their studies and libraries, relying for their material on the descriptions of earlier travellers to the scene. Malinowski decreed that anthropologists should live among the people they were investigating, eat their food, learn their language. Audrey Richards was the first woman to carry out these instructions in the 'queer mix-up' of people whom she found in what is now northern Zambia. Adam Kuper assesses her contribution to functionalist anthropology, her memorable personality, and her stout denials that she had ever encountered difficulties on account of her sex.

Honor Fell was a pioneer in cell biology and tissue culture, and the driving force behind the Strangeways Research Laboratory in Cambridge. The Strangeways was a place where people from thirty-two countries came to learn about organ culture, and Joan Mason shows how her unique combination of gifts, administrative, scientific and imaginative, was responsible for its success as a research institute. She too was elected an FRS relatively late in life, at the age of 52, and after some labour pains.

Finally Rosalind Franklin is here portrayed by her sister Jenifer Glynn in a memorable recollection. Her work on DNA has been given only late recognition, but as Sir Aaron Klug recalled, 'her work provided ingredients vital to the discovery of the Watson–Crick model of DNA, and vital to the concepts of structural molecular theory'. Her early death cut short a brilliant career.

These women deserve commemoration, and it is good that

Edward Shils conceived the idea of commemorating them in this book. They are examples of many more remarkable women, who in an ideal dimension of space and time should also have been included.

March 1995, Cambridge   CARMEN BLACKER

NOTE

I have relied chiefly on Rita McWilliams-Tullberg, *Women at Cambridge: a Men's University though of a Mixed Type* (London 1975); Christopher N. L. Brooke, *A History of the University of Cambridge*, vol. IV: *1870–1990* (Cambridge 1993); Anne Phillips (ed.), *A Newnham Anthology* (Cambridge 1979); Gordon Johnson, *University Politics: F. M. Cornford's Cambridge and his Advice to the Young Academic Politician* (Cambridge 1994); Gillian Sutherland, 'Emily Davies, the Sidgwicks and the Education of Women in Cambridge', in *Cambridge Minds*, ed. Richard Mason (Cambridge 1994). I am grateful too to Dr Elisabeth Leedham-Green, University Archivist, for permission to consult the file on the education of women, and to Kate Perry and Carola Hicks, Archivists to Girton and Newnham Colleges, for generous help.

POSTSCRIPT

As Edward Shils describes in his Introduction, the idea of a book on Cambridge women was originally his. It was a project dear to his heart during the last two years of his life, and on his visits to Cambridge from Chicago he would spend much time and energy, and green ink, in discussing its progress. It is with very deep regret therefore that we have to record his death in January 1995, before he could see the tangible results of his idea in the published book. But *Cambridge Women* may be accounted his last edited work, and a worthy successor to his own *Tradition, Center and Periphery*, and *Intellectuals and their Powers*. To all these books, and to the journal *Minerva* which he edited for thirty years, he brought to bear his unique intellectual gifts of total recall, pungent wit, large capacity for friendship, resolute dismissal of bogusness, and unwillingness to tolerate vapid academic fashions. That he accounted feminism in its fanatical form among such fashions may be inferred from the fact that readers will search in vain in this book for references to gendered types, female figurations and androcentric premises.

C.B.

INTRODUCTION

Edward Shils

Over the course of many years, I read *Reminiscences of a Student's Life* by Jane Harrison, *Paper Boats* by Eliza Butler, *What I Remember* by Mary Paley Marshall, Ada Keynes's *The Cambridge I Remember*. They formed a small gallery of distinguished learned women connected with the University. I had also read Eileen Power's *Medieval People* and her *Medieval English Nunneries* and R. H. Tawney's and John Clapham's obituaries of her. She too was educated and taught in Cambridge and she too took her place in the gallery of great Cambridge women, scholars and teachers. I had in addition the very good fortune to have been for many years a colleague and friend of Audrey Richards in London and Cambridge. What struck me, along with the impression of distinction of intellect and character of these remarkable individuals, was the contribution which they made to the ethos and tone of the great University which they served and from which they were for so long excluded. They contributed to the formation of modern Cambridge not only by their scientific and scholarly achievements but perhaps even more by the radiation of their bearing through their teaching and their hospitality. Alongside this was the utter absence of complaint about their standing in Cambridge or British society, their selfless devotion to intellectual life and to the institutions in which they were absorbed.

The academic women I had met were not like Professor Rosa in Angus Wilson's *Anglo-Saxon Attitudes*. They were not dowdy eccentrics, pursuing bees in their bonnets. They were elegant women, learned, steady and hard-working, witty and deep, generous to their colleagues and their students. I do not know that there was anything distinctively feminine about their learning or their reasoning although a few of them, like Eileen Power, often had women as their subject-matter. I must confess to seeing no difference between the learning of a female scholar and that of a male scholar. Entry into an academic career is always perilous for men or for women. Max Weber said the decision to enter an academic life 'ist ein wilder Hasard', especially for Jews. In his time in Germany women had not yet come within his horizon (although his wife merits notice). It was perilous for a young man; it was even more perilous for young women to try to pursue an academic career. The academic women whom I knew and whose writings I read did not complain, any more than the better academic men.

I am aware of the handicaps from which women have suffered in the efforts to find places in universities as well as other spheres of life. I am not a passionate feminist and dislike the tactics and rhetoric of the contemporary feminism. I have a good conscience in this matter since, when I had the power to influence appointments at the University of Chicago, I never paid any attention to the sex of the candidate and played a significant role in advancing the cause of a number of women candidates. I was not by any means indifferent to the situation of women in the university world. I was, therefore, all the more impressed by the fact that the academic women whose autobiographies I had read and those I knew personally, were not offensively aggrieved about the problems they encountered from their families, from their teachers – who in some cases were not the source of difficulties but in fact forceful agents in the encouragement and promotion of the learned careers of their outstanding women pupils.

But although not complaining is a genuine merit, it is only a negative one. Those who came to my attention were notable for much more, for their strong intellects, for their brilliant personalities, their openness of spirit, their great capacity for concentrated work under distracting circumstances, and their adamant refusal to be discouraged.

I doubt whether the learned women ever thought of themselves as a single group. That is a testimonial to their devotion to learning, to their colleges and to the University which until nearly half a century ago would not acknowledge them officially as members. They did not make common cause on grounds of their status in the University. (They were unlike the University Assistants' Association!) The only common cause they made was in the pursuit of truth about their respective intellectual interests.

Nevertheless, their portraits do belong in a single gallery. Of course, each of them has her proper place in the history of her discipline – disciplines which many of them helped to create – but they also belong together because they had something essential in common. That essence is difficult to define but anyone who reads this book will perceive and appreciate that essence. That is the justification for Dr Blacker's and my editing of this book.

I was led to undertake this volume by an experience which had only indirect but important relations to Cambridge. In 1991, in preparation for the centenary of the University of Chicago, I edited a volume entitled *Remembering the University of Chicago* (Chicago 1992). The volume consisted of short memoirs of notable scholars, scientists and teachers of the past three-quarters of a century, written each by a person who had been a pupil, friend or colleague of one of the persons portrayed. There was a considerable number of interesting, vivid and brilliant portraits among the nearly fifty which comprised the volume. What was striking to me was how small a part the University, beyond particular departments and beyond the academics and specialities, played in these recollections. The University of Chicago is generally reputed to be an extremely stimulating university but it suffers intellectually and socially from the practical absence of intellectual conviviality. Cambridge adds to its enormous intellectual distinction by its tradition of vivacious intellectual conviviality – I do not mean entertainments. Thinking back over my study of the history of universities and my experience as a teacher in London, Manchester and Cambridge, I thought that it was the Cambridge academic women who accounted for the difference.

It also occurred to me, quite separately from these reflections, that it would be a pleasure for many serious readers with an appreciation of character and respect for learning and for those with an interest in Cambridge to be able to read in a single volume a series of well-written portraits of learned Cambridge women based on long acquaintance with their works and, where it was still possible, with the individuals themselves. It would be an act of justice as well as a contribution to the personal history of the University of Cambridge and of universities generally to produce such a volume. That is how this book came about.

We have not been able to do justice to all the distinguished women who have been associated with Cambridge University. We have omitted Eliza Butler, Dorothy Garrod, Dorothy Needham, Barbara Wootton, Ada Keynes, Edith Chrystal, Muriel Bradbrook, Betty Behrens, Odette de Mourgues, Jocelyn Toynbee, Dorothy Whitelock, Dorothea Krook, and quite a few others. These are women whose portraits we were compelled to omit, partly because we could not discover authors who were able and willing to write about them, partly because we have been forced to limit, out of consideration of space, the number of portraits we could print in a small volume. There might also be some others who were overlooked through ignorance. They deserve to be remembered because there were numerous distinguished scientists, scholars and teachers among them.

I had already drawn up a list – very tentatively – of the women whose life, work, strong character might be portrayed, and a more tentative list of persons to be invited to collaborate. The proposal met with universal approval but no one wished to share in the editorial responsibility.

When I turned to Dr Carmen Blacker, her response was different. It was not only immediate and enthusiastic, but she was actually willing to do some of the work. She objected to my suggestion that she be the editor; she said she would be my assistant on the project. I refused that offer but said I would accept her as a co-editor. As it has turned out, she has done most of the work which has been entailed in producing this volume. Without her it would not have been done.

Chapter 1

ELEANOR MILDRED SIDGWICK
1845–1936

Helen Fowler

In Clough Hall, Newnham College, after contemplating the noble plasterwork of the walls and ceiling and the immense windows, the eye comes to rest on the formidable portraits which hang behind High Table: one of the College's founder, Henry Sidgwick, and those of his first Principal, Anne Jemima Clough, and the second Principal, Eleanor Mildred Sidgwick, his wife.

Hers is not a portrait one immediately takes to; it is as sober as the sitter, it reflects her stillness, her containment, her fastidious austerity. But it is after a while as haunting a portrait as that of her husband, masked by his beard but with a firmness of face and keenness of eye to remind one that he was one of the greatest figures of Victorian Cambridge and one who helped bring modern Cambridge into being.

Sidgwick's agnosticism or, at any rate, his inability to subscribe completely to an orthodox faith and ritual, stemmed not so much from a growth of doubt engendered by the spread of scientific knowledge as from his philosophical meditations. After years spent in painful questioning of his own religious faith and belief, he resigned his Fellowship at great personal risk in 1869 – and was promptly reinstated by Trinity as a College lecturer.

A professional doubter, uneasy sceptic and chronic waverer Henry Sidgwick might have been, but there were some things in which his abilities for practical administration and manoeuvre

7

were constantly involved: his concern for university reform and pre-eminently his part in the foundation of both Girton and Newnham. As far as Girton was concerned, his support, after its beginnings, was not wanted: Emily Davies and he had differing views on the ways women's education should be instituted; but, as for Newnham, it was he who found houses and furniture and Miss Clough, and no doubt the dusters that were hemmed in high-minded sewing bees by students and dons alike.

His other practical coup was to woo and marry Nora Balfour, not only a Balfour and a wealthy woman, but also a mathematician with a lifelong commitment to science. They probably met in London at a seance at her brother Arthur's house at 4 Carlton Gardens. Henry began to interest her in his plans and coaxed money from her for his College schemes and invited her to stay with Miss Clough to see for herself.

His contact with the Balfours went back to the time when he was Arthur's beloved tutor at Trinity. They had much in common in temperament: a dreamy detachment, a disinclination to be too intense, personal or committed. In both men, their gentle speculativeness masked powers of intellect and action. They had both been brought up by pious and widowed mothers. But their backgrounds were utterly unalike. Lady Balfour was a Cecil, at home with the kingmakers at Hatfield, a favourite goddaughter of Wellington's. Henry's father had been a clergyman and the headmaster of Skipton Grammar School. The house in Rugby where the family moved when Henry was a pupil at the school was a far cry from the Balfour estates at Strathconan in the Highlands, Whittingehame in East Lothian and Carlton Gardens, next to the Gladstones. Of all these great houses Nora had been châtelaine for many years after their mother's death.

The house Henry plucked Nora from was a world of its own. Whittingehame is still a noble pile dominating its park and policies with all the confidence of neo-classicism. Silent and empty now, it stands amongst trees above a dark bubbling river.

In its heyday it was a place echoing with music, argument and fierce debate, all initiated by Arthur.

Reputed to be one of the richest young men in England, he entered Parliament as a Tory in 1874 and became Prime Minister in 1902; in the years between he was in various Cabinet offices. His lounging air of indolence was deceptive: he was the longest serving Cabinet Minister ever. In love he was unlucky, but he had many friends of both sexes and was 'King Arthur', the leader of the Souls, that elitist and would-be intellectual group.

Life at Whittingehame was a jolly and noisy affair as mirrored in the diary of Mary Gladstone,[1] a frequent guest: gallops, glees sung after dinner, and snatches of oratorio to Arthur's accordion accompaniment, sandcastles built by grave and scheming adults, picnics on the beach. Nora never seems not to have joined in. Presumably she enjoyed it all, winking complicitly at her brother Arthur, who was always listening for her low voice in any conversation. Winking was a great Balfour accomplishment: no tell-tale twitch of the face.[2]

The Balfours were a large family: five sons and three daughters. Lady Blanche had been an austere woman (she made the girls dye feathers they had been given for their bonnets black to make them less conspicuous) but she had advanced ideas about bringing up children and had seen to it that her daughters were provided with independent fortunes under their father's will. She had also had Nora learn Euclid, provoking a priggish reply from her when asked by curious relatives what use it might be – 'I might some day want to cut an equilateral triangle out of some valuable material and then the first proposition would enable me to do so without waste.'

This was the beginning of mathematics for Nora. She developed a matter-of-fact approach to finance, not usually associated with Victorian women. No doubt that stemmed in part from her role in running three Balfour houses, but mainly it came from her love for and genius with figures. The professor with whom she

9

studied privately, for she never went to school, thought she would have made a High Wrangler had she been able to read for the Cambridge Tripos. She settled always into mathematical problems for pleasure.

Tradition has it that Henry and Nora became engaged in the dining room of Old Hall during a visit to Miss Clough. It is a pretty Victorian room, full of light, looking over the garden. The engagement not only gave great pleasure to their friends and family ('thundering bit of news' wrote Mary Gladstone) but uncharacteristic excitement to themselves. Henry spent part of every week at Terling, the house in Essex of Nora's sister who was married to Lord Rayleigh. ('I cannot but feel myself in the Garden of Eden – don't tell anyone that I get away for so long,' wrote Henry to a friend.) In Paris later Nora wrote every day, letters brimming with affection to her 'dear one', her 'dearest'. He was meantime busy finding a house for them while their own house, Hillside in Chesterton Road, overlooking Magdalene, was being built. 'I have written to take Fawcett's house – the drawing room is Green and Blue with plenty of plates,' Henry told his friend J. A. Symonds of the house in Brookside.

They were married at St James's, Piccadilly in April 1876 by Henry's brother-in-law, E. W. Benson, later to be Archbishop of Canterbury. She was 31 and Henry 37. Two Newnham girls stole up to London for the wedding and watched Nora walking down the aisle in an ivory-coloured wedding dress, shaking hands with her friends.[3] The Balfour Kitchen Account Book records a cake from Gunters and fruit for the wedding breakfast. There is no mention of anything else.

The honeymoon was spent in Paris and by May they were back in the Fawcett dining room at Brookside amongst the fashionable decor.

Life began very sociably; Nora had three brothers in Cambridge: two Fellows, one an undergraduate. This added to the 'social charm of life', in Nora's phrase.

The Sidgwicks had obviously contemplated marriage with warmth and anticipation. But various of Arthur Balfour's biographers assert Henry was impotent.[4] Without wishing to rummage too much in the steamy cupboards of Victorian sexuality, the nature of this famous marriage is interesting. One has no idea of the precise nature of Henry's impotence or whether there was any sexual element in their relationship. 'We are a gray people,' Nora said in an apt phrase. It is possible that for both Arthur Balfour and Nora the current of sexuality ran lethargically: for years he was known as 'Pretty Fanny', though his inclinations were heterosexual. Henry's inclinations were possibly more dubious. His slight appearance confirmed his lack of physical robustness, as did his high voice and his stammer. Nora, who confessed later in life not to have been much excited by anything, may not have been too disappointed in a *mariage blanc*.

It was an age of romantic and intense friendships, but the fact remains that many of Henry's closest friends were homosexual by inclination or practice. He had become an Apostle in his second year at Trinity: to the end of his life the Society and its band of brothers was almost his most intensely valued commitment. In those days the Apostles had a reputation for elitism, intellectual rigour and secrecy, but there was no homosexual colouring to its membership as there has been at times later.

The Sidgwicks settled comfortably into work and Hillside was now ready for them. A contemporary Cambridge figure, Professor Marshall, declared that 'marriage should never be an idea of living for each other but with each other for some end'.[5] The idea of marriage as a working partnership was unusual in general then. However, Cambridge pioneered several such alliances: the Fawcetts, Batesons, Peiles, Verralls, etc. Women's education and the end of celibacy for Fellows brought about a change; women's voices were beginning to be heard, in harmony or descant. Henry was busy at Trinity, Nora was running Newnham's finances and its mathematical teaching. They were obviously both happy. Henry's letters reflect this: 'I am horribly and disgracefully conscious of Bien-être.' 'Nora is doing mathematics in the intervals of time she can spare from the melancholy contemplation of our drawing room curtains, which have just come after a long delay and turn out to be so badly made that a beautiful cross stripe of brown velvet is unequally situated in the two halves.'

There were many visitors, including the irrepressible Mary Gladstone (and her sister Helen), who lists fellow guests: Joachim and Stanford, Oscar Browning, Robert Browning and Austen Leigh, who contributed to the tumultuous talk, dominated by Henry who paused once in long recitations from Pope and Tennyson to ask for 'a moment's consideration, only a moment, to this fish'.[6] George Eliot and G. H. Lewes stayed at Hillside; the former wrote endearingly to apologise for having left behind a pencil case, penholders and nail scissors.[7] J. W. Cross, Lewes's secretary, whom George Eliot eventually married, had a sister and brother-in-law living in Six Mile Bottom (in the house famous for an earlier tenant, Augusta Leigh, whose half-brother Byron frequently stayed there). Dinner and house parties there were great social occasions, frequented by the cream of Cambridge's intellectual society, including the Sidgwicks. Mrs Sidgwick and George Eliot used to visit the Newmarket stables to feed sugar to the horses. They were all, as one visitor wrote in his diary, 'a lively lot', but everyone had to wait for the end of any discussion for George Eliot to sum up like a presiding judge in a 'rather drawling satiny voice'.[8]

When the Rayleighs came to live in Cambridge in 1879 on his appointment to the Chair of Experimental Physics, extra dimensions were added to Nora's life, not just the proximity of a beloved sister, but her inclusion in Lord Rayleigh's research. He was working on the redetermination of measurements of electricity. Nora kept the notebooks and checked all the arithmetical computations and recorded the readings of the magnetometer.

Her name appears with Lord Rayleigh's on the three papers published by the Royal Society. (He was awarded the Nobel prize for physics in 1904.) Perhaps the origin of the Cavendish Laboratory's tea-parties can be traced back to that period when Lady Rayleigh and Mrs Sidgwick joined all the laboratory workers for tea and scientific chat.

The Sidgwicks' relationship with Newnham became even closer. In 1880, when the second hall, North (now called Sidgwick), was opened, it was thought sensible that Nora should take charge of it and become Vice-Principal of the College. So Hillside had to be left for two years or so. They moved into three rooms, Nora received no salary and they paid for their board and lodging. What the Sidgwicks lost in comfort and privacy, students gained. They had Henry to listen to at top table when they were in turn invited there: his talk was compared to a mountain stream, full and sparkling. Arthur Balfour came to Sunday lunch, adding distinction. Nora was always remote but 'like an exquisite alabaster vase with the soul shining through'. Her shyness was noticeable, but students met her in the corridors and garden and were aware of her friendliness, her cool impersonal judgements and her whole-hearted laughter. She could make her displeasure about rule-breaking silently known; students had to dress for dinner (woe betide anyone who omitted to do so), and they were not allowed to cut lectures, even to meet visiting fathers' trains.[9]

But life in college was for most a time of liberation, when like-minded young women could argue and discuss to their hearts' content. Later generations may smile at the famous evening cocoa parties, but they represented a social freedom from a possibly stifling home life. It was a time of innumerable societies and debate, with politics and poetry predominating.

In 1881 Girton took the initiative in agitating for women's admission to degree examinations. Emily Davies had always insisted on an absolute Cambridge model for her girls, including a rigid adherence to Littlego, the Previous examination *en route* for the Tripos, with compulsory Latin and Greek tests. Newnham had followed a flexible policy, letting girls come with Higher Local Certificates only and to stay only a year or two according to needs. Like the sewing parties which still formed part of its communal life, 'make do and mend' was characteristic of Miss Clough's and the Sidgwicks' style. They whittled away at the masculine walls and were pleased to dislodge a brick or two. Girton wanted to marshal a full siege battery. Therefore the Sidgwicks were reluctant to join Girton's campaign, much to Emily Davies's scorn. While she was anxious for their company on the orthodox path, she disdained 'complicity with your heretical way'. Henry had pleaded for sharing a united front and did not enjoy being rapped over the knuckles. 'I inadvertently assumed,' he wrote, 'that both Girton and Newnham were engaged in promoting the academic education of women.' Exchanges were bitter but what is surprising is that all the correspondence was on Henry's part; his wife seems to have assumed the silent role of any Victorian wife. Perhaps it was an agreed division of labour, but they were both much 'driven' by what was going on, by all the manoeuvring and lobbying.

In February 1881 women were indeed allowed to be admitted to examinations and placed on the official lists. Full membership of the University took another sixty-six years to achieve, but the passage of these graces was heralded as a famous victory and the impromptu party which followed became in subsequent years a formal commemoration. 'Nora went to Newnham to celebrate with speeches and dancing,' Henry wrote. Outwardly austere as she may appear to us, she always seems to have liked parties.

Frank Balfour, her beloved and brilliant younger brother, who held a new Chair of Animal Morphology, was killed in a climbing accident in the Alps. In his memory Nora and another sister bought land in Downing Place for the building of a laboratory, jointly for both women's colleges, despite Emily Davies's reservations. It would be an improvement on the cold little laboratory in Newnham garden, which was in itself better than the Sidgwicks' bathroom at Hillside, where Nora first conducted various classes and experiments.

The Sidgwicks stayed at North Hall until the autumn of 1882. At a time when they had been actively engaged in their academic and administrative works, they had also been closely involved in paranormal investigation. Release from residence meant they could spend more time on this. The Society for Psychical Research, the SPR, was founded in 1882 with Henry as its first President. Lord Rayleigh was a member; so too were many senior members of the University, including his old friends Frederick Myers and Edmund Gurney. Despite much sympathy, there were some who brought robust commonsense to bear, amongst them Lady Jebb, who wrote with true American independence of mind of the boredom of various table turnings and seances. 'Henry Sidgwick and Fred Myers are the head of the investigations as they call it, but both seem as easy to delude and as anxious to believe as any infant.'[10] All the Balfour family was interested in psychic phenomena, despite a bow to orthodox religion in their continued ritual of family prayers. But there is no evidence that Nora went to church and there is no chapel at Newnham. Arthur Balfour declared that while he himself was a sceptic, he would support the Church of England through thick and thin. Henry Sidgwick said, with the little stutter that enhanced his witticisms, that he would support it through thin.[11]

Science and religion had earlier in the century gone hand in hand; the Sidgwicks' labours in the field of psychical phenomena stemmed from a desire to give such matters scientific treatment and possibly unconsciously to fill the uncomfortable vacuum caused by their aching doubts. What had sapped the sureties of faith was scientific discovery; therefore the harnessing of scientific techniques to the exploration of the supernatural was a neat idea. Nora was the perfect practitioner in the collection and sifting of evidence. Her coolness and detachment infused all the activities of the Society and cast both a light of authenticity and a concomitant feeling of mild dullness and respectability over all its proceedings.

They both helped in the production of *Phantasms of the Living*, the SPR's first official publication by Myers, Gurney and Podmore, published in 1886. The 1,000 accounts Nora sifted for this work were as nothing compared with 17,000 replies about hallucinations which she dealt with later, over five years, during two of which she was Principal of Newnham. Her own paper, 'Phantasms of the Dead', was read in 1885. 'I fear it was disappointing to the audience, as it poured cold water on more than nine-tenths of our ghost stories.' The Sidgwicks visited many haunted houses themselves; no ghosts ever appeared. But they had many encounters with people who claimed telepathic and other powers.

An account of her attempts to bandage the eyes of one such claimant describes minutely what she did: 'I covered each eye with a piece of gummed paper. This was stuck both over the eyelid and down to the cheek. Over each eye a penny was placed and held there with a strip of gummed paper . . . over this a handkerchief was bound.' Nevertheless, she could not feel sure there was no chink and she tried the procedure on herself, with the conclusion 'that no bandages of the eyes can be made satisfactory'.[12] Nora became adept in detecting tricks and codes and learned about conjuring; she offered cool comments on various happenings: one has a familiar ring. 'Is it not possible that the dogs . . . in General Barker's narrative were afraid, not because they saw something but because they saw nothing?'

Even the Sidgwicks were taken in by the notorious Madame Blavatsky, whom they had to stay at Hillside despite her incessant smoking and racy language. 'If she is a humbug, she is a con- summate one.' Eusapia Paladino was another to-be-discredited medium with whom they spent much time. They were always bleakly candid when a deception was discovered and did not allow themselves to be as emotionally involved as did other SPR members. When the SPR cut itself off from the spiritualists, Nora wrote to Henry, 'people who fly into rages are such a bore . . . their spirit is theological, not scientific'.

The accusation that they glossed over their old friend Edmund Gurney's death as possibly accidental and not suicide after his discovery that he had been deceived by some well-known telepathists is substantiated by Nora's omitting various relevant passages from Henry's journal in her later Memoir.[13] They obviously suffered various conflicting emotions over this personally unhappy event. The pursuit of supernatural enquiry brought frustrations and disappointments and even sometimes boredom. Happily also mockery, on Henry's part anyway: 'He (L.A.) believes himself to be in continual close contact with his deceased wife, but yet has just married a second; spiritual bigamy it seems – but I understand his first approves.'

The Sidgwicks travelled extensively in the vacations, partly for pleasure, partly for the SPR. The hay fever which plagued them both made summer holidays by the sea or in the mountains essential. Henry has left a charming picture of a quiet stay near Aldeburgh in a borrowed house:

no front door but an outer staircase up to a verandah . . . into which three sitting rooms open. I live in one, Nora in the other, and we have meals in the third . . . I have read Political Economy and written part of my address for the British Association. Nora has edited the July journal of the SPR and written the report of the Theosophic phenomena . . . in the evening read bad novels and tried psychical experiments with cards. Isolation complete.

Christmas and New Year found them always at Whittingehame with a large, rumbustious, talkative house party, dominated by Arthur Balfour, who had by 1887 graduated from being 'Pretty Fanny' to 'Bloody Balfour' as Irish Secretary in Dublin.

Their comfortable life in Hillside came to an end in 1892 when Miss Clough died and it was unanimously agreed that Nora should succeed her. It was an invitation not lightly accepted. What seemed to have worried Henry most, and which seems surprising considering his commitment to the College, was that Nora would not now find time for the work of the SPR. In 1894 they moved into the Principal's flat in the newly built Pfeiffer, a building over the gateway linking two halls. A new road was constructed at the back of Clough and Sidgwick Halls after much negotiation, which meant that a public footpath right through the College could be closed. (Henry described the campaign as 'tears and wrath and long letters in the Cambridge papers and in short a first-class row'.) It was Nora's idea that plane trees should be planted in the new Sidgwick Avenue to mask the rawness of the red brick. She paid for them and their tending.

The scant six years they had left together seems to have been, judging from contemporary impressions, one of the most brilliant phases of the College, whose after-glow has cast a radiance down the years. For people who described themselves as 'gray' it was a triumph. Jane Harrison gave an account of the jollier side of that life:

There was the actual Cambridge academic circle – a brilliant circle, it seems to me, looking back. Cambridge society was then small enough to be one, and there were endless small, but not informal, dinner parties. The order of the University precedence was always strictly observed. Henry Sidgwick was the centre, and with him his two most intimate friends, Frederick Myers and Edmund Gurney . . . This was the Psychical Research circle; their quest, scientific proof of immortality. To put it thus seems almost grotesque now; then it was inspiring.[14]

Students were brought into contact not only with the life of the Sidgwicks, but with the worlds they both represented: in Henry's case the world of academic politics and learning; in Nora's of politics, great houses and great names. Some of this must have rubbed off onto students with a more modest range of experiences. The world they kept utterly separate was that of the SPR. What they succeeded in so effortlessly was to divide up their different concerns. They were skilled in leaving each other space; in the over-cosiness of Victorian relationships this was unusual.

Jokingly Henry considered that the position of Appendage to the Principal was one he was born to fulfil. It was one the students bidden to have tea with the Sidgwicks and baffled by Nora's capacity for silence were grateful for. Yet she is always described as shining like a star in any gathering.

It is surprising now to realise how closely she was involved not only with the accounts (chasing a missing twopence with pleasure) but with the actual housekeeping, with understandable anxiety about food (a constant source of complaint from 'fermented stewed fruit' and 'semi-tepid raw meat' to 'uninviting sausages and bacon')[15] and concerns about health and discipline. The rules for the student body remained unaltered for decades and did not encourage a very dashing style of life. The Vice-Principal had to be consulted about invitations, excursions and places of worship. Students had to be in college by 6.30 p.m. The Sidgwicks may have held unconventional views on many subjects but they did not tolerate unconventional behaviour in students. The place of women in Cambridge was too tenuous to allow any challenges to the social norm. However, in many ways Nora was enlightened. Lord Acton, one of her admirers (and who preserved even her invitations to dinner), was asked by her to have girls for his Trinity tutorials on the French Revolution, 'alone or with the men'. Trinity College, Dublin, approached her about her experience with mixed classes: she dispatched a brief questionnaire to all who had been teaching mixed classes in science, classics and modern and medieval languages: no difficulties reported, except with an occasional classical text; no chaperones needed.

The health of her girls and any stress or strain did concern her, perhaps because this was always raised by those who thought education bad for them. A journalist was ill-advised enough to claim in the *Pall Mall Gazette* that intellectual success could only be achieved by women at the cost of physical deterioration and the consequent weakening of the stock. Here was a challenge and another opportunity to produce killing statistics, which she did, with the help of a committee and over 500 questionnaires. Social historians would find the figures, however amateurish the questions, fascinating. The journalist was probably stunned by the seriousness of the response. Nora's passion for figures and interest in patterns of physique and heredity led her to another questionnaire and set of cards in the College archives: type of skin, colour of hair, height, weight, region of the country, etc. are meticulously recorded along with Nora's own card. She called her hair, so fine and straight in every photograph, 'curly'!

One of the ephemeral College productions in 1895 had relevant lines:

> Mrs Sidgwick she up an' sez 'Look at the fax
> . . . the one thing we ax
> Is – do treat a girl as a rational creature.'

The 'rational creatures' were beginning to ask again for degrees; schools were demanding qualifications for teachers, learned professions were opening up to women, new universities naturally gave degrees to them. This time Mrs Sidgwick joined in the fray and was provoked by a fly-sheet (a pamphlet setting out an opinion or argument) from Professor Marshall into answering him. She had acquired a known voice by now and a reputation in the educational world. Her argument has an unassailable confidence; she accused men of continually presenting different hurdles. As soon as women have proved that they could reach the highest places in the Mathematical and Classical Triposes, their feminine qualities are then thought to prevent them from vigorous mental work afterwards.

A grace to grant degrees to women was presented to the Senate in 1897, all MAs having a vote. Passions ran high; undergraduate opinion was (unusually) canvassed and was overwhelmingly against; a special train brought the cohorts of the faithful anxious to preserve the status quo; a tumultuous crowd gathered outside the Senate House armed with fireworks, flour and eggs. When the result was known (1,707 against to 661 for), the roar of the undergraduate mob advancing towards Newnham was heard anxiously in the College and the gates were quickly locked. What is odd is that no mention is made of this disturbing event in the Memoir.

Doubtless the Sidgwicks were wounded and disappointed, but what mattered was that the College should grow in stature and success and in numbers. Henry, fighting for other reforms in the university, was frustrated and overworked. The demands of the SPR had not diminished: Nora was doing practically a full-time job for them as well as carrying out her administrative and academic duties to the full. It must have been a relaxation for her when, on frequent visits to Terling, after her brother-in-law's retirement there in 1885, she could work and talk with Lord Rayleigh in his laboratory there.

Despite Henry's pleasure in living in Newnham and his rapport with students there and at Trinity, some dissatisfaction with Cambridge and a muted sadness about life in general surfaces in his letters.

In 1900 he wrote: 'I cannot persuade myself that Newnham would get on as well without my wife' and that they were both 'neither just as well as we would wish, sometimes mildly anxious about ourselves and sometimes about each other'. Anxiety about his own health led Henry to consult a specialist and to learn that he had cancer and little prospect of a full recovery after the necessary operation. In the sad weeks after this verdict he behaved with dignity and stoical grace, as did Nora, telling a few friends only and begging them to pray for him. He put his affairs in order, had the operation, convalesced by the sea and in spite of plans to proceed back to Cambridge via a visit to Terling, he became ill and died there in August 1900. In the event of there not being an Anglican funeral service for him (which there was) Henry left a sentence to be read over his grave, which has the unmistakable diffident Sidgwick note to it, 'Let us commend to the love of God with silent prayer the soul of a sinful man who partly tried to do his duty.'

The only ghost ever heard of as haunting Newnham is that of Henry, a happy spirit with flying beard and cloak.

Nora resumed her work in College and for the SPR. She immediately set about publishing Henry's papers and compiling a Memoir with his brother. Reading it deepens one's knowledge of her. She never obtrudes by so much as a phrase; the writing is cool and detached, she quotes appositely but never adds a personal note. Every word is thoughtfully weighed. One is reminded that she admonished someone who asked what she meant by a certain word, 'I never *mean* anything.' There is no doubt of the grief she felt for him, though checked by her watchful duty not to succumb to emotion. She wrote to Lady Rayleigh about 'a counting of the days to the holidays' and later confessed to a feeling of the 'fewness' of the coming years. She was to live for another thirty.

While Mrs Sidgwick wore solitariness like a garment, she was not a solitary. She was a vital part of an institution as well as of a large and gregarious family. She had been married to a man who loved parties – legend has it that their dinner parties had far better wine than food – and she continued to give them. She also belonged to a women's dining club, which gave good dinners in turn with wine (but not champagne) and provided topics for talk: the irrepressible Lady Jebb proposed 'sex' once. Visits, official and friendly, were undertaken. Nora went to innumerable stately dinners in London, particularly when Arthur was Prime Minister, in reputedly borrowed *grande tenue*. The unconventional and austere side to her is revealed in a comment to someone complaining how much space a dressing-gown took in a suitcase. 'I always wear my mackintosh,' said Nora.

There are various descriptions during the remaining years of her reign: 'tall, slightly bent, emaciated figure . . . a white face, with snowy hair covered by a delicate fragment of lace; the face was almost Chinese in its still, aloof absorption'; 'something was transmitted . . . some virtue passed from her to us; some whiff from the heights'; 'Colour seemed remote from her; yet the greys in which it was natural to see her drawn were so definite, so luminous and so subtle that . . . they could make vivid colour appear crude'.[16] Henry's nephew, A. C. Benson, went to call. 'Found Aunt Nora . . . like a graceful ghost or Prioress in her widow's dress . . . She is herself like a porcelain shadow.' Lytton Strachey one goes to for an opposite and yet confirming impression: 'a faded monolith of ugly beauty, with a nervous laugh, and an infinitely remote mind, which, mysteriously, realises all'. Frances Cornford records a tea-party given by Jane Harrison. 'I remember Mrs. Sidgwick there and the radiance which seemed to be around her enchanting ugly head. With her unique frank courtesy, she, like Jane, treated a young creature like an interesting equal.'

Unfleshly she may have appeared, but there was still steel in her bones. She complained to her students about rushing about and belonging to too many societies and blamed the few Firsts – only 5 out of 79 – on this. Attendance at societies flagged at once. Anyone professionally interested in the supernatural might be considered a soft touch for an old tale. So Violet Martin's story (one-half of the Somerville and Ross partnership) is unexpected. She tried to impress Mrs Sidgwick and her SPR secretary by her discovery of a leprechaun's tiny slipper on an Irish hillside. 'Did they think your evidence water-tight?' 'They did not! Those two white-headed old weevils would bore a hole in anything.'[17]

Nora's reaction to the well-known book, *An Adventure*, about ghosts at Versailles by Miss C. A. E. Moberley and Miss E. F. Jourdain was equally tart. She had used a French investigator to draw maps and comment on the topographical detail before she reviewed the book, which she describes as very readable, but 'we cannot honestly say that they appear to us to have added anything of interest on the positive side of Psychical Research', and 'too little allowance is made for the weakness of human memory'.[18]

Nevertheless, the book has exercised a continuing fascination. During the last decade of her Principalship she was both a member of the Council of the SPR and its President for a year.

Two new buildings were added to Newnham, named after benefactors, Kennedy Building and Peile Hall. A fund was started by her in 1903 to endow research scholarships as she believed in the importance of research for the intellectual health of the College. It was a time of expansion and consolidation in that glowing Edwardian era of hope. Degrees were no nearer, rules of chaperonage had not changed, independently minded girls chafed against restrictions, but it was a fruitful time for some of the College's most famous daughters as Fellows and students: Jane Harrison, Anna Paues, Ka Cox, Margaret Corbett Ashby, Lynda Grier, Ray Costello, Amber Reeves, to mention a few.

Mrs Sidgwick had become a public figure and a speech-maker sought after by conferences, Royal Commissions, schools and colleges. She was given honorary degrees by four universities. One is struck always by the gentle force of her implacable argument: 'Life has to be prepared for in view of alternative possibilities – marrying or not marrying.' 'Society has a right to expect that women, unmarried as well as married, should take a share in the work of the world . . . women themselves have a right to the kind of happiness which can only come from work.'

Nevertheless, when Helen Gladstone, the Vice-Principal, was summoned back by the family to help with her ageing parents, Nora commented, 'She was wanted at home and we cannot wonder at her feeling that her first duty was there.' 'Wanted at home!' That terrifying old phrase was accepted as conventional wisdom.

Her farewell talks to students (preserved in College archives) before they went down are models of 'fireside chats'. What characterises these talks, apart from their graceful conversational style, is her expectation of complete identification with the College: 'You will still belong to us and it is only through this parting that Newnham can do its work, it is like a plant shedding its ripe fruit around.' She quotes Jowett and the importance of doing silently some real work: 'for most of us the best work is silent and inconspicuous'. Nora saw her students as fighting against evil, unhappiness, ignorance. Her message and its resemblance to that given by Jowett to his young men has been recently explored. She stressed, as he did, the creation of an ambitious, aspiring and idealistic elite. No doubt she also realised that it was not just through their own careers, but through their husbands and children that Newnham ideals would trickle down.

This is part of what she gave to Newnham: its sense of identity. Interestingly, what she also gave to the College was the feeling of a great country house, with its library, gardens, comfortable architecture and civilised relationships. Nowadays one might scoff at this notion. Until the Second World War, it was still valid when the last of the little Fen maids, with their rough and jaunty ways, laid fires and made beds and Fellows came to hall in full evening fig and students changed into best dresses.

Nora also gave the College a great deal of money and a great deal of financial attention and advice. Pioneers have almost the happiest time of it. Those immediately after them have to continue creative progress with patient perseverance. Nora Sidgwick developed a powerful institution of learning and research and social influence from a beginning of amateur enthusiasm. She seems to have done this without ever raising her voice.

When she retired to her house in Grange Road, she still ran the accounts and watched what was going on. One hears her businesslike voice behind various official documents. Not all the younger dons cared for her perpetual presence. Even when, during the Great War, she went to live with her brother Gerald and his family at Fishers Hill near Woking, she came back for Council meetings to a very great age.

Naturally she was greatly interested in the campaign for

women's suffrage, though she was appalled at the actions of the suffragettes. She spoke at many meetings: Frances Partridge recalls her beautiful voice, which she fell in love with as a young girl. Her attitude remains one of her feeling about good behaviour at Newnham; women must never behave in an unladylike way in assailing male bastions: 'If in a rising tide we watch to see when a sandcastle will be overwhelmed, we shall see one little wave after another approaching and receding without apparently affecting anything . . . But the failure of these waves does not set back the tide . . . inevitably a wave does at length reach and overwhelm the castle.'

Perhaps she was remembering sandcastles on the beaches near Whittingehame on those jolly picnics of her youth. It was certainly an image one can associate with her feelings about women's education.

Her interest in the SPR never waned; the tough-mindedness which was irritating to a number of members softened in later years. In her presidential address in 1908 she did endorse experiments to prove continued existence. The fillip bereavement gave to spiritualism during the Great War depressed her, but in 1924 she wrote in a letter, 'people die very fast as one gets old and one feels that it is a parting for only a short time'. Perhaps the prospect of seeing 'my Henry' again imperceptibly changed her views. In 1936, the year of her death, her brother Gerald read her address to the SPR: 'I have Mrs Sidgwick's assurance, that upon the evidence before her, she herself is a firm believer both in the survival and in the reality of communication between the living and the dead.'

Her dearest Arthur had died in 1930; at 85, close elder sister to the last, she was holding his hand. Her houses had always been his and his hers. Comments she made about him seem applicable to her: 'his inner self has always been veiled', 'You may be ready to live and die for a cause without enthusiasm'. How lovable Nora Sidgwick seemed to any but her family is debatable, but they, especially the younger ones, confirm the affection she gave and generated in a close family circle.

In her 91st year, confused for once as to where she was and being told she was at Fishers Hill, almost her last words were: 'That is a very bold hypothesis.' One can imagine her with the illusion that she was back in Cambridge, her spiritual home. Her pursuit of gradual progress: 'Lente, lente', her disregard for comfort and cosiness, her liking for facts and figures, had their perfect setting there. 'Educated doubt' was stamped through her.

In the rose garden below Sidgwick Hall is a tiny fountain which has chimed through the lives of many Newnhamites. The circle which surrounds it is inscribed: 'The daughters of this house to those that shall come after commend the filial remembrance of Henry Sidgwick.' The daughters of the house remember Nora Sidgwick with gratitude also. The Sidgwicks have heirs innumerable.

NOTES

I am indebted throughout to the following sources of information: *Henry Sidgwick: a Memoir* by A. Sidgwick and E. M. Sidgwick (London 1906); *Mrs. Henry Sidgwick* by Ethel Sidgwick (London 1938); the Sidgwick Papers in Newnham College Library; and to the Balfour Papers in the Scottish Record Office.

1 Mary Gladstone, *Diaries and Letters*, ed. Lucy Masterman (London 1930).
2 Lady Frances Balfour, *Ne Obliviscaris* (London 1930).
3 Mary Paley Marshall, *What I Remember* (Cambridge 1947).
4 E.g. Kenneth Young, *A. J. Balfour* (London 1963), amongst others.
5 Mary Paley Marshall, *What I Remember*.
6 Mary Gladstone, *Diaries and Letters*.
7 G. S. Haight, *George Eliot* (Cambridge 1968).
8 Sedley Taylor's Letters, Cambridge University Library, Add. 6255(184).
9 Ann Phillips (ed.), *A Newnham Anthology* (Cambridge 1979).
10 M. R. Bobbitt, *With Dearest Love to All* (London 1950).
11 A. C. Benson, *Diary*, ed. P. Lubbock (London 1926).
12 *Proceedings of the SPR*, 1883.

13 T. H. Hall, *The Strange Case of Edward Gurney* (London 1964).
14 Jane Harrison, *Reminiscences of a Student's Life* (London 1925).
15 Catherine Holt, *Letters* (privately printed).
16 M. A. Hamilton, *Remembering My Good Friends* (London 1944).
17 Rosalind Heywood, *The Sixth Sense* (London 1959).
18 *Proceedings of the SPR*, 1911.

Chapter 2

JANE ELLEN HARRISON
1850–1928

Hugh Lloyd-Jones

The lives of scholars do not always throw light upon their work, and are often too uneventful to make interesting reading. Some modern attempts to ginger them up result in a product not very far removed from gossip-writing.[1] In recent times, a number of people have shown interest in Jane Harrison for the wrong reasons; in certain circles in America, she has been made a saint in a fashion that she herself would have deplored.[2] But she led a more interesting life than many scholars, and in her case some knowledge of the life does help one to understand the work. She was the first English woman to make a name in classical scholarship, and she was not only a scholar and a pioneer in scholarship, but something of a literary artist. Her writings had a distinct importance in the culture of her times, and a significant part of her achievement consisted in the remarkable effect which she had on gifted pupils and on distinguished colleagues. Gilbert Murray wrote in 1955 that few people would accept the whole of her conclusions, but that nobody could write about Greek religion without being influenced by her work, and that continues to be true.[3]

Jane Ellen Harrison[4] was born at Cottingham, near Hull, on 9 September 1850, the third daughter of Charles Harrison, a timber merchant, and his wife Elizabeth Hawksley Nelson. Her mother, whom she heard described as 'a silent woman of singular gentleness and serenity', died almost at her birth. Her father was an affectionate but a reserved and absent-minded parent; when she sent him her books, he never read them, but after his death she learned by chance that when he travelled he always took them with him. Mr Harrison would have agreed with Lord Melbourne that 'things have come to a pretty pass when religion is allowed to interfere with a man's private life';[5] but unfortunately he replaced her mother with a fervent Welsh revivalist, who taught her step-children and her own numerous offspring that they must be born again, and that 'God would have their whole hearts or nothing'.[6] This training must have had much to do with Jane Harrison's loss of Christian faith; when as a young woman she read Aristotle's *Ethics*, she found that 'it was like coming out of a madhouse into a quiet college quadrangle where all was liberty and sanity, and you became a law unto yourself'.[7] Like Nietzsche, she read *The Origin of Species* at the age of 20, and Darwin as well as Aristotle encouraged her to abandon Christianity.[8]

The Harrison family was not one in which advanced education for women was a high priority. When Jane Harrison as a small girl got hold of a Greek grammar and was seen to be enjoying it, an aunt asked what use Greek would be to her when she had a house and family of her own. Until she was 17 Jane Harrison was educated by a series of governesses, all of them in her words 'grossly ignorant'.[9] But one of them shared her eagerness to learn languages, and with her attacked German, Latin, the Greek Testament and even some Hebrew, before going off her head.[10] But her family must have recognised her unusual ability, because in the end she was sent to Cheltenham Ladies' College, which had been founded in 1853 by Frances Mary Buss and Dorothea Beale. From her memoir one gathers that Miss Harrison did not enjoy Cheltenham; whatever their initial relations may have been,[11] she ended up not entirely sympathetic to Miss Beale, who sided with Cromwell, ordained that no girl should buy a book, 'for fear of undigested reading',[12] and reprimanded her after intercepting a postcard sent her by a boy who was a friend of hers and with reference to a coming examination had asked her to give his love to the examiners.[13] Lessons in mathematics and chemistry interested her more than those in the humanities; but in spite of Miss Beale's prohibition she managed to read a good deal, and Miss Beale herself became fully aware of her exceptional ability.

For four years after leaving Cheltenham in 1870, Miss Harrison remained at home, teaching her brothers and sisters and making occasional trips abroad. Doubtless she continued her education by herself; and one of the books which she read at this time was D. F. Strauss's Hegelian life of Jesus (1835/6), translated (1846) by the young George Eliot, another of the books that helped to cure her of her Christian faith.[14] In 1874 she passed the entrance examination and entered Newnham College, Cambridge, which had been founded only three years before. Here she was happy. She was able to pursue her studies with resources that had not hitherto been available to her; and as she wrote later she 'liked to live spaciously, but rather plainly, in large halls with great spaces and quiet libraries'.

She made good friends among her fellow students, such as Margaret Merrifield, who married the ingenious but perverse Greek scholar A. W. Verrall, Mary Paley, who married the economist Alfred Marshall, and Ellen Crofts, who married the botanist Sir Francis Darwin. She was not beautiful, but she was tall and had a splendid figure, having profited, no doubt, from being made to lie on a backboard in early years. She became an elegant dresser in the fashion of the current avant-garde, whose taste she then shared; her favourite modern painter was Rossetti and her favourite modern poet Swinburne. Interesting social opportunities were open to a gifted Newnham undergraduate at this time. One of the leading figures in the foundation of the College and its early years was Mrs Henry Sidgwick, niece of one Prime Minister, the third Marquess of Salisbury, and sister of another, A. J. Balfour. It is clear that the great personal charm that finds expression in Jane Harrison's writing was already in evidence. She encountered various distinguished visitors to the new foundation, including Turgenev, Ruskin and Gladstone, whose daughter Helen was a fellow student; later, she stayed with Tennyson, met Browning, was friendly with Burne-Jones, and at the house of Walter Pater and his sisters frequently encountered Henry James. Most importantly for her, she met George Eliot, who entered her room at Newnham, lately repapered with William Morris wallpaper, and murmured, 'Your paper makes a beautiful background for your face.'

Jane Harrison had a passion for language, and is said to have known 'three Romance, three Scandinavian, German, three Oriental and five dead languages',[15] apart from her Russian, which we will come to later. In her seventies she learned Persian. She never managed to learn Greek with the accuracy that results from a strict classical education; but I do not think her work suffered greatly from this deficiency, as she had excellent Greek scholars available for consultation, and much of what she did could be done without great proficiency in the language. When G. S. Kirk writes that her books were 'utterly uncontrolled by anything resembling careful logic', he is a little too severe; Jane Harrison's main faults were faults often found in enthusiastic and imaginative people, a tendency to imprecision and a propensity to sweeping generalisation. The lively receptivity to new ideas that was one of her best qualities could cause her to be carried away too easily by seductive theories; the light-heartedness and playfulness that make her letters to Gilbert Murray so delightful could spill over into silliness and sentimentality, a tendency that became stronger as she grew older. Still, Jane Harrison combined a wide knowledge of Greek literature with a wide knowledge of Greek art in a most unusual fashion, and she possessed a rare kind of imaginative flair that has been denied to many persons with a firmer grasp of Greek grammar and of systematic thinking.

Although women were denied degrees at Cambridge until 1947, they were allowed to take the Tripos. When Miss Harrison did this in 1879, she was given second-class marks. At about this time Newnham College advertised a lectureship in classics, and she applied, but the post was given to her friend Margaret Merrifield. From 1880 Jane Harrison remained in London, where at the British Museum she was able to study under Sir Charles Newton, an archaeologist of very great distinction, who after many years of work in Greece, during which he excavated Cnidus, Halicarnassus and Didyma, had since 1861 been Keeper of Greek and Roman Antiquities and since 1880 Yates Professor of Archaeology. She devoted herself to the study of Greek art, particularly vase-painting, and before long made a considerable reputation as a lecturer on that subject. She spoke with great success at public schools, including Eton and Winchester; a boy at Winchester, asked if he had liked the lecture, said that he had not, but that he had liked the lady, who was like a beautiful green beetle. During this London period she made several visits both to Italy and to Germany. In London she met Wilhelm Klein, later Professor of Classical Archaeology in Prague, who introduced her to the work of many German archaeologists.[16] Not many English classical scholars of that period spoke and read German as fluently as Jane Harrison, and when she visited Germany she made valuable connections among German archaeologists. She got to know Ernst Curtius, the excavator of Olympia, Heinrich Brunn, the eminent authority on Greek sculpture, and Wilhelm Dörpfeld, who had begun as Schliemann's assistant and later became the greatest living expert on the archaeology of the early period.[17]

During this time she became acquainted with D. S. MacColl, nine years younger than herself, and at that time a leading art critic, who later was to become Keeper first of the Tate Gallery and later of the Wallace Collection. MacColl was a tough-minded Scot who from Glasgow had made his way to University College London, and later to Lincoln College, Oxford; he had a formidable scholarly equipment, and was fully alive to the decline of late Romanticism. Late in life, he was to produce a valuable study of the work of Steer, an artist very different from the Pre-Raphaelites and their followers. With him Jane Harrison established one of the *amitiés amoureuses* with a younger male scholar, involving a high degree of mutual intellectual influence, which marked her life. MacColl is said to have proposed marriage to her, but to have been rejected. Jane Harrison seems to have realised early that she was not meant for married life. But MacColl shattered her pattern of life by denouncing her *fin-de-siècle* aestheticism, at the same time pouring contempt on her highly successful but in his view effusive manner of lecturing. His criticism produced a severe depression, but effected a conversion whose results it is impossible to regret. She began to examine objects of Greek art more exactly and more objectively, and to pay close attention to products of the early period which earlier she might have despised as 'primitive'. In 1888 she visited Greece for the first time, in company with MacColl, and came away with a strong sense of the importance of the cults that lay behind the myths. Later, she wrote that she came from art to the study of religion because she became aware that the religion which she found displayed by early works of art did not correspond to the Olympian religion known from later art and literature.

In 1882 Jane Harrison had published *The Myths of the Odyssey in Art and Literature* and in 1885 *Introductory Studies in Greek Art*. The former work is original in that Miss Harrison showed herself conscious that artists did not necessarily work with a poetic version of the scenes or persons whom they represented, so that their works may be held to bear independent witness to a tradition.[18] But in these attractively written books she does not discuss critically the problems presented by the material, so that they have no great scientific value. No injustice, therefore, was done when Miss Harrison applied unsuccessfully for the succession to Newton in the Yates Chair of Archaeology at London University in 1888.[19] But in 1890 she published two books which show her moving in a new direction. One was a *Manual of*

Mythology in Relation to Greek Art, a translation from the French of Maxime Collignon; in her preface she warns the reader that 'if we would know the truth about the origin of mythological types, it is to archaic art we must look'. The other book was called *Mythology and Monuments of Ancient Athens: Being a Translation of a Portion of the 'Attica' of Pausanias*. A kind of ancient equivalent of Baedeker produced in the time of Hadrian by Pausanias is an important book for the study of Greek art, and the second work took the form of a commentary on the first book of Pausanias, which deals with the art and antiquities of Attica, and had been translated by Jane Harrison's friend Mrs Verrall.[20]

The most important early nineteenth-century school of interpretation of Greek myth[21] derives from the *Prolegomena zu einer wissenschaftlichen Mythologie* (1825) of Karl Otfried Müller (1797–1840), who approached the myths historically, being aware that myths have a history of their own and believing that they supply evidence for early history in the preliterary period. Müller may have exaggerated the historicity of myths, but he still made a great contribution to the subject. Following his eminent predecessor in the study of myth, Christian Gottlob Heyne (1729–1812),[22] he realised that Homer and Hesiod represent not a beginning but a comparatively late stage in the development of Greek religion, something that Miss Harrison was later to do much to make the English public understand. The extent of Müller's influence on her work is indicated by the obvious echo of his title in the title of her *Prolegomena*. But for a long time the most influential type of interpretation had been that of a much inferior school of thought, which explained myths in terms of meteorological and cosmological phenomena. This view was popularised in England by Max Müller (1823–1900), a German Sanskrit scholar who migrated to that country, where he was absurdly overrated,[23] and obtained a chair at Oxford. Miss Harrison did much to cure the English public of its addiction to this unprofitable stuff.

Beginning in the 1860s, a different trend was inaugurated in Germany by Wilhelm Mannhardt (1831–90) in a series of studies of vegetation, grain and wood spirits, which helped to bring the study of myth nearer to reality. The school of interpreters of ancient religion founded by Hermann Usener (1834–1905), who became a professor in Bonn in 1866,[24] deprecated excessive emphasis on myths and emphasised the importance of rites and customs and the value of ethnology and anthropology to the student of ancient religion. In England Sir Edward Tylor's *Primitive Culture* (1871) used the anthropological data that had now accumulated to make people aware that the study of primitive culture might throw light on early religion. From the 1880s on, the nature myth theory was challenged in England by Andrew Lang (1844–1912), who argued that myths were designed to explain something in the real world. In Germany there appeared Erwin Rohde's great book *Psyche*, whose two parts were reviewed by Miss Harrison in 1890 and 1894. Dealing as it did with beliefs about chthonic cults, about the soul and immortality, and about ecstasy and mysticism, this work made against an excessive concern with the Olympian gods and with myths and their interpretation.

The work of K. O. Müller, Mannhardt, Tylor and Lang was known to Jane Harrison when she wrote the preface to her Pausanias commentary in 1890. She wrote (p. iii):

I have tried everywhere to get at, where possible, the cult as the explanation of the legend. My belief is that in many, even in the large majority of cases, *ritual practice misunderstood*[25] explains the elaboration of myth . . . Some of the loveliest stories the Greeks have left us will be seen to have taken their rise, not in poetic imagination, but in primitive, often savage, and I think always *practical* ritual . . . The *nomina numina* method [she means the nature myth theory of people like Max Müller] I have utterly discarded.

The stress on the importance of cult and ritual was at that time in the air. A year earlier, in 1889, William Robertson Smith (1839–94) in his *Religion of the Semites* had argued that to understand religion one must work back from beliefs and concepts to 'fundamental institutions', and in particular 'ritual institutions'.[26] In 1890 J. G. Frazer (1854–1941), a Fellow of Trinity College who was four years younger than Jane Harrison, published the first edition of *The Golden Bough*, dedicated to his friend Robertson Smith. After losing his chair at Aberdeen, partly for having doubted that Moses wrote the Pentateuch, Robertson Smith had become Professor of Arabic in Cambridge in 1883. With immense learning Frazer studied rites and institutions, whose evolution from primitive religion to rational thinking he believed could be traced, using the concept of a 'survival' as a link between successive stages. Robertson Smith, in spite of being accused of heresy in Scotland, had remained a Christian; Frazer was a sceptic, whose evolutionary approach was obviously influenced by the work of Darwin.

It is by no means certain that Jane Harrison read Robertson Smith at an early date; and though she must have read *The Golden Bough* soon after the appearance of the first edition in 1890, and in her preface to a translation of a German manual of mythology published in 1892[27] she associates its author with Andrew Lang as an exponent of 'the Folklore Method', it is doubtful whether she had at this time been influenced by Frazer.[28] But she had clearly been moving towards the view expressed in the preface to her book ever since her visit to Greece in 1888.[29] Her change of attitude corresponds to a movement of taste which can be seen at work in other cultural spheres about this time; it often happens when such changes are occurring that several people make the same discovery simultaneously and independently. When Jane Harrison lectured at Clifton in the early 1880s, one of her hearers had been Roger Fry. People who had been brought up on Rossetti and Burne-Jones were now beginning to admire primitive art.

The commentary on Pausanias is intended as a guidebook for students, and does not contain much original material; later Miss Harrison considered most of it to have been superseded for scholars by Frazer's great commentary on the whole of Pausanias and for ordinary people by E. A. Gardner's handbook *Ancient Athens*, and in lieu of a second edition brought out in 1906 to a small book called *Primitive Athens as Described by Thucydides*, in which she was able to argue for Dörpfeld's view of certain topographical problems. In 1894 the Yates Chair was again vacant by the resignation of R. S. Poole, and when the vacancy was to be filled in 1896 Miss Harrison again applied for the succession. She got as far as a short-list of two; but again she was defeated by a candidate who answered more adequately the requirements of the post, in this case E. A. Gardner, who undoubtedly excelled her in general proficiency in archaeology.[30] But in 1898 she was given an opportunity much better suited to the kind of work on which she had now embarked, when she was elected to a Research Fellowship of Newnham College. Here she was free to move on from archaeology to the study of Greek myths and Greek religion.

Miss Harrison had never lost touch with her friends in Cambridge, and on returning she was enthusiastically welcomed back to Newnham. She was particularly well suited to a college life. She had, she wrote later, 'a natural gift for community life'. In Newnham College she had an excellent opportunity to indulge this taste. She had many friends in Cambridge; a number of them were scholars with whom she could discuss her subject, and Jane Harrison was the kind of scholar to whom learned discussion made a great difference. In 1892, Mrs Henry Sidgwick had succeeded Anne Jemima Clough as Principal of Newnham; her husband, the distinguished philosopher, Miss Harrison wrote later, was the centre of the academic circle. Other members were the three gifted sons of Charles Darwin, the eminent legal historian Frederic Maitland, and Sir Richard Jebb, Regius Professor of Greek, and his superb and formidable American wife. She was able to carry on her friendly battle with the wild, learned, eccentric, one-eyed Irishman Sir William Ridgeway. She was acquainted with Bertrand Russell, who once offered to provide her with a bull, on condition she and some of her women friends would guarantee to tear it to pieces. Several members of this group were interested in psychical research; the philosopher Edmund Gurney had died in 1888, but Mrs Sidgwick's brother Gerald Balfour and F. W. H. Myers were still active. Jane Harrison's old friend Margaret Verrall and her husband shared this interest.

One of her great friends in Cambridge was R. A. Neil, Fellow of Pembroke, whose edition of Aristophanes' *Knights* (1901) is still valuable. It appears[31] that she was actually engaged to Neil when he died suddenly, at the age of 49, in 1901. Like MacColl, Neil was a Scotsman and a thoroughly sound scholar; 'his sympathetic Scotch silences', Jane Harrison wrote later, 'made the dreariest gathering burn and glow'. In the Preface of her *Prolegomena* (p. xiii)[32] she acknowledged that in the first two chapters she owed much, as regards philology, to Neil: 'his friendship and his help', she added, 'were lost to me midway in my work, and that loss had been irreparable'. Certainly a cautious Scotsman with an excellent knowledge of Greek must have been a far better counsellor for Jane Harrison than the irresponsibly speculative Verrall. Here clearly we see another of her intellectual *amitiés amoureuses* with a younger male scholar, in this case only two years younger, that punctuate her career. Would she really have married him? If she had, it might have been a mistake; later she wrote that she was not cut out for married life,[33] and if one considers what would have been expected of a wife in the Cambridge of that time, one cannot think that she was mistaken.

In 1900 she met in the Verralls' house Gilbert Murray,[34] who a year earlier had resigned owing to ill health the chair at Glasgow that he had occupied since 1889. Luckily he and not Verrall became her chief counsellor after Neil's death; but *Prolegomena* is dedicated to the Verralls, and Verrall continued to exert a harmful influence. Gilbert Murray was a very gifted Greek scholar indeed, and, like Miss Harrison herself, an inspiring and imaginative person, so that there was an immediate sympathy between them. Not that Jane Harrison ever became emotionally involved with Murray as she did with some of her other male collaborators. She managed to maintain friendly relations with Murray's aristocratic, Liberal and alarming wife, born Lady Mary Howard, daughter of the ninth Earl of Carlisle and his terrifying consort.[35] Unfortunately, Murray too was not immune to Verrall's influence; some of the qualities that he shared with Jane Harrison made them in certain respects bad for each other. At about the same time Harrison received a fan letter after a lecture from a fourth-year undergraduate at Trinity College, F. M. Cornford, later Fellow of Trinity and finally Laurence Professor of Ancient Philosophy. From that moment Cornford became a close associate of hers, and indeed Miss Harrison struck up with him one of the deep intellectual relationships that played such an important part in her career.

Miss Harrison seems to have had little personal contact with Frazer. This may have been partly due to the watch kept by another alarming scholar's wife, Lady Frazer; but despite initial sympathy Frazer moved away from the position she adopted with regard to ritual. All the same, in many ways Frazer's work was more closely related to hers than that of A. B. Cook, whose credentials as a member of the group are to some extent dubious.[36] Cook was a very learned man, and he and Miss Harrison corrected each other's proofs and helped each other in several ways; but he was an Evangelical Christian with a strong belief in monotheism and in several ways their outlooks differed.

Between 1899 and 1904 Jane Harrison published in the *Journal of Hellenic Studies* three substantial articles on Greek religion.[37] Much of their content was repeated or summarised in her first major work, *Prolegomena to the Study of Greek Religion*, published in 1903.

In the preface Miss Harrison warns the reader against assuming that the picture of Greek religion presented by Homer represents our earliest evidence for Greek religion; behind the splendid surface of Homeric religion, she writes, lies a 'substratum of religious conceptions at once more primitive and more permanent'. In this she was following in the footsteps of such scholars as Heyne, K. O. Müller, F. G. Welcker (1784–1868) and Rohde (1845–98);[38] but to many of her English readers it will have come as a revelation. 'Had ritual received its due share of attention,' she continues, 'it had not remained so long neglected.' Miss Harrison explains that she is not indifferent to literature, and that she has indeed investigated primitive rites in order to come to a better understanding of some forms of Greek poetry. But she had come to see that her favourite subject was religion, which she took to be a kind of art.

At the start of her first chapter Jane Harrison quotes words of Ruskin about the Greeks: 'there is no dread in their hearts; pensiveness, amazement, often deepest grief and desolation, but terror never'. Greek religion as described in Greek from Homer to the great writers of the fifth century appears, in her words, 'a thing of Joyful confidence', whose festivals and sacrifices gave pleasure to all and whose deities required only service, 'a sort of tendance', in order to benefit the community. *Do ut des*, 'I give that you may give', is the watchword of this kind of religion; but it is balanced by another kind of religion whose watchword is *do ut abeas*, 'I give that you may go away', and whose central element is not that of tendance, but that of aversion. This is because it is directed to powers that are capable of doing harm, and its attitude towards them is expressed by the Greek word *deisidaimonia*, which means literally 'the fear of spirits'.

The Greeks themselves on occasion distinguish between the Olympian gods, the gods of the sky, and the chthonic gods, the gods who live below the earth. The importance of the latter, Miss Harrison points out, will emerge clearly from an examination of some of the Greek festivals. The first example which she gives is that of the Diasia, an Athenian festival which honours Zeus; but the Zeus whom it honours is not the Zeus of Olympus,

but Zeus Meilichios, 'the gentle'. This Zeus is honoured not with
the kind of sacrifice usually made to the Olympians, at which the
sacrificers got their share of sacrificial meat, but by a holocaust, by
which the victim's entire body was consumed. That title is an
example of the conciliation of dangerous powers by giving them
euphemising names; the Erinyes, the avenging goddesses, are
often called the Eumenides, 'the kindly ones'. Zeus Meilichios is
represented in certain works of art as a great snake; snakes, which
can move between the upper world and the world below the earth,
are often associated with the chthonic powers. Miss Harrison
argues that a chthonic power called Meilichios, 'the gentle one',
was later identified with Zeus; but from early times the god of the
underworld, more often called Hades or Pluto, could also be
called the Zeus of the earth.

In the next three chapters Miss Harrison examines the
principal Athenian festivals. She rightly concentrates on Athens,
because of the festival calendars of the various Greek cities,
the Athenian is by far the best known to us, and it had been the
subject of much detailed work by German scholars which she
could make use of.[39] If one considers these chapters as if they
amounted to no more than an attempt to prove that in every case
in which a ritual is connected with a myth the latter has been
generated by the former, they cannot be thought to be successful.
In most cases, as G. S. Kirk remarks in the course of a careful
investigation of the question, 'we find that *pre-existing* myths, or
faintly plausible details from them, are dragged in as *aitia*, which
is a very different process from solid mythological invention'.[40]
'The rituals' as he writes in another place,[41] 'do not seem to
generate myths except in rare and exceptional cases. What they
more frequently do is to encourage half-baked *aitia* in the form of
loosely applied or ill-chosen details from other and obviously
independent tales.' A good deal of work has been done on this
subject since Miss Harrison's time, and as a scholarly account of
the festivals her chapters have long been superseded. But her main

object in these chapters is not so much to insist that all myths are closely associated with or derived from rituals as to show how small a part was played in the rituals associated with the religious festivals by the Olympian gods with whom they were officially associated. She insists that aversion plays a more important part than tendance in these rituals, and she is above all eager to show how different the earliest religion must have been from the Olympian religion as it is presented by Homer, Hesiod and the later poets. In this she has surely been successful.

The fifth chapter is entitled 'The Demonology of Ghosts and Sprites and Bogeys'. It is an attempt to indicate the nature of the shadowy powers which the rites of aversion were originally to avert, and, in the words of Jean-Pierre Vernant,[42] 'to connect them all to the same "primitive" religious base and make them different types of "Keres"'. Not all the varied kinds of spirit which the chapter describes offer much positive evidence. The Keres are spirits of death, which appear first in high poetry; Miss Harrison is not the only scholar to have thought that they originated as ghosts, but this remains a guess, for the evidence that has been thought to point to this view is slender.[43] Some take the Sirens also to be spirits of death, but others have argued that they originated as a personification of the soporific heat of the midday sun.[44] The mythical Gorgons developed from the hideous face depicted for apotropaic purpose;[45] and the Graiai belong to myth rather than to popular belief. The Sphinx – originally Phix or Sphix – was a mythological monster, which came to be identified with the woman-lion of Oriental art.[46] The Erinyes belong in a rather different category. Miss Harrison held that they were originally the ghosts of murdered persons; Rohde before her and Nilsson after her were of that opinion, and it is shared by the author of the fourth-century commentary on an Orphic poem that is preserved on the papyrus found during the sixties of the present century at Derveni in Macedonia.[47] But even if this is how the Erinyes began, they became, or they came to be identified with, earth-goddesses, at one stage perhaps not very different from Demeter and Kore, and like all earth-goddesses could do men good or harm.[48] One must agree with Vernant that Miss Harrison's attempt to make all these creatures Keres is unsuccessful; she ignores obvious differences between them. None the less, the surmise that in early times the Greeks or their ancestors feared mysterious spirits rather than gods is by no means unreasonable.

In the sixth and seventh chapters, 'The Making of a Goddess' and 'The Making of a God', Jane Harrison sets out to show how religion began with spirits, at first nameless. A spirit, which she thought was denoted by the word *daimon*,[49] might gradually become a god, in Greek *theos*, worshipped far beyond the place where his or her worship had originated. For her monotheism existed before polytheism, which came into being only when the many single gods of individual localities were brought together. In the early period, she believes, goddesses were more prominent than male gods. She had been encouraged in this belief by the new knowledge of Minoan art, in which female deities play the major part. She points out that if we examine local cults we see that certain deities are specially important in certain places. For example, in Argos, and also in Samos, Hera is the main divinity, and we hear little about Zeus. In Athens the main deity is Athene, who may well have taken her name from the city; the legend was that she had defeated Poseidon in a contest for that honour. In the cult of Eleusis there are two goddesses, Demeter and her daughter, who in that place is seldom called by her name, Persephone, Persephassa or in Attic dialect Pherephatta, but simply Kore, 'the Maiden'; Jane Harrison well observes (p. 274), referring, of course, to the early period, that 'they are, in fact, merely the older and younger form of the same person'. Besides the two-fold Mother and the Maiden, there are trinities of goddesses – Charites (Graces, originally fertility spirits), Moirai (Fates), Horai (Seasons), and the Muses are three times three. Jane Harrison was already acquainted with the Cretan discoveries of

Sir Arthur Evans, made known in 1900; she visited Crete several times, and it had great significance for her. She identifies the goddesses shown in Cretan art with the Mistress of Animals (Potnia Theron), some of whose attributes were later taken over by Artemis; in fact there seem to have been several different goddesses. One might have expected that Aphrodite, having been imported from Syria by way of Cyprus, would have interested Jane Harrison less; but she suggests that Aphrodite's birth from the sea has features of the rising from the earth, the *anodos*, of an earth-goddess. She describes the vases that show an earth-goddess rising up from beneath the ground; the name Pandora belonged originally to such a deity. Goddesses, she argues, started as local heroines. Many female deities never acquired full divine status; for example Diktynna and Britomartis were taken over by Artemis, Aphaia by Athene. Helen counted as a mere local heroine in most of Greece, but in Sparta she was a goddess, sister of the divine twins, Castor and Polydeuces.

Into this world dominated by goddesses of the earth burst the Olympians, with whom Miss Harrison had little emotional sympathy, regarding them as glorified mortals, lacking in the numinous quality that could inspire awe. The notion of an Olympian take-over, we must observe, is not supported by historical evidence; as Albert Henrichs has remarked, 'what is lacking in Harrison's reconstruction of primitive Greece is a concrete chronological framework'.[50] From the chilly north come the cold Olympians; earth-goddesses are replaced by divinities of the sky, matriarchy is displaced by patriarchy.[51] This belief cannot be sustained by historical evidence;[52] later Miss Harrison was to exchange the term 'matriarchal' for the less objectionable 'matrilinear'.[53] Zeus, who began as the Indo-European sky-god, marries Hera and tries to subordinate her; he or his brother Hades rules in the underworld. At Delphi Apollo displaces the Earth-Goddess, sometimes identified with Themis, Divine Wisdom or Divine Justice. Gods take over the shrines of old heroes; Zeus displaces Meilichios and Apollo displaces Hyakinthos. Some heroes become minor gods – Helen's brothers, the healer Asklepios, the mighty warrior Herakles. This brings her to the special case of Dionysos, a son of Zeus by a mortal woman, who becomes a major god. The rest of the book is taken up with the discussion of Dionysos and the related figure of Orpheus.

The modern period in the understanding of Dionysos dates from the year 1872, when Nietzsche published *The Birth of Tragedy*. Although Rohde seldom mentions his former friend, his treatment of Dionysos and Orpheus in *Psyche* betrays his influence. In that same year A. Rapp distinguished the violent maenadism of myth from the subdued maenadism of cult;[54] Miss Harrison took account of Nietzsche, but not of Rapp. Like almost all scholars at that time, Miss Harrison believed that the cult of Dionysos had been introduced to Greece from Thrace, a belief that had been refuted even before the appearance of his name on tablets written in the Linear B script; like other scholars she mistook the legend of the cult's introduction for the record of its history. But she had read Nietzsche and Rohde,[55] and understood the importance of the god's connection with ecstasy;[56] and her survey brings out the importance of each of the three main spheres of Dionysiac activity, wine, maenadism, and the afterlife. But it has certain weaknesses. First, she fails to follow Rapp in distinguishing between the maenadism of literature, whose most important manifestation is in Euripides' tragedy the *Bacchae*, and the innocuous maenadism of cult.[57] In speaking of omophagy, the way in which the maenads are depicted as tearing apart animals and eating their raw flesh, she repeatedly uses the Christian term 'sacrament';[58] she argues that originally the maenads were eating their god so that his power would enter into them. She argues for this by connecting the omophagy with the myth in which Dionysos has the alternative name or cult title Zagreus. The story figured in one of the rhapsodies attributed to Orpheus and composed as early at 500 BC, but probably existed earlier. This myth told that Dionysos, who in this connection has the additional or alternative name Zagreus, was the son of Zeus by his own daughter Persephone. Seen from the perspective of the pre-Olympian period, 'Zeus' and 'Persephone' can mean simply the ruler of the underworld and his consort; both Homer and Aeschylus call the ruler of the underworld 'Zeus' as an alternative to 'Hades'. The infant Dionysos was cut to pieces and swallowed by the enemies of Zeus, the evil Titans. But his heart was preserved by Athena, and Zeus swallowed it and then had intercourse with the Theban princess Semele, so that Dionysos was born again. Zeus destroyed the Titans with his thunder, and from their ashes mankind came into being. Man thus partakes not only of the nature of the Titans, who were evil, but also of the divine nature of Dionysos, son of Zeus. Many scholars have protested against the sacramental theory, but others have adopted it from Miss Harrison, including E. R. Dodds in writings that still exert great influence.[59]

From the sixth century on, some part of Dionysiac worship is involved with the mysterious figure of Orpheus;[60] Orpheus again is involved with the almost equally mysterious figure of Pythagoras. Miss Harrison, putting too much faith in writers of the imperial period, clings to the belief that Orpheus was a real man. That view is understandable as a reaction against the opinion put forward in 1895 in a learned book by Ernst Maass[61] that he was a *daimon* of the underworld. But it is hardly tenable; the evidence indicates that he was a legendary poet and musician, first mentioned in the second half of the sixth century BC, supposed to be the author of poems of a religious and cosmological character, and associated with mysteries whose initiates practised vegetarianism and other forms of austerity.[62] Material discovered since Miss Harrison's time has increased our knowledge of Orphism. For example, we now have more of the tablets inscribed with Orphic poetry that were placed in tombs, some of which she discusses; some of these contain allusions to Dionysos which justify Miss Harrison and others who have thought the poems to be connected with the worship of that deity.[63] They have not confirmed Miss Harrison's belief that the soul of the initiate became identical with Dionysos; but they have shown that the soul was believed to have a particle of divine being which made it possible for its existence to continue after death. She believed that the Dionysiac and Orphic mysteries had a genuine religious element that was lacking in the worship of the Olympians. Renate Schlesier[64] has acutely observed that 'she is at once attracted and repelled by ecstasy and asceticism'; her sympathies are divided between the ascetic Orpheus, preacher of vegetarianism, and the ecstatic maenads, eaters of raw flesh, who tear him to pieces. In the religion of Dionysos as she conceives it, she would seem to have found a way of preserving those elements of Christianity which appeal to her while eliminating others.

Some accounts of the influence of *Prolegomena* leave the impression that its main importance consisted in its advocacy of the theory that all myth was derived from ritual; others find its main importance to lie in its account of the worship of Dionysos. But that element by no means exhausts the value of the book. Building on the results of the important German work of the preceding century, Miss Harrison introduced English readers to a side of Greek religion of which few of them can previously have had much notion. A particularly notable feature of the work is the way in which its author uses art, as well as literature, to explain religion.[65] Its author's elegant and highly individual style marks it off from the work of most classical scholars. That style has several features characteristic of the *fin-de-siècle*. The modern reader may not care for all of these; in particular for the translations into rhyming verse of the late Romantic type, by Gilbert Murray and others, in which Greek poetry is quoted. These are singularly remote from the nature of the original. The book has some of the disadvantages, as well as the advantages, of being in its way a work of art.

In the years after the publication of *Prolegomena* Miss Harrison's relationship with Cornford was especially close; their regular bicycle rides together were the occasion of an especially fruitful exchange of ideas. It is clear that Cornford's marriage in 1909 caused her great emotional distress. Cornford's wife was Frances Darwin, daughter of Sir Francis Darwin by his first wife, formerly Ellen Crofts, who had been one of Jane Harrison's closest friends since they had been undergraduates at Newnham together. Mrs Cornford, who was a minor poet not without talent, was devoted to Miss Harrison, whom she had known all her life, and was eager for the bicycle rides and the intimacy that accompanied them to continue. But the strain of this situation became too great for all those concerned, and Jane Harrison went through a period in which ill health was accompanied by emotional distress. It was at this time, in 1909, that Augustus John painted the remarkable portrait of Jane Harrison now in the Combination Room at Newnham College; in this the marks of that distress can be discerned. 'Did it never occur to you', Mrs Cornford once asked her husband, 'that she might be in love with you?' 'No, never,' Cornford replied. 'She meant a great deal to me, but she was old enough to be my mother.'[66] It seems to me that this and other passions of Jane Harrison were not passions of a sexual kind; indeed, it may well be that her early experience with her step-mother and her many children had made it difficult, if not impossible, for her to entertain ordinary sexual feelings. But emotional intimacies like those which played so great a part in Jane Harrison's life and work could cause jealousy and distress no less than those occasioned by sexual passions.[67] In the same year of 1909 there came up to Newnham Hope Mirrlees, the last of the persons to whom Jane Harrison became devoted.

During this period Jane Harrison maintained intense intellectual activity, and she had by no means lost her youthful sensitivity to new impressions. Indeed, that sensitivity seems to have become almost febrile. She was carried away by Henri

Bergson's *L'évolution créatrice*, which had appeared in 1907; his emphasis upon *l'élan vital* and his exaltation of intuition greatly appealed to her, as did his concept if *la durée*, the time during which perpetual motion and change subsist. In 1909 lectures given at Cambridge by A. R. Radcliffe-Brown made her acquainted with the sociology of Emile Durkheim. His main work, *Les formes élémentaires de la vie religieuse*, came out in the same year as her own *Themis*, but his view that religion originated as the expression of the collective mind of societies had been made clear enough by his earlier writings.[68] At almost the same time Sigmund Freud brought out his *Totem and Taboo*, another work that powerfully influenced her. Freud's emphasis on sexuality distressed Miss Harrison, who had been horrified by the obscenities in Joyce's *Ulysses*; but Freud's view of totemism was in accord with her theory of the origin of religion and the sacramental character of sacrifice.

The difficult word Themis is usually taken to mean 'divinely instituted order';[69] the personified Themis, according to Hesiod, was the first consort of Zeus and by him the mother of Dike (Justice), Eirene (Peace) and Eunomia (Law-abidingness). The book *Themis*[70] derived its initial impetus from the discovery in 1904 at Palaikastro in eastern Crete of a stone inscribed with two copies of a Greek hymn; the inscription dates from the second century AD, but the hymn itself must be much earlier, perhaps written during the fourth century BC, and based on religious notions that go back very much earlier. The hymn is addressed to Zeus, but the Zeus whom it addresses is very different from the classical Greek Zeus; he is a god of fertility, who has disappeared during the winter months, and is now urged to return and leap into flocks, crops, houses, cities, ships, citizens and into Themis (but the word Themis may have been qualified with an adjective that limits its meaning to 'order' of some particular kind). In the translation which Gilbert Murray supplied to Miss Harrison, the expression I have rendered by 'leap into' is mistranslated as 'leap for'. But in general her interpretation is not very different from that of M. L. West, the latest scholar to publish a critical examination of the hymn;[71] indeed, if West is right in thinking that 'the greatest Kouros, the son of Kronos' is said to have 'gone to earth', her interpretation is strengthened.[72] This remarkable evidence that the god who was to become the greatest of the Olympians was in Crete identified with a spirit of fertility encouraged Miss Harrison to believe that *all* Greek gods had started as such spirits. From the Cretan hymn she goes to the myth of Zagreus, which this time has a different function in her scheme.

Just as the Kouros is the projection of the band of his worshippers, Miss Harrison argues, so is Dionysos the projection of his *thiasos*, the band of his worshippers. 'Omophagy', in the words of Albert Henrichs,[73] 'is now seen as the constitutive act of a totemistic organization which established "group-unity". The Zagreus myth is no longer the explanation for a sacramental meal, but a blueprint for an initiation of a tribal group.' Like their god, those initiated into the mysteries of Dionysos experience death and rebirth. In the use made of the concept of initiation here we see the influence of Arnold van Gennep's famous book *Les rites de passage*, which had appeared in 1909; but the notion of the god as a projection of the band of worshippers is in accordance with Durkheim's theory of the origin of religion. Miss Harrison's attempt to link the *thiasos* of Dionysos with the Kouretes by an impossible etymology, taking the name of the dithyramb, a song honouring Dionysos, to have meant originally 'the song that makes Zeus to beget' did little to recommend her interpretation.

She now draws attention to a fragment of the *Cretans* of Euripides[74] in which the chorus describe themselves as initiates of Zeus of Ida – this means the Cretan mountain – and of the thunder of night-wandering Zagreus, who have feasted on raw meat and held up torches to the Mountain Mother and with the Kouretes have been consecrated and received the name of

Bakchos, a name of Dionysos that could be applied to those initiated into that god's mysteries. From the identification of Zeus with the 'greatest Kouros' of the Palaikastro hymn, Miss Harrison goes on to identify not only these deities, but *all* the Greek gods and heroes with the Spirit of the Year, the Eniautos Daimon, as she calls him, putting together two words which are not combined to form this expression in any extant text.

A god, in Miss Harrison's view, is not essential to a religion; following Durkheim, she points to the example of Buddhism. 'Collective emotion, *mana*, sacramentalism,' she wrote (p. 488), '... all existed before they blossomed into the figure of a god. The spirit, the *daimon*, who may later develop into a god, originates as a projection of his band of worshippers.' In the case of Dionysos, his usual band of worshippers, the maenads, were female; but this difficulty was disposed of by recalling that maenads were ritual 'mothers of the holy child'. Ritual and myth, the *dromenon*, the thing that is done, and the *legomenon*, the thing that is said, are now said to originate together; 'ritual is the utterance of an emotion, a thing felt in *action*, myth in words or thoughts'. Anthropomorphism, Miss Harrison argues, is a late development in religion; in the beginning the spirit is imagined in the shape of his totemic animal. In eating that animal, the worshipper eats his god; he does this in order to possess his magical power, his *mana*. Just as Dionysos died and was resurrected, so the initiate in his mysteries undergoes symbolic death and resurrection. Poems written on tablets found in tombs in Italy and in Crete – more such tablets have been discovered since – seemed, as Miss Harrison had already argued in *Prolegomena*, to indicate that in virtue of the divine element in the composition of man, an initiate might attain life after death. This theory of sacrifice and its accompanying ritual could be made use of to explain the origins of certain religious institutions. The book *Themis* includes a chapter by Cornford in which he puts forward a theory of the origin of the Olympic Games in the race that accompanied sacrifices at the grave of the hero Pelops. It also includes an excursus by Murray in which he argues that tragedy originated in a ritual dance relating to the death and resurrection of Dionysos, and in a book published in the same year as *Themis*, Cornford put forward a similar theory of the origin of Attic comedy.[75]

Although Miss Harrison sees the history of Greek religion in terms of evolutionary theory, and the Olympian gods represent a comparatively advanced stage of evolution, her emotional sympathies continued to be all on the side of the earlier stages of that history. The Olympians are simply idealised humans, and she dislikes what she calls their 'chill remoteness'. When she speaks of them, her streak of silliness comes out; Zeus is called 'bourgeois', Apollo is called 'a parvenu' and 'a prig'. 'It is when religion ceases to be a matter of feeling together,' she writes (p. 487), 'when it becomes individualized and intellectualized, that doubts gather on the horizon.' What Matthew Arnold had called 'the power not ourselves making for righteousness' becomes identical with Themis, who is 'the "herd instinct", the collective conscience, the social sanction' (p. 485). 'To say that life and force are the same as moral good,' writes Miss Harrison on the last page, 'and to label the mystical marriage of the two "God", is to darken counsel. It is to deny that very change and movement which *is* life, it is to banish from a unified and sterilized universe "l'Evolution Créatrice".'

In the April of 1912, the year of the publication of *Themis*, Miss Harrison's close friend and collaborator, Gilbert Murray, gave the lectures at Harvard which appeared the same year with the title *Four Stages of Greek Religion*.[76] After a chapter about the beginnings of Greek religion very much on Miss Harrison's lines, and featuring the Eniautos Daimon, Murray came to the Olympians, whom he defended as having reduced the horrors, such as superstition and indecency, which in his view were part of the earlier religion, 'brought order into the old chaos', adapted religion to new social needs, and 'worked for concord and fellow-

feeling throughout the Greek communities'. He obviously shared
Miss Harrison's feeling that the Olympian religion was deficient
in religious quality; yet he did not regret this, for he believed that
it led the way towards the kind of enlightened scepticism that he
approved of.

But if the study of religion in Homer, Greek lyric and Greek
tragedy by the scholars of the last half-century has shown
anything, it has shown that that religion, far from being the
frivolous and superficial affair that Miss Harrison thought it,
represents human life and the working of the universe in a
manner which, although it is not at all like that of Christianity,
cannot be thought lacking in profundity.[77] That impression is
confirmed by the art of the period in question; the sculptures of
the temple of Zeus at Olympia and of the Parthenon cannot
lightly be dismissed as lacking power to arouse strong emotions.

Themis made less of an immediate impression than *Prolegomena*.[78]
This was partly because the outbreak of war in 1914 distracted
attention from such matters. But sociological theory was not
acceptable to all, and the speculative elements in the theories of
Durkheim and Bergson inevitably provoked criticism. In France,
it is true, it received a notable and appreciative review in the *Revue
de l'histoire des religions* from Adolphe Reinach, a member of
Durkheim's school, who later perished in the war; and in 1928
Miss Harrison's work was made use of in an important article
by Louis Gernet, who, though not properly esteemed by his
contemporaries, is now recognised to have been a scholar of great
distinction.[79] But in general the school of Durkheim gave *Themis*
a cold reception; its Bergsonian element did not appeal to them.[80]
In Germany the book made little impact. During the war Murray
managed to convey a copy of it to the greatest living Greek
scholar, Wilamowitz, who wrote in reply that he respected Jane
Harrison but was 'not disposed to explain the perfect structure by
the embryo nor Plato by the superstitions of his grandmother'.[81]
Until the end of his life Wilamowitz remained strongly resistant

to the use of ethnology and the comparative method to investigate early Greek religion.

Miss Harrison's dependence on Durkheim was in several ways unfortunate. First, his view of totemism was based almost entirely on the study of the aborigines of the southern part of Central Australia. He considered these people to be the simplest of the extant communities, and inferred that they had preserved most features of the earliest communities, by no means a safe inference. Soon after the publication of *Themis* his theory of totemism was exploded;[82] totemism is only one among many methods of classification. In the words of Robert Lowie,[83] 'totemism is a widespread but by no means universal phenomenon, while the belief in spiritual being is universal; precisely those rudest tribes which have a decisive bearing on the question are non-totemic animists'. Next, the sharp dichotomy between the sacred and the profane which Durkheim drew is a mistake; in many cultures they shade into each other.[84] Further, in Durkheim's theory, which Miss Harrison took over, the belief in supernatural beings is quite a late development. There may indeed be rituals which have come into being without belief in a spirit or a god; but surely such beliefs, starting perhaps with fear of ghosts, are of very early origin. Albert Henrichs in a valuable series of studies of Dionysos and his worship has protested against interpretations which ignore the fact that Dionysos was not thought of by his worshippers as a projection of his *thiasos*, but as a god.[85] Durkheim is a great figure in the history of sociology, and his view of religion as the cement of primitive communities can hardly be contested. But his theory of the origin of religion, with its high degree of generalisation, hardly does justice to the immense variety of human behaviour, and takes insufficient note of the importance of belief in the supernatural.[86] Walter F. Otto,[87] never sufficiently appreciated by English-speaking scholars, who gave the Olympian religion full credit for its achievements, in discussing origins spoke not of 'myth and ritual' but of 'myth and cult', thus avoiding the implication that all ritual at first lacked any connection with belief.

Among classical scholars, the extreme claims made for the Eniautos Daimon were the subject of much criticism. Throughout his long career, in the face of strong opposition, Murray continued to defend it, but for all his prestige his defence had little success. His own theory of the origins of tragedy was in 1927 severely criticised by Sir Arthur Pickard-Cambridge, whose still valuable book *Dithyramb, Tragedy and Comedy* should be read in the original edition of 1927 and not in the travesty presented in 1962 as a 'second edition' by T. B. L. Webster; someone ought to reprint the original book. The cause of the Eniautos Daimon was not helped by the enthusiastic activity of minor writers who took up the theories of the group in popular books, some of them of very dubious quality.[88] On the whole, the group's credit, least among classical scholars, between the end of the Great War and about 1960 did not stand high. Even E. R. Dodds, always a loyal pupil of Murray, was wary of quoting Jane Harrison, even in the course of an account of Dionysiac religion in Euripides' *Bacchae* in which he upheld the sacramental theory.[89]

The war utterly changed most English people's lives, and Jane Harrison was no exception. She had always been fascinated by Russia, the fascination being connected in her mind with her eccentric and at times sentimental passion for bears, which she regarded as her own totem animals.[90] She now threw herself into war work designed to alleviate the sufferings of Russians, and at the same time she studied the Russian language with passionate enthusiasm. A striking feature of the verbs of Russian and other Slavonic languages is the contrast between perfective forms, which present an action considered as completed, and imperfective forms, which consider an action as being in progress; thus in the sentence 'They hunted the stag all day' the verb would be rendered by an imperfective and in the sentence 'They hunted down the stag' a perfective would render the expression 'hunted down'. This distinction seemed to her perfectly calculated to bring out Bergson's notion of *la durée*, and in her pamphlet *Aspects, Aorists and the Classical Tripos* (1919) she suggested that the best possible humanistic education could be attained if Russian were to be studied in the Tripos together with Greek. There was something unbalanced about this extreme Russophilia; like A. A. Milne, Miss Harrison tended to forget that bears have several unpleasant habits. Prince Mirsky, a great admirer of Jane Harrison, wrote that 'her love could make you, if you were a Russian, quite uncomfortable, so undeserved and unjustified did it seem'.[91] At this time she turned away from her former studies; she wrote in her introduction to the second edition of *Themis*, which appeared in 1925, that for nearly ten years she never opened a Greek book.

Yet after the war her college life in Cambridge resumed its course, and according to Mrs Stewart it 'had never been fuller or more appreciated' than at this time. She took up the study of Persian; she became a magistrate and enjoyed sitting regularly on the bench; in 1920 she visited Spain, where she delighted in the elaborate ceremonial of the cathedral of Seville. On this trip she was accompanied by Hope Mirrlees. 'In my old age,' Jane Harrison wrote in her autobiography, 'Fate has sent me, to comfort me, a ghostly daughter, dearer than the children of the flesh'.[92] Hope Mirrlees was a keen student of Russian, and in 1926 the two brought out a joint work, *The Book of the Bear*.

In 1922 Jane Harrison surprised all her friends by leaving Cambridge and taking off, in company with Hope Mirrlees, to live in Paris. She left, she wrote in her memoirs, 'with infinite regret'. 'I began to feel', she wrote, 'that I had lived too long the strait academic life with my mind intently focussed on the solution of a few problems. I wanted before the end came to see things more freely and more widely, and, above all, to get the new focus of another civilisation.' Before she left, she destroyed most of her papers, including all Gilbert Murray's letters. Russia, luckily for her, was closed to her, so she went to France instead. Before leaving England she brought out in 1921 her *Epilegomena to Greek Religion*, in which she set out 'to summarize as briefly as possible the results of many years' work on the origins of Greek Religion, and to indicate the bearing of these results on religious questions of today'.

Again Miss Harrison strongly insists that 'the discovery of its social origin is the greatest discovery yet made in the scientific study of religion'. Totem, taboo and exogamy are presented as closely linked facets of group unity, and the importance of initiation rites and their connection with groups like the Kouretes and the *thiasos* of Dionysos is strongly stressed. In course of time the group comes to be dominated by a single person, the medicine man or king-god; in consequence there comes into being the spirit, later the god. Fertility rituals, several examples of which from different cultures are adduced, lead to the creation of tragedy and comedy as they had been envisaged by Murray and Cornford. Myth and rite are 'practically inseparable'; 'the *daimon* is born of the rite'. C. G. Jung, whose *Psychology of the Unconscious* had appeared in English translation in 1919, had distinguished 'directed thinking', which means thinking of the kind ordinarily used in scientific research, from 'dream or phantasy-thinking', which 'turns away from reality and sets free subjective wishes'. Primitive theology and mythology spring from dream-thinking, but later theology of the kind we find in Homer spring from directed thinking. Since a god of the *daimon* type is too near, too intimate to bring relief to men who have passed beyond the primitive stage and are struggling with the conflict against their environment, this kind of theology is now treated more sympathetically than it had been treated in Miss Harrison's earlier works. In her preface to the second edition of *Themis* (1925) Miss Harrison wrote that the psychology of Freud had taught her that the full-blown god, the Olympian, had a biological function which could never be adequately filled by the *daimon*. But in the religion of today, she writes, there has been a kind of movement backwards towards the belief of early times. The Pope, at that time Pius XI, is quoted as having said that the essence of Modernism is Immanence, and nowadays God is no longer envisaged as external, but is sought by men within their own souls. Rather surprisingly, Jane Harrison deduces from this that 'the core and essence of religion today is the practice of asceticism'. Since physical life has now been secured by civilisation and by modern science, 'religion turns not to the impulsion of life but its betterment, and the betterment of life involves asceticism – the expulsion of evil'. It would seem that the Russian influence is responsible for this victory of Orpheus over the maenads; the Russian philosopher Vladimir Soloviov is quoted as thinking that 'shame is the sign manual of human consciousness, and shame issues in asceticism'. Miss Harrison hastens to add that the kind of asceticism she means is not mere negation; she insists that it must be consistent with the cultivation of the Bergsonian *élan vital*.

Jane Harrison, accompanied by Hope Mirrlees, lived for three years at the American Women's Club in Paris, where she found that though the people were kindness itself, 'intellectually they were just nowhere'. It was here that she wrote her brief but delightful autobiography, which was published in 1925, in an attractive small volume, by the Woolfs' Hogarth Press; Virginia Woolf admired Miss Harrison, and had visited her in Paris in 1923. In that year they returned to England; they found a very small house in Mecklenburgh Street, in Bloomsbury, where Miss Harrison died on 15 April 1928.

Near the end of her memoirs she wrote:

Life does not cease when you are old; it only suffers a rich change. You go on loving, only your love, instead of a burning, fiery furnace, is the mellow glow of an autumn sun. You even go on falling in love, and for the same foolish reasons – the tone of a voice, the glint of a strangely set eye – only you fall so gently; and in old age you may even show a man that you like to be with him without his wanting to marry you or thinking you want to marry him.

Jane Harrison was prone to fall in love, and her love-affairs were closely connected with her work. But as the passage I have quoted implies, she was old-fashioned enough to connect sexual relations with marriage, and she came to realise early on that marriage was not for her. She tells us all this with a calm dignity that should make the matter clear enough to anyone who is not concerned to identify her with modern causes or to make up a melodrama about her life.

For some fifty years after the First World War, the work of Miss Harrison and that part of the work of her collaborators that stood in close relation to her was not highly valued by students of Greek religion. True, her influence and that of her friends spread to the study of Middle Eastern religions by scholars like S. H. Hooke and Theodore Gaster in the learned book *Thespis*, to which Murray wrote an introduction. In France scholars influenced by the school of Durkheim, like Louis Gernet[93] and Henri Jeanmaire, were influenced by her treatment of groups of worshippers and initiates. Of course the activity of the group, together with that of the German school founded by Usener, had helped to bring about a concentration on ritual rather than on myth that continued throughout the period between the wars. Fieldworkers in anthropology were grateful for the model with which that concentration provided them; thus Bronislaw Malinowski in his essay 'Magic, Science and Religion' of 1925 made an approving reference to Miss Harrison and Cornford, although Frazer's work meant more to him. The same concentration is found in the work of the scholars who during that period dominated the study of Greek religion. But the leading lights among those scholars, such as the Swede Martin Nilsson, the German Ludwig Deubner and the Canadian settled in Scotland, H. J. Rose, were all averse to the group's ethnological approach to Greek religion. I have already mentioned the attitude of Wilamowitz.

But it was not until about 1960 that Miss Harrison's reputation made a notable recovery. Among her favourite topics the most fashionable at the moment is that of initiations and *rites de passage*, but it was Van Gennep and not she who was the most important pioneer in this matter. The main reason why her stock has risen is that there are once more notable scholars who have found the courage to try to understand the early stages of Greek religion, a field in which speculation can hardly be avoided and certainty can hardly be attained. During the 1960s Walter Burkert produced a series of important studies of such rites; in Italy Angelo Brelich and his school and in France Pierre Vidal-Naquet handled the same topic, which has continued to be much discussed. Vidal-Naquet and also such colleagues of his as Jean-Pierre Vernant and Marcel Detienne are heirs, through Louis Gernet, of Emile Durkheim. Durkheim is one of the ancestors of structuralism, of which they have made use, sometimes with great effect.[94]

Although Jean-Pierre Vernant and his colleagues do not accept Miss Harrison's sacramental theory of sacrifice, they are, like her, among the heirs of Durkheim, and their theory[95] agrees with hers in accepting the notion, developed by Durkheim's followers Henri Hubert and Marcel Mauss,[96] that sacrifice is a bridge between the sacred and the secular. But her theory is closer to that of Burkert, who in 1972 brought out his now famous book about the origins of sacrifice, *Homo Necans*.[97] 'To a field still largely dominated by philological-historical positivism or by the residue of the Tylorian approach in Nilsson and Deubner,' he wrote in the translation of that book which appeared in 1983 (p. xiii), 'it brought a comprehensive and consistent application of the myth-and-ritual position; it introduced, after Harrison's *Themis*, functionalism to the study of Greek religion; it used a form of structuralism in interpreting the complexes of mythical tales and festivals; and it made a first attempt to apply ethology to religious history.' Burkett's theory of sacrificial ritual indeed owes less to Jane Harrison than to the work of the Swiss scholar Karl Meuli, who has traced back its origins to the longest period in human history, the age before the introduction of agriculture and pasturage, when man sustained himself by hunting. This brilliant hypothesis has a good deal more historical justification than that of Miss Harrison, though like her theory it can hardly claim to have established indubitable facts. Burkert has also put forward a theory of the origin of tragedy which has a point of contact with that of Murray and Miss Harrison; if tragedy gets its name from the sacrifice of a goat to Dionysos, as Burkert argues, then in his words 'whether we are entitled to see in the goat Dionysus himself impersonated, or to understand both goat and Dionysus as representing an "eniautos-daimon" or even the dying king, is difficult to assess'.[98] For Burkert, myth and ritual while close together are not necessarily dependent upon each other.[99] He has considerably refined the concept of ritual both by means of a structuralism that analyses what is actually done without assuming any original meaning and by using the analogy of animal rituals offered by the ethology of Konrad Lorenz and Sir Julian Huxley. But his acknowledgement of Jane Harrison as a predecessor is significant.[100] It is the fate of scholars that their writings are quickly superseded, and Jane Harrison is no exception to that rule. But even if we do not read our predecessors, we stand upon their shoulders, and Gilbert Murray's remark that nobody can write about Greek religion without being influenced by the work of Jane Harrison seems truer now than when he made it nearly forty years ago.[101]

NOTES

Abbreviations

Ackerman   'Jane Ellen Harrison: the Early Work', in *Greek Roman and Byzantine Studies* 13 (1972), 209–30.

AO   Jane Ellen Harrison, *Alpha and Omega*, 1915.

CRR   *The Cambridge Ritualists Reconsidered*, ed. W. M. Calder III, 1991.

EH   *Entretiens de la Fondation Hardt*.

HSCP	*Harvard Studies in Classical Philology.*
Peacock	Sandra J. Peacock, *Jane Ellen Harrison: the Mask and the Self,* 1988.
Prolegomena	Jane Ellen Harrison, *Prolegomena to the Study of Greek Religion,* 1903; 2nd edn, 1908; 3rd edn, 1921.
RSL	Jane Ellen Harrison, *Reminiscences of a Student's Life* (1925).
Stewart	Jessie Stewart, *Jane Ellen Harrison: a Portrait from Letters,* 1959.
Themis	Jane Ellen Harrison, *Themis: a Study of the Social Origins of Greek Religion,* 1912; 2nd edn, 1927.
Versnel, *TRMR*	H. S. Versnel, *Inconsistencies in Greek and Roman Religion: Transition and Reversal in Myth and Ritual* (1993).

1 Just as the polite term for *Quatsch* is *Geistesgeschichte,* so the polite term for this is *Wissenschaftsgeschichte;* the history of scholarship can be written effectively only by a real scholar.

2 Tina Passman, 'Out of the Closet and into the Field: Matriculture, the Lesbian Perspective, and Feminist Classics', in *Feminist Theory and the Classics,* ed. Nancy Sorkin Rabinowitz and Amy Richlin (1993), p. 181, discusses Jane Harrison in a paper in which she wishes to 'question the objection of traditional contemporary classics to the possibility of the existence of early matricentric culture'. 'This denial within the classics profession', she continues, 'is an aspect of a broad heteropatriarchal attitude that opposes the ultimate goal of feminism: the dismantling of patriarchy for an egalitarian, nonhierarchical ethic of self-governance and interaction between persons, groups and nations. At stake are two views of humanity: one that insists upon a hierarchy of values and persons, and sees the world in terms of dichotomous, "either/or" thinking, and one that asserts that all persons and opinions have value, conceiving of the world in terms of "both/and" thinking.' 'The real problem', she writes, 'is that Jane Harrison wrote like a dyke and lived like a dyke.'

3 In a letter quoted by Stewart (p. xi), quoted by Schlesier (p. 226, n. 130).

4 In the less than a hundred pages of her *Reminiscences of a Student's Life* (1925), a small book, beautifully produced by Leonard and Virginia Woolf at the Hogarth Press in 1925, Jane Harrison has given a delightful and illuminating account of her life and work. Her former pupil, Jessie Stewart, the widow of H. F. Stewart, Fellow of Trinity College, Cambridge, and an expert on French literature, in 1959 published *Jane Ellen Harrison: a Portrait from Letters* (1959) (henceforth

Stewart), a biography which contains a selection of Jane Harrison's letters to Gilbert Murray. Mrs Stewart does not pretend to evaluate Jane Harrison's work, but she knew her well for many years, and not only offers valuable material in the letters, but provides a lively and appealing account of her by a person who responded eagerly to the inspiration she gave to friends and pupils. Robert Ackerman, 'Jane Ellen Harrison: the Early Work', *Greek, Roman and Byzantine Studies* 13 (1972), 209–31 (henceforth Ackerman), is an excellent study by the biographer of Frazer. I was too severe in applying the adjective 'awful' (*Classical Review* 42 (1992), 236) to Sandra J. Peacock's book *Jane Ellen Harrison: the Mask and the Self* (1988); I had not then seen Ms Passman's production. The biography contains a fair amount of information of some value, particularly that which derives from the author's study of matter contained in the archives of Newnham College, some of it deposited by the companion of Jane Harrison's last years, Hope Mirrlees. But it is long-winded and diffuse, suffering from its author's naive Freudianism, preoccupation with social status, and whimpering feminism of the school that sees women as victims. She is not well qualified to assess the significance of Jane Harrison's work, nor is she able to get the feel of her country and her period. *The Cambridge Ritualists Reconsidered*, ed. W. M. Calder III (1991) contains besides other relevant matter a valuable article by Robert Ackerman called 'The Cambridge Group: Origins and Composition' (pp. 1–19). It also contains a learned and intelligent account of Jane Harrison's work by Renate Schlesier, called 'Prolegomena to Jane Harrison's Interpretation of Ancient Greek Religion' (pp. 185–226). For the bibliography of Jane Harrison's work, see Shelley Arlen's *The Cambridge Ritualists: an Annotated Bibliography of the Works by and about Jane Ellen Harrison, Gilbert Murray, Francis M. Cornford and Arthur Bernard Cook* (1990).

5 *RSL*, pp. 17–18; Jane Harrison did not get the words quite right.
6 *RSL*, p. 19.
7 *RSL*, pp. 80–1.
8 Darwin continued to be important for Jane Harrison; see her pamphlet *The Influence of Darwin on the Study of Religions* (1909, later reprinted in *Alpha and Omega* (1915), pp. 143–78).
9 *RSL*, p. 22.
10 *RSL*, p. 27.
11 Peacock, pp. 24f.
12 *RSL*, p. 35; F. C. Steadman in her life of Miss Beale was unable to find any other evidence for the existence of this rule (see Peacock, p. 29).
13 *RSL*, p. 29.

14 Peacock, pp. 28, 30.

15 See Ackerman, p. 210, n. 2.

16 Schlesier, *CRR*, p. 193, n. 33.

17 For succinct accounts of all these famous archaeologists, see A. Rumpf, *Archäologie I; Einleitung: Historischer Uberblick* (Sammlung Göschen, vol. 538, 1953); cf. *Archäologenbildnisse: Porträts und Kurzbiographien von klassischen Archäologen deutscher Sprache*, ed. R. Lullies and W. Schiering (1988).

18 Schlesier, *CRR*, pp. 192f. has rightly made this point, noting that even today many scholars fail to observe it.

19 W. M. Calder III, *CRR*, pp. 37–59, tries to demonstrate this fact by examining the persons who wrote in support of Jane Harrison and their credentials; but what matters is the quality of the work that she had so far published.

20 It is greatly to Jane Harrison's credit that though she had carefully read the attacks upon Pausanias by Wilamowitz and his follower A. Kalkmann, she defended her belief that Pausanias' book is 'the careful, conscientious, and in some parts amusing and quite original narrative of a *bona-fide* traveller' (p. vii). This view has been ably defended by Christian Habicht, *Pausanias' Guide to Ancient Greece* (1485); compare the recent editions of Book 1 by Domenico Musti and Luigi Beschi (1982) and by Michel Casevitz, Jean Pouilloux and François Chamoux (1992).

21 For excellent brief sketches of the study of Greek mythology in the nineteenth and twentieth centuries, see Walter Burkert, 'Griechische Mythologie und die Geistesgeschichte der Moderne', in 'Les études classiques au XIX et XX siècles: leur place dans l'histoire des idées', *Entretiens de la Fondation Hardt* (1980), 159–207 and Fritz Graf, *Griechische Mythologie* (1985) = *Greek Mythology*, tr. Thomas Marier (1993).

22 Heyne's *De causis fabularum seu mythorum veterum physicis* appeared in 1764; Friedrich Schlegel's history of Greek and Roman poetry of 1798 has chapters called 'Orphische Vorzeit' and 'Vorhomerische Periode des griechischen Zeitalters'; and Friedrich Creuzer (1771–1858) wrote 'Wer vom homerischen Olymp ausgeht, der ist gerade auf dem Weg, um die Uranfänge des religiösen Lebens unter den Griechen zu verfehlen' (the last two works are cited by Albert Henrichs in his brilliant Thyssen lecture *Die Götter Griechenlands: ihr Bild im Wandel der Religionswissenschaft*, given at Munich in 1986, first printed as a pamphlet, then reprinted in *Auseinandersetzungen mit der Antike*, ed. H. Flashar (1988), pp. 39f.).

23 See my review of Nirad Chaudhuri's life of him, reprinted in *Blood for the Ghosts* (1982), pp. 155–64. Delusions about this person are still prevalent; Ian Morris in *Cultural Poetics in Archaic Greece*, ed. Carol Dougherty and Leslie Kurke (1993), p. 19, tells us that Müller was 'one of the leading classical scholars of the day'.

24 On Usener's work on Greek religion, see Maria Michela Sassi in *Aspetti di Hermann Usener filologo della religione*, ed. A. Momigliano (1982); cf. Roland Kany, *Mnemosyne als Programm* (1987).

25 Fritz Graf, *Griechische Mythologie*, p. 44 = p. 40, has observed that the notion of a misunderstanding recalls Max Müller's belief that myth originated from 'a disease of language'; cf. Schlesier, in *CRR*, p. 189, n. 19.

26 An attempt to minimise the importance of Robertson Smith has been made by Morton Smith in *CRR*, pp. 251–61. But there can be no doubt about his influence on Durkheim and on Freud; see Sir Edward Evans-Pritchard, *Theories of Primitive Religion* (1965), pp. 51f. and *History of Anthropological Thought* (1981), pp. 69f.

27 A. H. Petiscus, *The Gods of Olympos* (1st edn, 1863; 20th edn, tr. Katherine Raleigh, 1892), p. vi; on this preface, see Ackerman, pp. 227ff.

28 See Ackerman, p. 227.

29 See Ackerman, pp. 216f.

30 See Calder in *CRR*, pp. 53f.

31 See Peacock, pp. 107–8.

32 *Prolegomena to the Study of Greek Religion* (1903; 2nd edn 1908; 3rd edn 1921).

33 *RSL*, p. 88.

34 See my Jane Ellen Harrison Lecture on Gilbert Murray in *Blood for the Ghosts* (1982), pp. 195–215 and R. L. Fowler, *CRR*, pp. 79–96.

35 See Dorothy Henley, *Rosalind Howard Countess of Carlisle* (1958).

36 An excellent account of the work of A. B. Cook is given by Hans Schwabl in *CRR*, pp. 227–49.

37 *Journal of Hellenic Studies* (henceforth *JHS*) 19 (1899), 205–51; 'Delphika'; 20 (1900), 99–114, 'Pandora's Box'; 23 (1903), 292–324, 'Mystica Vannus Iacchi 1'; 24 (1904), 241–54, 'Mystica Vannus Iacchi 2'. Jane Harrison amusingly describes (*RSL*, p. 57; cf. Stewart, p. 21) how the famous botanist Sir Francis Darwin chided her for writing about a *vannus* without knowing what it was; for an authoritative explanation, see Sir Roger Mynors's note on Virgil, *Georgics* 1, 166.

38 Albert Henrichs, in *Friedrich Gottlieb Welcker: Werk und Wirkung*, Hermes Einzelschriften, part 49, 1986, pp. 194–8, shows how Welcker saw that an earlier period of religious history had preceded Homer, but

in describing it employed 'the naive concept of a coherent religion of Nature that presented no problems', and how Rohde, stimulated by Nietzsche's criticism of that view, assigned special importance during the early period to the chthonic powers and the cult of the dead. Cf. also Henrichs, *Harvard Studies in Classical Philology* (henceforth *HSCP*) 88 (1984), 205–40.

39 E.g., August Mommsen, *Feste der Stadt Athen* (1898).

40 *The Nature of Greek Myths* (1974), p. 231.

41 Ibid., p. 235.

42 'Death in the Eyes: Gorgo, Figure of the Other', in *Mortals and Immortals*, ed. F. Zeitlin (1991), p. 115; originally *La mort dans les yeux: figures de l'autre en Grèce ancienne* (1985). See this essay (pp. 115–38), and also 'Feminine Figures of Death', in the same volume, pp. 95–110 = 'Figures féminines de la mort en Grèce', in *L'individu, la mort, l'amour: soi-même et l'autre en Grèce ancienne* (1989), pp. 131–52.

43 See M. P. Nilsson, *Geschichte der griechischen Religion*, p. 224.

44 Nilsson, *Geschichte*, p. 228 takes the former view; for the latter, see K. Latte, *Kleine Schriften* (1968), pp. 106–11.

45 See Vernant, 'Death in the Eyes'; cf. W. Burkert, *Greek Religion: Archaic and Classical*, p. 104.

46 See C. Robert, *Oidipus* (1915), II, pp. 16f., n. 4; A. Lesky s.v. Sphinx, Pauly-Wissowa, *Real-Enzyklopädie* III (1928), pp. 1703f.

47 See H. Lloyd-Jones in *Owls to Athens: Essays on Classical Subjects Presented to Sir Kenneth Dover*, ed. E. M. Craik (1990), pp. 205–6, with nn. 7 and 8.

48 See A. Henrichs, 'Namenlosigkeit und Euphemismus: zur Ambivalenz der chthonischen Mächte im attischen Drama', in *Fragmenta Dramatica: Beiträge zur Interpretation der griechischen Tragikerfragmente und ihrer Wirkungsgeschichte*, ed. H. Hofmann (1991), pp. 162–201.

49 As Schlesier, *CRR*, pp. 207f., points out, this use of the word is inaccurate. *Daimon* is commonly used of any supernatural agency that cannot be identified, and is often used to mean 'god'.

50 Albert Henrichs, *HSCP* 88 (1984), 231. Burkert, *Greek Religion* (1985), pp. 199–203, points out that there is no reason to believe that the chthonic divinities as a body were earlier than the Olympians.

51 Schlesier, pp. 231f., points out that at p. 261, n. 3 Miss Harrison understood by 'matriarchy' not 'the rule of females' but 'matrilinearity', and for an explanation referred not to the most famous advocate of belief in early matriarchy, the Swiss scholar J. J. Bachhofen, whose *Mutterrecht* appeared in 1861, but to Tylor. Miss Harrison does once quote Bachhofen, but the writers who first interested her in matriarchy are

more likely to have been Tylor and Sir Henry Maine, whose *Ancient Law* also came out in 1861.

52 See Simon Pembroke, 'Women in Charge: the Function of Alternatives in Early Greek Tradition and the Ancient Idea of Matriarchy', *Journal of the Courtauld and Warburg Institutes* 30 (1967), 1–35.

53 See Schlesier, *CRR*, pp. 213–18.

54 A. Rapp, 'Die Mänade im griechischen Cultus, in der Kunst und Poesie', *Rheinisches Museum* 27 (1872), 1–22 and 562–611.

55 See Schlesier, *CRR*, p. 222, n. 121.

56 This had been pointed out, before Nietzsche, by Welcker; see Henrichs, *Friedrich Gottlieb Welcker*, p. 22, with n. 189.

57 See A. Henrichs, 'Die Mänaden von Milet', *Zeitschrift für Papyrologie und Epigraphik* (hereafter *ZPE*) 4 (1969), 223–41; 'Greek Maenadism from Olympias to Messalina', *HSCP* 82 (1978), 121–60; 'Changing Dionysiac Identities', in *Jewish and Christian Self-Definition* III, ed. B. F. Meyer and E. P. Sanders (1982), pp. 137–60 and 213–36, especially pp. 143–7 with nn. 51–4; 'Loss of Self, Suffering, Violence; the Modern View of Dionysus from Nietzsche to Girard', *HSCP* 88 (1989), 205–40; Jan Bremmer, 'Greek Maenadism Reconsidered', *ZPE* 55 (1984), 267–86.

58 See Schlesier, *CRR*, p. 219, with n. 114, who points out that in connection with Orphism she uses words like 'sin', 'hell', 'evil', 'atonement', and 'church'.

59 As an appendix to *The Greeks and the Irrational* (pp. 270–82), Dodds reprinted his article 'Maenadism', which first appeared in the *Harvard Theological Review* 33 (1940); see also the introduction to his commentary on Euripides' *Bacchae* (1944; 2nd edn, 1960).

60 The first Greek author to mention this person is Ibycus, fr. 25 = 306 in Malcolm Davies, *Poetarum Melicorum Graecorum Fragmenta*; Ibycus was active in the second half of the sixth century.

61 *Orpheus: Untersuchungen zur griechischen, römischen, altchristlichen Jenseitsdichtung und Religion* (1895).

62 See Fritz Graf, 'Orpheus: a Poet among Men', in *Interpretations of Greek Mythology*, ed. Jan Bremmer (1987), pp. 80–106; also the volume *Orphisme et Orphée en l'honneur de Jean Rudhardt*, ed. Ph. Borgeaud (1991), especially Jan Bremmer, 'Orpheus: from Guru to Gay', pp. 13–30.

63 See H. Lloyd-Jones, *EH* 17 (1985) 269f. = *Academic Papers* I (1990), pp. 96f.; F. Graf. 'Dionysian and Orphic Eschatology: New Texts and Old Questions', in *Masks of Dionysus*, ed. T. Carpenter and C. A. Faraone (1993), pp. 239–58.

64 *CRR*, p. 224.

65 Albert Henrichs in the Thyssen Lecture, *Die Götter Griechenlands* (4 = 117), writes: 'Bebilderte Darstellungen der Geschichte der griechischen Religion sind aber bedauerlicherweise immer noch die Ausnahme, obwohl bereits 1903 die Engländerin Jane E. Harrison in ihrer *Prolegomena* auf so bahnbrechende Weise den Anfang gemacht hatte.'

66 Stewart, p. 112.

67 Even such an intelligent writer as H. S. Versnel has misunderstood this. In *Inconsistencies in Greek and Roman Religion*, vol. 1: *Transition and Reversal in Myth and Ritual* (1993) (henceforth *TRMR*), p. 24 he writes of Jane Harrison: 'She led an unorthodox life, which gave rise to many rumours, with such standard ingredients as libertinism in matters of sex and religion, more or less pronounced feminism, and hovering between the extremes of esthetic refinement on the one hand and the "beastly devices of the heathen" on the other.'

68 Notably by 'De la définition des phénomènes religieux', in *L'Année Sociologique* 2 (1899).

69 For a learned account of Themis, see R. Hirzel, *Themis, Dike und Verwandtes: ein Beitrag sur Geschichte der Rechtsidee bei den Griechen* (1907; reprinted, 1966).

70 *Themis: a Study of Social Origins of Greek Religion* (1912; 2nd edn 1927).

71 *HS* 85 (1965), 149–59.

72 H. S. Versnel, *TRMR* (1993), p. 27, n. 25, in the course of a learned discussion of the question of myth and ritual, calls West's conjecture 'very improbable'; but *pankrates ganos* and *pankrates ganous* both seem to me very difficult, and the conjecture gives good sense. 'To my mind,' Henrichs writes in a personal communication, 'the real problem with West's reading is the proleptic position of *gan*. One expects an adjective in this position, followed within the relative clause by the corresponding noun, as in Sophocles, *Antigone* 1118.' If I were worried by this consideration, I would suggest emending to *gan esbebekas*. But I am not; cf., e.g., Aristophanes, *Thesmophoriazusae* 315f.: *chrysolyra te Delon hos echeis hieran.*

73 *HSCP* 88 (1984), 231. See that article, and also Henrichs, 'Der rasende Gott; zur Psychologie des Dionysos und des Dionysischen in Mythos und Literatur', forthcoming in *Antike und Abendland* 40; also D. Obbink, 'Dionysus Poured out: Ancient and Modern Theories of Sacrifice and Cultural Formation', in *Masks of Dionysus*, ed. T. H. Carpenter and C. A. Faraone (1993).

74 Fr. 472 Nauck = fr. 3 Cantarella = fr. 79 Austin.

75 *The Origin of Attic Comedy* (1912), reprinted in 1993 with an introduction by Jeffrey Henderson.

76 The book became *Five Stages of Greek Religion* in the second edition of 1925.

77 See, for example, H. Lloyd-Jones, *The Justice of Zeus* (1971; 2nd edn, 1983); Jasper Griffin, *Homer on Life and Death* (1980). Vernant's conception of the Olympian religion as a coherent system in which each deity has his or her place and function supplies a further warning against the facile dismissal of Olympianism by people whose notion of religion is entirely based on Christianity or on some of its features; see 'La société des dieux', in *Mythe et société en Grèce ancienne* (1974), pp. 103–20 = *Myth and Society in Ancient Greece* (1980), pp. 92–109, and Vernant's inaugural lecture at the Collège de France of 5 December 1975 (English version in *Mortals and Immortals* (1991), pp. 269–89).

78 This was observed by Gilbert Murray in his Jane Ellen Harrison Memorial Lecture of 1928 (p. 13), although he himself thought that it marked a great advance on *Prolegomena*.

79 'Les frairies antiques', *Revue des études grecques* 41 (1928), 313–59, reprinted in *L'anthropologie de la Grèce antique* (1968), pp. 23–61. I do not mention the inaccurate English translation of this book that appeared in 1981.

80 See R. di Donato, 'L'uso e abuso dell'antropologia', in *Giornate Pisane: Atti del IX Congresso della F.I.E.C.*, 24–30 August 1989 (*Studi Italiani di Filologia Classica* 85 (1992), 1175–87).

81 Gilbert Murray, 'Memories of Wilamowitz', *Antike und Abendland* 4 (1954), 12. On Wilamowitz's treatment of Greek religion, see Albert Henrichs, '"Der Glaube der Hellenen": Religionsgeschichte als Glaubensbekenntnis und Kulturkritik', in *Wilamowitz nach 50 Jahren*, ed. W. M. Calder, H. Flashar and Th. Lindken (1985), pp. 263–505.

82 By A. Goldenweiser, 'Religion and Society: a Critique of Emile Durkheim's Theory of the Origin and Nature of Religion', *Journal of Philosophy, Psychology and Scientific Methods* 12 (1917) and 'Form and Content in Totemism', *American Anthropologist* NS 20 (1918); A. van Gennep, *L'état actuel du problème totémique* (1920).

83 In *Primitive Religion* (1936), cited by Evans-Pritchard, *History of Anthropological Thought* (1981), p. 162.

84 See Robert Parker, *Miasma* (1983), pp. 150f.

85 See the articles of Henrichs cited in nn. 57 and 71, and also his 'Male Intruders among the Maenads: the So-Called Male Celebrant', in *Mnemai: Classical Studies in Memory of Karl Hulley*, ed. H. D. Evjen (1984), pp. 69–91 and 'Between Country and City: Cultic Dimensions

of Dionysos in Athens and Attica', in *Cabinet of the Muses*, ed. M. Griffith and D. J. Mastronarde (1990), pp. 257–77.

86 See the criticism of Durkheim by Sir Edward Evans-Pritchard, *Theories of Primitive Religion* (1965), pp. 48–77, and *A History of Anthropological Thought* (1981), pp. 153–69.

87 *Die Götter Griechenlands* (1929; tr. M. Hadas, as *The Homeric Gods*, 1954); *Dionysos: Mythos und Kultus* (1933; tr. R. B. Palmer, as *Dionysus, Myth and Cult* (1965).

88 These drew heavy fire from Joseph Fontenrose, *The Ritual Theory of Myth* (1966); cf. G. S. Kirk, *Myth: its Meaning and Functions in Ancient and Other Cultures* (1970), p. 13; Versnel, *TRMR*, pp. 37–41.

89 See Albert Henrichs, *Jewish and Christian Self-Definition* (1982), pp. 137–60, and Dirk Obbink, in *Masks of Dionysus*, ed. T. Carpenter and C. A. Faraone (1993), pp. 65–86. Henrichs (p. 235, n. 216) writes: 'It is inexcusable that Dodds, while expressing a debt to "Gruppe's view" [the allusion is to O. Gruppe, *Griechische Mythologie und Religions-geschichte* (1906), pp. 729–37] of sacramental omophagy ['Maenadism', p. 166 = *The Greeks and the Irrational*, p. 277] nowhere revealed the full extent of his indebtedness to Jane Harrison . . . Instead, he advised his readers that her *Prolegomena* "should be used with caution".' True, but should one throw caution to the winds when reading *Prolegomena*?

90 See Albert Henrichs, 'Gott, Mensch, Tier', in *Klassische Antike und Neue Wege der Kulturwissenschaften: Symposium Karl Meuli* (1991), p. 151, n. 69.

91 D. S. Mirsky, *Jane Ellen Harrison and Russia* (The Jane Ellen Harrison Memorial Lecture, No. 2, 1930), p. 9.

92 Notice the word 'daughter'; there is no excuse for the gross language of Ms Passman, quoted in n. 3 above.

93 See n. 78 above. On Gernet and his relation to Durkheim, see S. C. Humphreys, *Anthropology and the Greeks* (1978), pp. 76–106 and R. di Donato's postscript to Gernet, *Les grecs sans miracle* (1983), pp. 403–20.

94 Most strikingly, for example, in Vernant's interpretation of the two versions of the myth of Prometheus in Hesiod's *Theogony* and *Works and Days* (*Mythe et société en Grèce ancienne* (1974), pp. 177–94 = *Myth and Society in Ancient Greece* (1980), pp. 168–85). But their use of structuralism has its dangers; see my essay 'Psychoanalysis and the Ancient World', in *Freud and the Humanities*, ed. P. Horden (1985), pp. 152–80 = *Academic Papers* (1990) ii, pp. 281–305 = *Greek in a Cold Climate* (1991), pp. 172–95.

95 See Vernant, 'Sacrifice et mise à mort dans la *thysia* grecque', *EH* 27

(1980), 1–39 (translated into English, but without the appended Greek text of Porphyry, *De abstinentia* II, 28, 4–30 and without the discussion that followed the reading of the paper, in *Mortals and Immortals* (1991), pp. 290–302).

96 *Essai sur la nature et la fonction du sacrifice*, in Année Sociologique 2 (1898), 29–138 = Mauss, *Œuvres* I (1968), pp. 193–307; translated as *Sacrifice; its Nature and Function* (1964).

97 English translation by Peter Bing, 1983; see also *Anthropologie des religiösen Opfers* (Munich 1983).

98 See *Greek Roman and Byzantine Studies* 7 (1966), p. 113, with n. 61 = *Wilder Ursprung* (1990), p. 38, with n. 61. It is worth noting that the author of a less convincing theory of sacrifice, René Girard, *Violence and the Sacred*, tr. Patrick Gregory (1977; French original, 1972), who does not mention Miss Harrison or any of her associates, can write (p. 306): 'All religious rituals spring from the surrogate victim.'

99 'Einen entscheidenden Fortschritt in der Theorie vollzog Jane Harrison im Alleingang, indem sie die von Durkheim entwickelte soziologische Betrachtungsweise übernahm': Burkert, in 'Griechische Mythologie und die Geistesgeschichte der Moderne', *EH* 26 (1980), 175. See the first two chapters of Burkert's *Structure and History in Greek Mythology and Ritual* (1979), and also the discussion of the problems concerning myth and ritual by Versnel, *TRMR*, pp. 15–88, with full discussion of its more recent phase.

100 I am most grateful for Renate Schlesier's learned discussion of Jane Harrison's work (cited in n. 2 above), to which the present essay is much indebted. But when she writes of Jane Harrison (p. 226, n. 130), 'Aside from rare (and generally negative) references to her work, a *damnatio memoriae* prevails, accompanied by a silent acceptance or rejection of her ideas', I would remind her of the works of Burkert, Henrichs and Versnel mentioned above.

101 I would like to thank Professor Albert Henrichs for his helpful comments.

Chapter 3

MARY PALEY MARSHALL

1850–1944[1]

John Maynard Keynes

Mary Marshall deserves a record of piety and remembrance, not only as the wife of Alfred Marshall, without whose understanding and devotion his work would not have fulfilled his fruitfulness, but for her place in the history of Newnham, now nearly three-quarters of a century ago, as the first woman lecturer on economics in Cambridge, and for her part in the development of the Marshall Library of Economics in Cambridge in the last twenty years of her life.

She came of that high lineage from which most of virtue and value in this country springs – yeoman farmers owning their own land back to the sixteenth century and beyond, turning in the eighteenth into thrifty parsons and scholars. The Paleys had been thus settled at Giggleswick in Yorkshire for many generations. Her great-great-grandfather took his degree at Christ's College, Cambridge, in 1733, and was headmaster of Giggleswick Grammar School for fifty-four years. Her great-grandfather, born just over two hundred years ago, was William Paley, Fellow and tutor of Christ's and 'the delight of combination rooms', Archdeacon of Carlisle, author of the *Principles of Moral and Political Philosophy*, which anticipated Bentham, and of what is generally known as 'Paley's Evidences' (*Natural Theology, or Evidence of the Existence and Attributes of the Deity Collected from the Appearances of Nature*), the reading of which a generation later by another Christ's man, Charles Darwin, put him on the right track.

She has bequeathed to the writer of these pages the small picture of the great Archdeacon which always hung in her room, and she once showed him a small packet, in an embroidered case, of the love-letters of this most unromantic of philosophers. One of the Archdeacon's grandsons was F. A. Paley, Greek scholar of the mid-nineteenth century, another was Mary Marshall's father, Rector of Ufford near Stamford, an evangelical clergyman of the straitest Simeonite sect. Her mother was a member of the Yorkshire family of Wormald.

In the last years of her life Mary Marshall put together short biographical notes which she called *What I Remember*.[2] She kept them by her chair down to her last days, and would, from time to time, add new passages as she sat there alone and another echo from the past came back to her. It will be published, for there is no more tender and humorous record of the early days of Newnham and the newly married Cambridge which blossomed from the desert when the ban on marriage was removed in 1882. Meanwhile I will steal from it here and there in what follows as much as is permissible, perhaps more, though much less than would be in place if the Notes themselves were not due to be soon published as she wrote them.

In these Notes she recalls her upbringing in the country rectory, where she was born on 24 October 1850. 'These twenty years were spent in a rambling old house, its front covered with red and white roses and looking out on a lawn with forest trees as a background, and a garden with long herbaceous borders and green terraces. I did not realise the beauty of the place until I visited it years later, as an old woman.' Reading her memories of those years in the same week as Coulton's records of his upbringing in Norfolk not much later (he, too, from yeoman farmers in Yorkshire, with records back to the sixteenth century, turned parsons and lawyers), is to understand what the world has lost in the atmosphere of plain living and high thinking and strictly restrained beauty and affection, which is the only

Eleanor Sidgwick, 1845–1936

Jane Harrison, 1850–1928

Mary Paley Marshall, 1850–1944 (on right)

Helen Cam, 1885–1968

education worth much. Perhaps no one who was not brought up as an evangelical or a nonconformist is entitled to think freely in due course – which means that before long no one will be so entitled, as is, indeed, obvious to see. Mary Marshall, by living for ninety-four years without decay of the grace and dignity and humour of character and sensibility which nurture as well as nature had given her, was able to show to the youngest student in her Library the beauty, the behaviour and the reserve of an age of civilisation which has departed.

But what a very odd, and sometimes terrible, thing are strict principles! Why can an age only be great if it believes, or at least is bred up in believing, what is preposterous? The Simeonite rector's beliefs were so strict that he could not even be intimate with any neighbouring clergyman; he thought Dickens a writer of doubtful morality (perhaps he was); when his dear Mary escaped from the narrow doctrine, it was a fatal breach between them; and she has recorded of her childhood – 'My sister and I were allowed dolls, until one tragic day when our father burnt them as he said we were making them into idols; and we never had any more.'

Yet he allowed his Mary to go up as a student to Cambridge when such a thing had never been done before. He had been the loving playmate of his children, and who could wish a better education than he devised for them as Mary Marshall recalled it to her mind eighty years later?

I can't remember much about our education till I was nine years old except that Mrs Markham's History of England was read aloud to us and Geography was learnt from two books *Near Home* and *Far off*, and that we played scales on the piano. In 1859 a German governess came and more regular lessons began. History, it is true, was chiefly dates and we learnt them by a Memoria Technica, beginning 'Casibelud Boadorp' etc., and Geography was chiefly names of Towns and Rivers. But we were taught French and German pretty thoroughly and the family talked German at meals. Science we learnt from *The Child's Guide to Knowledge* and *Brewer's Guide*. All I now remember of these is the date at which black silk stockings came into

England and 'What to do in a thunder storm at night', the answer being 'Draw your bed into the middle of the room, commend your soul to Almighty God and go to sleep.' We did a little Latin and even Hebrew with my father and some Euclid. As to story books, we read *The Wide, Wide World*, *Holiday House*, *Henry and his Bearer*, and *Sandford* and *Merton*. On Sundays we learnt the Church catechism, collects, hymns and Cowper's poems, there was a periodical called *Sunday at Home*, and we read and re-read the *Pilgrim's Progress* and the *Fairchild Family*. This had a prayer and a hymn at the end of each chapter, and some children I knew took all the prayers and hymns at a gulp, so as to get them over and then freely enjoyed that entertaining book. But our chief knowledge of literature came in the evenings when my father read aloud to us. He took us through *The Arabian Knights*, *Gulliver's Travels*, the *Iliad* and *Odyssey*, translations of the Greek dramatists, Shakespeare's plays and, most beloved of all, Scott's novels. These we acted in the garden and called ourselves by our heroes' names. The evening hour was looked forward to all day long and its memory has followed me through life. One point about this reading has always puzzled me. Though Scott was approved Dickens was forbidden. I was grown up before I read *David Copperfield* and then it had to be in secret. I suppose that there is a religious tone in Scott which is absent in Dickens.

In 1869 the Cambridge Higher Local Examination for Women over 18 came into being, and in the warmth of this newly risen sun the country chrysalis prepared to spread her wings. She and her father worked together at divinity and mathematics; her French and German were already good; and she went up to London for the examination. 'Professor Liveing invigilated and Miss Clough came and comforted me when I was floored by the paper on Conic Sections and was crying over it.' As a result of her performance in the examination she was offered a scholarship if she would go to Cambridge with Miss Clough. 'My father was proud and pleased and his admiration for Miss Clough overcame his objections to sending his daughter to Cambridge (in those days an outrageous proceeding). My father and she became great friends and in later years when we had dances at Merton Hall I can see them leading off in Sir Roger de Coverley.' He cannot have associated her too closely with her free-thinking brother, the poet, Arthur Hugh Clough, Matthew Arnold's Thyrsis. Indeed, her careful ways were more akin to her ancestor, Richard Clough, the famous agent of Sir Thomas Gresham in the reign of Elizabeth (who, it is curious to remember, was also the ancestor to Mrs Thrale). Between Mary herself and Anne Clough there was a deep and lasting affection.

Thus in October 1871 Mary Paley was one of the five students who went up to Cambridge to live with Miss Clough at 74 Regent Street (now the Glengarry Hotel), which became the nucleus of Newnham College. In the next year the industrious virgins became twelve and moved to Merton Hall 'with its lovely garden where the nightingales kept us awake at nights and with its ancient School of Pythagoras supposed to be haunted, though the only ghosts which visited us were enormous spiders'. It was terribly important that there should be no scandal, and the strictest discipline and propriety were enforced by the friends of the new movement of which Henry Sidgwick was the leader. But they were not a dowdy lot, as *Punch* of that day probably assumed. Mary Paley herself had noble features, lovely hair and a brilliant complexion, though she does not record that. And

there was my chum, Mary Kennedy, very beautiful with Irish eyes and a lovely colour. This caused Mr Sidgwick some anxiety. In after years Mrs Peile, a devoted friend, amused us by describing how in those early days of the movement he walked up and down her drawing-room wringing his hands and saying 'If it were not for their unfortunate appearance'. Some of the Cambridge ladies did not approve of women students and kept an eye on our dress. Mr Sidgwick heard rumours that we wore 'tied back' dresses (the then fashion) and he asked Miss Clough what this meant. She consulted us as to what was to be done. Could we untie them?

This characteristic passage, just as she used to talk of the old days, was written by Mrs Marshall in about her ninety-third year.

Three years went by, and then the grand excitement of two women, Mary Paley and Amy Bulley, sitting, as Newnham's first pioneers, for a man's Tripos, the Moral Sciences Tripos of 1874, the only examination at that time of which political economy

77

formed a part. It all had to be very informal by agreement with the examiners. I give the story of the last lap in Mary Marshall's own words:

We were examined in the drawing-room of Dr Kennedy's house in Bateman Street, the Kennedy of the Latin Grammar. He was rather excitable and hot tempered (we called him the purple boy).

The Tripos papers came by 'runners', as we called them, who after getting them at the Senate House hurried to Bateman Street: among these runners were Sidgwick, Marshall, Sedley Taylor and Venn. At the Examiners' Meeting there was at that time no chairman to give a casting vote, and as two voted me first class and two second class I was left hanging, as Mr Sidgwick said, 'between heaven and hell'[3] and Dr Kennedy made the following verses:

> Though two with glory would be cramming her
> And two with fainter praise be d—— her,
> Her mental and her moral stamina
> Were certified by each examiner.

> Were they at sixes and sevens? –
> O Foxwell, Gardiner, Pearson, Jevons!

As we were the first two of Miss Clough's students who attempted a Tripos we were made much of. The Miss Kennedys gave us very delicate light lunches, and after it was over they took us to stay with them at Ely until the results were known for fear that the excitement might be too great for us.

All the 'runners' were familiar Cambridge figures of my youth. Apart from Marshall, they were all very short, and had long, flowing beards. Though, perhaps, their beards were not as long then as when I knew them twenty-five years later. I see them as the wise, kind dwarfs hurrying with the magical prescriptions which were to awaken the princesses from their intellectual slumbers into the full wakefulness of masculine mankind. As for 'her mental and her moral stamina', succeeding generations for another seventy years were going to be able to certify that.

Next year, 1875, Sidgwick invited Mary Paley to come into residence at the Old Hall at Newnham, where Miss Clough had now assembled about twenty students, to take over from Marshall the task of lecturing on Economics to women students. What a galaxy of eminent and remarkable women were assembled at Newnham in those early days! Mrs Marshall in her notes mentions among those early students 'Katherine Bradley, "the Newnham poetess" (better known along with her niece as Michael Field), Alice Gardner, Mary Martin (Mrs James Ward), Ellen Crofts (Mrs Francis Darwin), Miss Merrifield (Mrs Verrall) and Jane Harrison', not one of them without at least a touch of genius. The mention of Jane Harrison led her to run on:

This was the Pre-Raphaelite period, and we papered our rooms with Morris, bought Burne-Jones photographs and dressed accordingly. We played Lawn Tennis and Jane Harrison designed the embroidery for our tennis dresses. Hers was of pomegranates and mine of Virginia Creeper and we sat together in the evenings and worked at them and talked. I had known her as a girl and even then she was called the 'cleverest woman in England'. Though in the end she read for the Classical Tripos she was nearly persuaded to read Moral Science by Mr Marshall, and she always afterwards called him 'the camel' for she said that she trembled at the sight of him as a horse does at the sight of a camel. She used to declare that she had brought about my engagement to him by stitching clean, white ruffles into my dress on that day.

For in the following year, 1876, Mary Paley and Alfred Marshall became engaged to be married. So far as she was concerned, it had been, I suspect, a case of love at first sight five years before. In her first term in Cambridge at 74 Regent Street she recalls:

My first recollections of Mr Sidgwick and Mr Marshall are the evenings when we sat round and sewed the household linen in Miss Clough's sitting-room. This was my first sight of Mr Marshall. I then thought I had never seen such an attractive face with its delicate outline and brilliant eyes. We sat very silent and rather awed as we listened to them talking to Miss Clough on high subjects.

In her first term she began to go to his lectures – in the coach-house of Grove Lodge, which had been lent for lectures to women. 'Mr Marshall stood by the blackboard, rather nervous, bending a quill pen which took flight from between his fingers, very earnest and with shining eyes.' Mrs Bateson, wife of the

Master of St John's, gave a small dance in the Hall of the Lodge. 'Seeing that Mr Marshall seemed rather melancholy, I asked him to dance the Lancers. He looked surprised and said he didn't know how, but he consented, and I guided him through its mazes, though being shocked at my own boldness. I did not speak a word, and I don't think he did either.' Next an invitation to tea in his rooms, the highest in the New Court of St John's, chaperoned by Miss Clough. There is a fascinating account of Marshall's lectures, one extract from which I cannot forgo:

In these lectures he gave us his views on many practical problems, e.g., dancing, marriage, betting and smuggling. As to marriage. 'The ideal of married life is often said to be that husband and wife should live for each other. If this means that they should live for each other's gratification it seems to me intensely immoral. Man and wife should live, not for each other but with each other for some end.'

To which Mrs Marshall added the comment, 'He was a great preacher.'

Meanwhile she had promised Professor Stuart to write a textbook for the Extension lectures. After the engagement he began to help her with it.

It was published in our joint names in 1879. Alfred insisted on this, though as time went on I realised that it had to be really his book, the latter half being almost entirely his and containing the terms of much that appeared later in the *Principles*. He never liked the little book for it offended against his belief that 'every dogma that is short and simple is false,' and he said about it 'you can't afford to tell the truth for half-a-crown'.

It was, in fact, an extremely good book; nothing more serviceable for its purpose was produced for many years, if ever. I know that my father always felt that there was something ungenerous in Marshall's distaste for this book, which was originally hers, but was allowed to go out of print without a murmur of complaint from her when there was still a strong demand for it. The book which replaced it in 1892, under a similar title and over his sole name, was of quite a different character, being mainly an abridgement of the *Principles*. The 1879 volume, so great an advance when it came out on what had gone before, is the little book in green covers, not the thicker one in blue Macmillan cloth.

In July of 1877 they were married. But their real honeymoon came, I think, in 1881, when, after four years as Principal of University College, Bristol, Marshall's health broke down and she took him for a long rest cure to Palermo. I fancy that this was the period of most unbroken happiness and perfect contentment in her life. Recalling it sixty years later she wrote:

We were five months at Palermo, on a roof, and whenever I want something pleasant to think about I try to imagine myself on it. It was the roof of a small Italian hotel, the Oliva, flat of course and paved with coloured tiles, and upon it during the day Alfred occupied an American chair over which the cover of the travelling bath was rigged up as an awning, and there he wrote the early chapters of his *Principles*. One day he came down from the roof to tell me how he had just discovered the notion of 'elasticity of demand'.

This is the beginning of a fascinating chapter which describes the Sicilian scene. Marshall, who was suffering from a stone in the kidney, was not unduly ill. His powers were at the height of their fertility. There was no controversy, no lectures, no tiresome colleagues, none of the minor irritations to his over-sensitive spirit which Mary was to spend so much of her life soothing away. Nature was kind and lovely. 'From the roof we had a view of the *conca d'oro*, the golden shell of orange and lemon groves stretching a few miles inland, and of the mountains which met the sea on either side and formed a semicircle of varied shapes.' They looked down upon a little court.

It was a small court but the most was made of it. The trellis work over the pathways was covered with vines loaded with grapes, and there was a lemon tree and an orange tree and plenty of flowers. The houses around had their balconies paved with coloured tiles, which especially near Christmas time were inhabited by turkeys, whilst pigeons lived in holes and corners.

She loved the morning visit to the market to buy fruit. All her life down almost to her latest days, Mary Marshall was a gifted amateur water-colourist, never so happy as when sketching. Whilst Alfred composed the *Principles* on the roof, Mary went out with her brush and colours.

The place I cared for most and in which I spent many hours, trying to make a picture, was the Cappella Palatina. It is small and dimly lighted by slit-like windows so that on entering from the sunlight hardly anything could be seen but a mass of dim golden shadows. Gradually, however, the wonderful beauty of outline and detail emerged. The outlines are Norman, and Saracenic workmen filled in the rich colour and oriental devices. Most beautiful of all was the golden apse, out of which loomed the great Christ's head.

They were months of perfect bliss.

For the next forty years her life was wholly merged in his. This was not a partnership of the Webb kind, as it might have become if the temperaments on both sides had been entirely different. In spite of his early sympathies and what he was gaining all the time from his wife's discernment of mind, Marshall came increasingly to the conclusion that there was nothing useful to be made of women's intellects. When the great trial of strength came in 1896 over the proposal to grant women's degrees he abandoned the friends of a lifetime and took, whatever his wife might think or feel, the other side. But Mary Marshall had been brought up to know, and also to respect and accept what men of 'strict principles' were like. This was not the first time that her dolls (which she was in risk of making into idols) had been burnt by one whom she loved.

Yet it was an intellectual partnership just the same, based on profound dependence on the one side (he could not live a day without her), and, on the other, deep devotion and admiration, which was increased and not impaired by extreme discernment. Nothing escaped her clear, penetrating and truthful eye. She faced everything in order that he, sometimes, need not. By a gift of character and her bright mind and, I think one should add, a sort of natural artistry, of which I have never seen the like, she could charm away the petty or the irritating or the unnecessary with an equable, humorous loving-kindness. Neither in Alfred's lifetime nor afterwards did she ever ask, or expect, anything for herself. It was always in the forefront of her thought that she must not be a trouble to anyone.

Thus splendidly equipped, she now merged her life in his. Both at Bristol and at Oxford, where they were soon to go, she lectured on Economics, and when they returned to Cambridge she resumed her lectureship at Newnham, where she was in charge of the students for many years. She kept a watchful eye over the proofs and the index of the early editions of the *Principles* and there are other ways of influencing the course and progress of a great book than open or direct criticism. The degree of D.Litt. of the University of Bristol was conferred on her. But she never, to the best of my recollection, discoursed on an economic topic with a visitor, or even took part in the everlasting economic talks of Balliol Croft. For the serious discussion she would leave the dining-room to the men or the visitor would go upstairs to the study and the most ignorant Miss could not have pretended less than she to academic attainment. Her holiday task was not to debate the theories of the Austrian economists, but to make water-colour sketches of the South Tirol. Indeed, her artistic gift was considerable. She seldom showed her work to her friends, but she exhibited regularly with the Cambridge Drawing Society, and has left to Mr C. R. Fay, who has deposited them with the Marshall Library, a substantial selection of the scenes, where she sat with her sketching stool and easel whilst the Master, on his '"throne" with an air cushion and a camp stool which when opened against a pile of stones made a comfortable back to lean against', defined, in a hand less steady than hers, the Representative Firm.

On their return from Palermo there was one more year in Bristol. In 1889 Marshall succeeded Arnold Toynbee at Balliol as lecturer to the Indian students in Oxford. At Oxford he had larger classes than at any other time, since 'Greats' men as well as the budding Indian Civilians attended his lectures. She records:

At that time Henry George's *Progress and Poverty* roused much interest. Alfred gave three lectures on it at Bristol which Miss Elliott said reminded her of a boa constrictor, which slobbers its victim before swallowing it. At Oxford he encountered Henry George in person, York Powell being in the chair and Max Müller on the platform. Shortly after another duel took place with Hyndman, who called forth Arthur Sidgwick's *Devil take the Hyndman*. Bimetallism and Home Rule were also raging about that time and were subjects too dangerous to mention at a dinner party.

The short interlude at Balliol, then at its highest point of brilliance and of fame, certainly introduced Alfred Marshall to a larger world than he had known previously. He became one of Jowett's young men. Jowett, who was on the Council of Bristol University, first came across him there, and the time at Oxford confirmed a friendship with both the Marshalls, whom he would afterwards visit at Cambridge. Mrs Marshall records:

My first sight of the Master was at a dinner party given by the Percivals. He and Henry Smith were on the Council of the College, they came regularly three times a year to its meetings and generally stayed at our house and these visits were a delight. They were such a well-fitting pair and seemed so happy together, for though Jowett was rather shy and silent unless with a congenial companion, he was quite at his ease with Henry Smith who was the most brilliant and humorous talker I have ever met. I used to sit up with them and Alfred till well after midnight. It took me about five years to feel quite at ease with Jowett, for his shyness was a difficulty, but after a while we got on quite well and only talked when we wanted to. I sometimes took walks with him and he would make a remark now and then and fill up the gaps by humming little tunes.

Thus the Marshalls easily took their place in Balliol and Oxford society. Evelyn Abbot, Lewis Nettleship, Andrew Bradley, Strachan Davidson, Albert Dicey and Alfred Milner were Fellows of Balliol.

The Women's Colleges had recently started and I had the great good fortune of getting to know Miss Wordsworth, the first head of Lady Margaret Hall.

She was wise and witty, her bon-mots were proverbial and walks with her were a joy. Then Ruskin was at Oxford giving drawing lessons, lecturing to crowded audiences and inciting undergraduates to make roads. Toynbee Hall was being founded and the Barnetts often came to Balliol to stir up the young men to take an active part. The Charity Organisation Society had just started. Mr Phelps was Chairman and Mr Albert Dicey and Miss Eleanor Smith (accompanied by her dog) regularly attended its meetings. There was also a Society led by Mr Sidney Ball for the Discussion of Social Questions, so the four terms of our life at Oxford were full of interest and excitement.

And there were Jowett's dinner-parties:

He enjoyed bringing his friends together and almost every week-end during Term he asked people to stay at the Lodge who he thought would like to meet one another or would be likely to help one another. His plan was to have a rather large and carefully arranged party on the Saturday which Arthur Sidgwick used to call a 'Noah's Ark' dinner, for so many strange animals walked in in pairs. One amusing pair was Lady Rosebery, a large lady, and the small Prince of Siam. There were the Goschens, the Huxleys, the Matthew Arnolds, Robert Browning, 'Dam Theology' Rogers, an Australian Prime Minister, Sir Robert Morier, Cornelia Sorabji and the Alfred Greys among many others. He liked to spend a quiet evening with his friends. He came once to meet Albert Dicey and Eleanor Smith, the sister of Henry Smith, who was as well known for her brusque home-truths as he for his genial humour. Another time he brought Ruskin, who told funny stories and made us laugh with quaint rhymes about little pigs, and Miss Smith who knew him well said she had never seen him merrier. Alfred happened one day to meet Professor Vinogradoff and was so much fascinated that he asked him to dine with us and meet Jowett who had arranged to come that night. There was a little stiffness at first, as Jowett had not met Vinogradoff and as usual was shy with strangers, but as the evening went on talk became more and more free; after dinner we sat out in the little back garden under the birch tree and a full moon and then it became what Jowett called 'good', on philosophy and poetry. I never heard him talk as freely as he did that evening and I would give much to be able to recall that conversation. He enjoyed discussing economic questions with Alfred and would bring out his little notebook and take down a remark that specially interested him. He once told me that Alfred's talk was the best he knew. At another time he said 'Alfred is the most disinterested man I have ever known.' Our faithful old servant 'Sarah' interested him and he was the only person to whom she would speak of her religious difficulties. When he stayed with us at Cambridge he would sit with her in the kitchen and talk them over.

The return to Cambridge in 1885 is best described in Mrs Marshall's own words:

By the end of four Terms we had quite settled in at Oxford. The small house and garden in Woodstock Road suited us well. I taught the women students, Alfred enjoyed teaching his big classes, and though he always felt that Cambridge was his true home, he thought that our future would lie in Oxford. However, in 1884 Fawcett died and Alfred was elected in his place, the only serious competitor being Inglis Palgrave, and in January 1885 we went to Cambridge, hired a house in Chesterton Road for a year and in 1886 Balliol Croft was built and we settled down there for good. In 1885 prices were still low and the contract for the house was £900, though on account of a mistake on the part of the architect it cost £1,100. For several years it was the only house in Madingley Road and we chose the site chiefly for its forest trees. Alfred took immense pains in planning the house and in economising space, especially in the kitchen department. He was anxious to have his study on a higher floor as he thought that in Cambridge it was well to live as far from the ground as possible. However J. J. Stevenson the architect persuaded him to be content with the first floor and a balcony.

It is a commentary on the change in the value of money that after Mrs Marshall's death, Balliol Croft, with nearly sixty years of its lease expired, was sold to another Professor migrating to Cambridge from Balliol for £2,500. It was part of Mrs Marshall's small inheritance still preserved from the Archdeacon's large profits as author, from the long Headmastership of Giggleswick in the eighteenth century, from the yeoman farmers of Yorkshire back into the mists of time, which was invested in this house; and has now filtered through to the University of Cambridge for the Marshall Library, the first-fruits of the bequest being the purchase in June 1944 of the original MS of Malthus's *Political Economy*.

For the next forty years 'one year passed much like another'. The Marshalls had a very small house and one faithful servant, but were endlessly hospitable not less to the rawest undergraduate than to visitors from the great world. The 'one faithful servant' deserves a separate word. For forty-three years Sarah, and after her death Florence. Sarah (Mrs Marshall wrote) 'nearly always gave warning in November, that most trying month, but I paid no attention, for I knew she would not leave'. She belonged to the Plymouth Brethren, the gloomiest sect of a gloomy persuasion.

She became an excellent cook and loved having great responsibilities. Though she considered it wrong to 'enjoy' herself she used to say that the happiest week in her life was when the British Association met at Cambridge and when there were about twelve at each meal; she ran the whole concern and would lie awake at nights considering the menus for the next day. At one time she was troubled by the feeling that she was not being of enough use in the world, but was consoled when she realised that by good cooking she was keeping Alfred in health and was enabling him to write important books.

Mrs Marshall knew how to win devotion. She recalls how Lady Jebb, who, coming 'to England in the 'seventies as a young American widow, took the place by storm, and don after don fell before her', once when the conversation was about servants, said that she believed very much in praise, and ended by 'Just think how much praise is required by the Almighty'.

In the earliest days of the Labour Movement the Marshalls used to invite the working-class leaders to stay. 'Ben Tillett, Tom Mann and Burnet were among our visitors and a specially delightful one was Thomas Burt.' Edgeworth would often be there. 'We had of course many visits from Economists from USA, Germany, Italy, France and Holland. We were very fond of Professor Pierson and his wife who stayed with us several times and of Professor and Mrs Taussig.' And, of course, we his pupils would be forever lunching there when there were interesting visitors for us to see, or taking tea alone in the study for the good of our souls and minds.

But apart from visitors the Cambridge society of those days formed a remarkable group:

I became a member of a Ladies' Dining Society of ten or twelve who dined at one another's houses once or twice a Term, the husbands either dining at their Colleges or having a solitary meal in their studies. The hostess not only provided a good dinner (though champagne was not allowed) but also a suitable topic for conversation, should one be required, and she was allowed to introduce an outside lady at her dinner; but it was an exclusive society, for one black ball was enough to exclude a proposed new member. Its members were Mrs Creighton, Mrs Arthur Verrall, Mrs Arthur Lyttelton, Mrs Sidgwick, Mrs James Ward, Mrs Francis Darwin, Baroness von Hügel, Lady Horace Darwin, Lady George Darwin, Mrs Prothero and Lady Jebb.

'There seem,' Mrs Marshall reflected in her extreme old age (and, I fear with justice), 'to be fewer "characters" now than in by-gone days.'

Most of the long vacations were spent in South Tirol, especially with Filomena, who kept the small wayside inn at Stern in Abteital.

One year we discovered that in the next village were assembled a large part of the 'Austrian school' of economists. The Von Wiesers, the Böhm Bawerks, the Zuckerkandls and several others. We boldly asked the whole company to a tea party in our enormous bedroom, which was the largest and most desirable room in the inn, and we afterwards adjourned to the tent shelter in the field nearby. Filomena was proud of having such distinguished guests and got up at 4 a.m. to make fresh butter and various delicacies for the entertainment. Von Böhm Bawerk was a wiry and agile little man, an ardent mountaineer who climbed a dolomite almost every day. This somewhat exhausted his economic energies and he did not want to discuss the Theory of the Rate of Interest, a subject which I had rather dreaded as he and Alfred had recently been corresponding warmly upon it. Professor Von Wieser was a noble-looking man and a delightful companion with a wife and daughter to match and I much enjoyed the return tea party which the Austrian School gave at the beautiful old peasant's house where they were spending the summer.

In 1920 a last, and rather disastrous, attempt was made to travel abroad. And after that the end of this sweet partnership was not far off.

The next three summers we spent in a lovely and lonely Dorset cove called Arish Mell, where he worked away at his third volume. But after *Industry and Trade* had been finished in 1919 his memory gradually became worse and soon after his doctor told me quietly that 'he will not be able to construct any more'. And it was so, though fortunately he did not know it. For in the old days he used to come down from his study and say 'I have had such a happy time, there is no joy to be compared to constructive work'.

Yet after Alfred Marshall's death there were still another twenty years of Mary Marshall of serene beauty and of deeper intimacy with Alfred's old pupils and their wives.

Forty years ago specialised lending libraries for students, from which they could take books away, were rare. It was an essential part of Marshall's technique of teaching to encourage his pupils to read widely in their subject and to learn the use of a library. To answer a question on price index numbers, a third- or fourth-year student would not be expected just to consult the latest standard authority. He must glance right back at least to Jevons and Giffen, if not to Bishop Fleetwood; he must look at any articles published on the subject in the *Economic Journal* during the last twenty years; and if he is led on to browse over the history of prices since the Middle Ages, or to compare the price of wheat in terms of wages in the times of Solon and of Charles II, no harm will have been done. A favourite pupil would be made to feel unworthy (i.e., of his great mission to be an economist and carry on the tradition of this high clerisy) if his eyes had scanned less than ten to a dozen volumes before his answer was shown up. He had three ways for making this possible. First of all, he established in his lecture-room a library of the more obvious books, small but, of course, much more extensive than any undergraduate's stock. When he resigned from his Professorship he passed this collection on to his successor. I think that I was its first official librarian and prepared its first printed catalogue. Beyond this was his own extensive collection, from which the pupil, after tea at Balliol Croft, would be expected to take away as many volumes as he could carry on the way home along the Madingley Road. Finally, he had long ago adopted a practice of breaking up learned journals, for which purpose he would sometimes acquire an extra set, so as to collect and bind the articles according to subjects. A great number of such volumes now lie in the Marshall Library, and this was a source which, together with its footnotes, could lead the raw student from one reference to another, until, if he persevered, he became, for that week at least, a walking bibliography on the subject. The preparation of these volumes, and subsequently the cataloguing of the items by author and subject in 'the brown boxes', had been for time out of memory, the special task of Mrs Marshall.

With all this, as a means of education and personal contact and inspiration, Mrs Marshall had been passionately in sympathy. The book-laden departing visitor would have a word with her down-stairs before he left, and she would see him out of the door and along the drive with the deepest satisfaction in her eyes. So when Alfred passed beyond her care, to preserve this tradition and to keep *his* books still living in the hands of the succeeding gener-ations of students became her dearest aim.

First of all, his library passed to the University for the use of students in *statu pupillari*, to be amalgamated with the existing students' library just mentioned, to become the Marshall Library of Economics. Next she set up a substantial endowment fund by payments under covenant, which she supplemented by paying into it an annual sum from the royalties of his books, the sale of which for some years after his death, so far from diminishing, increased. (In her will she has left the Library a further £10,000 and all her husband's copyrights). But above all she decided to become herself in her proper person the tutelary goddess of the books and of the rising generation of students. So in her seventy-fifth year, defying the University Regulations, by which it is now thought proper that we should all be deemed to be deceased at sixty-five, she was appointed Honorary Assistant Librarian of the Marshall Library of Economics; and so she continued for nearly twenty years. Every morning till close on her ninetieth year, when, to her extreme dissatisfaction, her doctor prohibited her (partly at her friends' instigation, but more on account of the dangers of the Cambridge traffic even to the most able-bodied than to any failure of her physical powers), she bicycled the considerable distance from Madingley Road to the Library (which in 1935 was moved to the fine and ample building, formerly the Squire Law Library, adjoining the Geological Museum in Downing Street), wearing, as she always did, the sandals which were a legacy of her Pre-Raphaelite period sixty years before. There she spent the morning in charge of the Library, first of all assisted by an undergraduate, afterwards, as the scale of the work grew, by a professional under-librarian, Mr Missen, from 1933 onwards; thus relieving of routine duties the successive Marshall librarians, Dennis Robertson, Ryle Ray and since 1931 (with an interval) Piero Sraffa. Keeping up 'the brown boxes' remained her special and most favourite task. She always spoke of the place as 'My Library'. Her heart and her head, as was the way with her, were equally engaged, and it became her main contact with the flow of life and the pulse of the Cambridge School of Economists which had begun to beat so strongly in Balliol Croft sixty years ago.

On 7 November 1936,[4] there was a small function in the Library when she presented a copy by William Rothenstein of his portrait of Marshall, which hangs in the hall of St John's College. Thereafter she sat at the head of the Library at a small central table under the portrait. (There is, fortunately, a most characteristic photograph of her so seated.) In 1941, when she was ninety-one, bronchitis began, for the first time, to make her attendance irregular. In 1942 she was not able to be there, except on 14 November, when she was present at the celebration of the centenary of her husband's birth[5] and made a speech in full vigour of mind, telling those present what happiness and delight her husband had drawn from the labours of his study. On 7 March 1944, she died, and her ashes were scattered in the garden of Balliol Croft.

Modest as morn; as Mid-day bright;
Gentle as Ev'ning; cool as Night.

NOTES

1 First published as an obituary in the *Economic Journal* 54 (1944), 268–84.
  Reprinted in *Essays in Biography* (New York: Horizon Press, 1951).
2 Mary Paley Marshall, *What I Remember*, with an introduction by G. M.
  Trevelyan (Cambridge 1947).
3 This is literally borne out by the parchment certificate of the Tripos
  results which has been found amongst Mrs Marshall's papers. It actually
  records that two examiners placed her in the first class and two in the
  second, and leaves it at that!
4 See *Economic Journal*, December 1936, p. 771.
5 Ibid., December 1942, p. 289.

Chapter 4

HELEN MAUD CAM
1885–1968

Janet Sondheimer

Helen Cam lived and worked in Cambridge for twenty-seven years (1921–48). She was already in her mid-thirties when she came to Girton, initially as a Research Fellow but clearly destined, as a medievalist, to fill the gap in College teaching left by the departure of Eileen Power. Helen Cam's election in 1927 to a Staff Fellowship brought her closer to the centre of College affairs, and her appointment in the same year to a University lectureship in the Faculty of History was something of a triumph, since this was one of the posts for which, under the University's new Statutes (1926), men and women were eligible to compete on equal terms. Some of Helen Cam's most notable and most recondite contributions to scholarship date from this inter-war period. These were also the years when from her study of local records and through keen-eyed observation she amassed the wealth of information – topographical, architectural, economic, social and political – which afterwards found its way into 'The City of Cambridge', the masterly full-length survey which she contributed to the *Victoria County History* (completed by 1951, published 1959). Helen Cam's interest in civic Cambridge was not purely historical. An ardent supporter of the Labour Party, she played a part, at times a very active part, in local politics and served on public bodies, chiefly those which had at heart the interests of young people, in or out of school. Even so, it was in the role of 'dedicated woman don' that Helen Cam made her deepest impression on Cambridge, both at Girton, where in 1940 she became Director of Studies in History, and in 1944 Vice-Mistress, and on the Faculty Board of History. In 1948, when it must have seemed that Helen Cam would see out the rest of her career, if not her days, in Cambridge, she suddenly took wing, crossing the Atlantic to become the first, and highly acclaimed, Zemurray Radcliffe Professor of History at Harvard. On her retirement six years later she settled down, not in Cambridge or in any other place where she had lived before, but in Sevenoaks.

Helen Cam was born on 22 August 1885 in Abingdon where her father, the Reverend William Herbert Cam, was headmaster of Roysse's School. The family surname derives from the River Cam in Gloucestershire where William had his roots. Maud, the second Christian name he and his wife Kate chose for their fourth child and second daughter, came straight out of Tennyson; Helen was perhaps in honour of the sainted mother of the Emperor Constantine the Great, dedicatory of the nearby church in Abingdon whose feast day falls on 18 August. But home as Helen remembered it was Birchanger in Essex where her father became rector in 1893. In the rectory and in the surrounding countryside she and the three younger sisters next in line received their education not from a governess but from their parents, in Helen's own words 'my first and best teachers'. William taught the girls mathematics and the art of observing natural phenomena, whether in the heavens or in the ground at their feet: astronomy and botany were among Helen's lifelong interests. From Kate, whose mother, sisters and aunts had been school-teachers or governesses, the girls learned to read, progressing from English to French and German, taking in history and geography on the way. Kate insisted on accuracy but still more on honesty: 'we were not allowed to pretend we understood anything if we did not'. Some of Kate's methods might be regarded today as dangerously progressive: 'if we asked her a question on some general or ethical

matter she would say: "What do you think about it yourself?"'
Haphazard as it may appear, the Birchanger curriculum was
geared to the Oxford Local Examinations which the girls took
from the age of 10, travelling to Oxford for the purpose. These
visits, which Helen described as 'a delightful break in the ordinary
routine', no doubt reinforced her ambition to follow in the footsteps of her father and two maternal uncles, Walter and George
Scott, who were Oxford graduates. But with a total of three sons
and six daughters to launch on the world her parents could not
afford to send her to Oxford unless she won a scholarship.
Although she was awarded a place at an Oxford college (reputedly
Somerville), it was a college attached to London University, Royal
Holloway, which offered her the needful scholarship.

At Royal Holloway, where she read for the single honours
degree in history recently introduced by London University,
Helen Cam met with well-deserved success, winning prizes and
further scholarships and graduating in 1907 with a First. Margaret
Hayes Robinson, the young, universally beloved Oxonian in
charge of the History Department, seems to have encouraged her
brightest students to note down 'subjects for investigation',
presumably with an eye to future research. Helen's list, unfortunately not dated, names topics which range in time from 'The
continental relations of the Anglo-Saxon kings' to 'A translation
of the correspondence of Pope Pius II', and in geographical
spread from 'A history of the Caucasian region' to 'A history
of Birchanger'. For her London MA dissertation she settled
eventually on a subject, 'Local government in Francia and
England', which had more to do with institutions than with kings
and so pointed forward to the studies in medieval administration
and jurisdiction in which she would later make her reputation.
The award for the year 1908–9 of a Fellowship in history at Bryn
Mawr College, Pennsylvania, enabled her to make contact, while
working on her thesis, with American medievalists of her own and
the preceding generation and introduced her to the resources of a

well-organised graduate school. She took advanced courses in Anglo-Saxon (the rudiments she had learned at Royal Holloway) and in other disciplines needed to support her research. Characteristically, she also seized the opportunity to inform herself about American history. With her sister Norah, who had enterprisingly enrolled as an undergraduate at Bryn Mawr, she travelled about, savouring the variety of the American landscape and falling in love with America.

Returning to England in 1909, Helen Cam successfully presented her MA thesis (published in 1912) and looked for a job. She is known to have applied for a university post at Sheffield, but when this failed she was happy to accept an appointment to the staff of Cheltenham Ladies' College, where she stayed for three years. Even if she had not planned it, this spell of schoolteaching was not a mere interlude. The life at Cheltenham, with its 'University' and Teacher Training Departments and its thousand or more pupils, was as far removed as could be from Helen's own girlhood experience and afforded her some precious insights into the workings, not only of the schoolgirl mind, but of a great institution. Although anecdotal evidence suggests that she taught chiefly (and brilliantly) the most senior girls, her curiosity was undoubtedly aroused by staffroom discussions of syllabuses and teaching methods appropriate to pupils of all ages; once captured, her interest in educational affairs led to an involvement with adult education and ultimately, by way of politics, to a disapproval of fee-paying schools such as Cheltenham; for Cheltonians, however, she always had a soft spot.

Helen Cam's return in 1912 as a lecturer to Royal Holloway College marked the true beginnings of her career as a full-time academic. In the ten years that followed she dedicated herself with equal zeal to her research, the focus of which shifted from the earlier to the later Middle Ages, and the education of her students. As a member of the University of London Graduates' Association she opposed proposals for university reorganisation under which teaching activities would have been concentrated in central London, thus depriving students, and resident students in particular, of the 'close intellectual intercourse' with their tutors they currently enjoyed. For some students, close encounters with Helen Cam could be overpowering; but if her erudition was alarming, her candour was appreciated and reciprocated, at least by bolder spirits. As one such, in later life a distinguished head-mistress but who arrived at Holloway 'very raw', long afterwards recalled: 'She was most encouraging and said I might get a First. I, being very socially-minded, said that a Second and all the other activities was preferable.' The student got her wish. Helen, too, engaged in 'other activities'. She remembered, for example, playing the Honourable Jane in a colleague's 'juicy parody' of *The Rosary*, an ultra-sentimental Edwardian novel, and she was a keen supporter of the College Political Society, to which she had offered 'A proposed solution to the Irish question' while still an undergraduate. At that time (1905) her thinking was conservative. But as she was afterwards to explain to successive generations of Girton students, 'In those days' (that is before women had the vote) 'one was only an academic politician.' Also 'academic' was her initial reaction to the women's suffrage movement, in the sense that it impelled her to examine the basis of political rights. Converted to votes for women 'as soon as I began to think about it', before long she was driven by the horrors of the First World War (in which her youngest brother was killed) to conclude that 'the only possible basis for political life was the equal right of each human being *as* a human being to life, liberty and the pursuit of happiness'. Enfranchised for the first time in 1918, she cast her vote for Labour.

It was during her second sojourn at Royal Holloway College that Helen Cam began her research on local government in the thirteenth century, taking as her starting point 'the so-called Hundred Rolls of 1274–5'. To equip herself she attended the London-based classes in palaeography and diplomatic conducted by the two greatest living experts, Hubert Hall and Hilary Jenkinson, and then worked intensively on the printed and manuscript materials to be found in specialised libraries and in the Public Record Office. The monograph setting out her preliminary findings was accepted by Professor Paul Vinogradoff, Corpus Professor of Jurisprudence at Oxford, for inclusion in his series 'Oxford Studies in Social and Legal History' and was published under the title *Studies in the Hundred Rolls: Some Aspects of Thirteenth-Century Administration* in 1921. Satisfied that the evidence of the Hundred Rolls, rightly interpreted, could be as useful to scholars interested in non-feudal local administration as it had been to 'students of feudal customs, of topography, and of genealogy', and conscious that her detailed studies had so far been restricted to two, possibly unrepresentative counties, Helen Cam now needed time in which to pursue her investigations. Fortunately for her and for Girton (and ultimately for Cambridge) the solution was at hand. In May 1921 she made successful application for the Pfeiffer Research Fellowship offered by Girton, having assured the electors that exploration of the Hundred Roll evidence from two more counties would adequately occupy the allotted three years.

Helen Cam did not come to Girton as a total stranger. Her youngest sister Marjorie (Natural Sciences Tripos 1921) had just gone down, and among the dons were former colleagues from Royal Holloway and Cheltenham, most notably M. G. (Gwladys) Jones, who had succeeded Eileen Power in 1920 as Director of Studies in History. She and Helen had met when M. G. Jones was in charge of the Training Department at Cheltenham; and although Helen perhaps always remained a little in awe of 'M.G.', who was her senior both in years and for a long while in the College hierarchy, they became the firmest of friends. Exactly when Helen came into residence at Girton is uncertain, but whether it was October 1921 or, as seems more likely, January 1922, the timing of her debut as a 'Cambridge woman' was inauspicious, coinciding as it did with the defeat of proposals to admit women to full membership of the University.

Helen's progress with her research over the next three years can be traced from her annual reports and the record of her publications: four articles were already in print by the end of her first year and a further three had been accepted for publication. To her original project, namely investigation of the Hundred Rolls of Cambridgeshire and Suffolk, she added the topic of the Private Hundred and was soon reporting that, while the material on these two points was still not exhausted, she had accumulated material on many others. In December 1924, with an ever-growing array of sources needing to be searched – Assize Rolls, Sherriff's Accounts, monastic cartularies (important for the light they shed on the administration of the Private Hundred) – she had to admit that the material was practically inexhaustible. The nature of her subject made it difficult, as she said, 'to *complete* any piece of work, as the same records have to be searched for material on different topics and different localities' – a problem that would nowadays be cracked by a computer. In the book she published in 1930, *The Hundred and the Hundred Rolls*, Helen Cam provided students with a guide to the three printed volumes of Hundred Rolls and Quo Warranto Pleas produced in the early nineteenth century and with an outline of local government practices in the reign of Edward I. It was not a treatise, and it touched on only some of the topics she was pursuing in her current work. There were to be no more full-length books (apart from the paperback *England before Elizabeth*, published in 1950 for a popular audience), but this did not matter. Through her prolific output of articles and papers to learned societies (some of the most important were reprinted in the collection she published in 1944 under the title *Liberties and Communities in Medieval England*) and through her extensive correspondence with fellow scholars, Helen Cam was recognised from the mid-1920s onward as the leading authority on medieval local government.

Girtonians who read for the Historical Tripos at any time between 1925 and 1948 could hardly fail to encounter Helen Cam. Even when her chief speciality, 'English Constitutional History to 1485' ceased in the mid-1930s to be a compulsory paper, the subject remained popular, above all with intending lawyers and schoolmistresses: 'without your explanations', said one former student faced with teaching medieval history in an emergency, 'I would be lost indeed'. Yet Helen Cam was equally at home, or so it seemed, with medieval Europe and with post-medieval England, the most modern period not excluded. In all matters affecting students she collaborated in perfect harmony with M. G. Jones. Interviews with prospective students were conducted jointly, as one of Helen's earliest students who afterwards became a close friend, later recalled:

In 1927, an awed schoolgirl of seventeen, I went up to Girton for my entrance interview. Too nervous to be conscious of anything except the formidable figure of M. G. Jones, I sat on the edge of my chair trying to make the best impression I could. 'I think we should ask my colleague,' said M.G. at one point. 'Let me introduce you.' Startled, for I was unaware that there was a third person present, I turned round and saw Helen Cam. The impression of some medieval figure was immediate; wrapped in a black cloak, for it was cold, and silhouetted against the light, her head down, Helen's attention was given wholly to the papers in her lap.

Anyone who saw Helen at work will immediately recognise the attitude of hunched concentration; she could assume it instantly and anywhere, reading proofs while waiting for a bus or at an airport, in the course of supervisions. An alliterative account of a mock election staged at Girton in the 1920s shows Helen Cam in an entirely different but equally recognisable posture:

> Loudly laughed Labour
> Fiercely she fought
> Questions flew quickly
> Flashed fiery answers . . .
>
> (*Girton Review* 1923)

Going about the College on her ordinary occasions she could seem unapproachable. But the knotted brow and stern expression, the 'serious and matronly mien', were signs it was easy to mis-interpret. The impression of severity was due in large part to her natural cast of countenance, the knotted brow denoted as often as not preoccupation with some knotty historical problem. Her style of dress was undeniably sober (she was not much interested in clothes) and her figure matronly. But no more than a short acquaintance was needed to call forth the beaming smile, the solicitous enquiry, or on special occasions the maternal embrace.

Throughout her time at Girton Helen Cam had two homes. She spent the vacations with her family, based from 1926 in Oxford, seizing the opportunity to work in the Bodleian. 'There she was to be seen', in C. R. Cheney's memorable description, 'as one passed by the carrels of Duke Humphrey's Library, sitting squarely by a window – sharp eyes, sharp nose, heavy eyebrows – intent on her books, looking rather like a broody hen in a nesting box, placid and comfortable, but ready to peck if occasion demanded. Some of her best articles must have been hatched there.' The first-floor set of rooms she occupied in Girton lay at the far end of a corridor and overlooked the small garden she her-self had created (and tended 'only rather sporadically' according to a colleague) which was designed to be seen from above. The furnishings of her room were simple and the general effect a little sombre, relieved only by the brilliant colours of the Polish medieval peasants' calendar hung above the fireplace. To teach she sat in an upright hard-backed armchair; the seating arrange-ments for others were a shade more comfortable: an old-fashioned settee and a blue-cushioned window seat, provided it was not occupied by books and other academic clutter, and provided also that the cushions had not been commandeered to accommodate a superfluity of pupils or guests on the floor. Bookshelves lined the walls and there were more in the corridor outside, to house the books students were free to borrow: the books deemed essential, or merely recommended, for the next week's essay, but also historical novels from the famous collection Helen later donated to the college library and the stridently jacketed volumes of the Left Book Club. Directly under Helen's rooms was a loggia where she kept her bicycle, always her preferred mode of transport. She used it to explore places of historical or archaeological interest and on at least one occasion, in order to accompany her nephew on an architectural tour, she took it to France. In term-time she bicycled regularly to and from Cambridge, always arriving in time for her thrice-weekly lectures, which by her own choice started at 9 a.m.

The hour at which she lectured somehow suited her subject, known for short as 'Early Constitutional'. In tracing out for undergraduates the medieval origins and development of the great institutions of state, Helen Cam constantly invoked the two supreme authorities of an earlier generation: Bishop Stubbs, whose pioneering three-volume *Constitutional History of England in its Origin and Developments* was the only secondary work thought fit for inclusion in the University's list of books 'recommended for study'; and F. W. Maitland, the legal historian, indeed the historian *tout court*, venerated by Helen Cam above all others, amongst other reasons for his 'habit of seeing and stating the general problem in terms of the ordinary individual'. Her lectures were thoroughly prepared and continually updated to take account of recent scholarship; and they were delivered with a vocal assurance, product no doubt of the 'reading aloud' the Cam family indulged in for entertainment, which held the attention of her audience. By this means her scholarly influence spread beyond her own college and produced new recruits for medieval research, some of whom pursued their postgraduate studies under her direction. But the relationship did not have to be thus formal. Helen Cam's scholarly expertise was available to anyone who needed advice or merely encouragement: to a 'lapsed' historian, for example, wishing to resume her research on religious houses in Cambridge, or to an army sergeant, an estate agent in civilian life, wanting to keep up his antiquarian interests during the war.

At Girton, where her teaching followed a regular round of supervisions, document classes and essay-marking, Helen Cam's attitude to her students was both kindly and critical. She would admire, and sincerely admire, an ingenious theory but then came the facer: 'Can you prove it?' Nor did she waste words. 'This is nonsense, think again', or an eloquent 'Oh!' in the margins of an essay said all that was needed to convict the careless or the ignorant of their misdoing. Her own methods of study stood partially revealed in the margins and end papers of books from her working library, which were filled with pencilled-in annotations, cross-references, emendations, genealogies, sketch-maps, or whatever else was needed by way of clarification or correction. The message was clear: in reading, as in writing, the first require-ment for a historian was to be rigorous in regard to fact, evidence, and honesty of argument. As a fount of knowledge, and not just of historical knowledge, Helen Cam was seemingly inexhaustible (and when in full flow unstoppable); this was an asset in more ways than one, since with her vast range of interests she could always find some common ground on which to draw out the most diffident student, whether in supervisions or on more hospitable occasions. The latter, although sometimes graced by visiting celebrities, were unpretentious affairs with coffee as the main refreshment. Talk was the object, keeping up with the hostess a distinct challenge. Yet there were more than a few moments of sheer hilarity, when no effort was required. Inevitably, there were some students with whom Helen Cam never managed to strike the right note, just as there were others, not necessarily the most academic, who discovered affinities which led to a lifelong friendship.

In 1937, with an ever-growing corpus of learned publications to her credit, Helen Cam submitted a successful application for the Cambridge Litt.D., or more precisely for the title of the Litt.D., representing the halfway status accorded to Cambridge women when their admission to full membership had been voted down in 1921. Dr Helen Cam was the first woman to earn the distinction (although Dr Marjory Stephenson of Newnham had advanced a year earlier to the parallel distinction of Sc.D.), and her achievement, which was at the same time a non-achievement, served to emphasise the absurdity of the position. One leading academic who wrote to congratulate her admitted his confusion: 'Can't hope to see you clothed in scarlet – or is this an exception?' (It was not, at least so far as University occasions were concerned.) The comment of another, 'What an extraordinary result from a London University upbringing!', was probably a teasing reference, allowable between friends, to Helen's unswerving and oft-proclaimed loyalty to her first *alma mater*, although whether it was received in that spirit is open to doubt. Gaillard Lapsley, University Reader in Constitutional History and the colleague whose scholarly interests came closest to her own, went straight to the point; his recognition of her achievement in bringing her subject into 'the mainstream of English history' must have warmed her heart. Lapsley drew inspiration, as she did, from ideas bequeathed by Maitland and there was the further bond that both had come as outsiders to Maitland's university (Lapsley, a Harvard graduate, had been teaching in Cambridge since 1904). It may have been Lapsley's work on the dynamics of medieval government, or more precisely on the developing relations between the parliamentary and executive bodies at the centre and the communities in the localities, which encouraged Helen Cam to direct her attention increasingly towards the representative aspect of local institutions and to the role of their representatives in Parliament.

Helen Cam's 'political other self', as Herbert Butterfield once termed it, took her among people whose preoccupation was with the present. She gave badly needed financial support to the Romsey Town Labour Club, which in the dispiriting climate of the early 1930s was struggling to bring 'some wideness' into the lives of working men and women. When asked by the secretary to suggest possible speakers, she may well have responded in person, and not merely from a sense of duty: a natural performer, Helen Cam enjoyed making contact with audiences of all kinds, having at her disposal an extensive repertoire of subjects which ranged from 'How local government works' to 'Some less obvious aspects of Kipling, illustrated by recitations from his poetry'. Helen's support for another project, Hillcroft College for Working Women at Surbiton, dated back to its foundation in 1920 by Fanny Street, a close friend at Royal Holloway. Hillcroft's principles, as Helen Cam expounded them with an almost missionary fervour to Girtonians, coincided with some of her most deeply felt convictions: 'That education is spiritual in its basis, that manual labour is as honourable as intellectual, and that the organisation of a college for adults must be democratic' (*Girton Review* 1929). Fundraising apart, much of Helen's work for Hillcroft was done behind the scenes. Her activities on behalf of the Labour cause in Cambridge were more conspicuous. She served for ten years (1925–35) on the Executive Committee of the Cambridgeshire Trades Council and Divisional Labour Party and for a while represented the Committee on the County of Cambridge Juvenile Employment Subcommittee. At one point, in 1928, she was put up as a candidate for the County Council but was not elected. Her absence from Cambridge in 1936–7 on sabbatical leave granted by her College seems to have been followed by a withdrawal from the political scene, to which she would nevertheless return in force as a doughty champion of the Labour candidate in the General Election in 1945.

The travels of Helen's sabbatical year took her to places as far distant as Madras, Rangoon, where her sister Avice was a medical missionary, Isfahan and Jerusalem. The charms of 'going abroad' had first been revealed to her on a euphoric springtime visit to Italy in her late teens. By contrast, travels in Germany and Austria shortly after the First World War brought her face to face with the human miseries of post-war Europe, and for several years thereafter she regularly donated money, food and clothing to an Austrian relief organisation. Never insular in her outlook, Helen Cam was a keen participant in the quinquennial deliberations of the International Congress of Historical Sciences, under whose auspices she visited Oslo, Warsaw and Zurich; in June 1939 she presented a paper, in French, to a more specialised group of legal historians meeting in Dijon. Well-equipped linguistically – she read French and German without difficulty and spoke both languages with the 'decent accent' she had acquired at her mother's knee – Helen Cam felt at ease with continental scholars. She was drawn in particular to a multi-national group of medievalists whose members were dedicated to the study of representative assemblies from a correspondingly multinational standpoint, but hopes of continuing collaboration were dashed for the time being, although not permanently, by the outbreak of war.

Helen Cam's task during the war, like that of many others just beyond middle age or older, was to carry on normally in abnormal circumstances. At Girton, where she became Director of Studies in History in 1940, the students were no less numerous than before; the Faculty of History, depleted as it was, depended all the more heavily on the services of those still on the spot. Efficient in the discharge of the routine jobs that now came her way, Helen Cam was roped in (or perhaps she volunteered) to assist with the conferences laid on in Cambridge for 'University Professors and Lecturers of Allied Countries'. Her efforts were especially appreciated by Polish, Czech and other allied historians driven into exile who were treated, like all her foreign visitors, to a personally conducted tour of Cambridge past and present. Meanwhile, pressing on with her parliamentary studies, she subjected to close analysis the varying meanings in medieval sources of the key phrase *in pleno parliamento*, presenting her findings in a paper, 'From Witness of the Shire to Full

Parliament', which she read to the Royal Historical Society in January 1943. Rather more than two years later, in June 1945, she delivered the Raleigh Lecture before the British Academy. Her chosen subject, 'The Legislators of Medieval England', had a certain topicality, as she clearly intended. With the imminent General Election in mind, the first since 1935, she evoked 'the experimental period in the evolution of the legislative process', stretching from Magna Carta to the Reformation, in an attempt to answer her own question, 'Who made the laws?' The preponderant role of the ruler and the judicature in the enactment of laws is not denied; but 'the most abundant source of lawmaking' turns out to be 'public demand, direct or indirect, implicit or explicit'. Parliaments, to which self-interested groups of men and individuals brought their grievances became as time went on the place where they asserted claims to law and justice, and as the result of 'common action in pursuit of a dimly realised common good', came at length to be recognised as the 'embodiment of national unity'.

The outcome of the General Election gave Helen Cam's 'other political self' enormous satisfaction and she hailed with especial glee the unprecedented return of a Labour candidate as Member of Parliament for Cambridge. A source of personal satisfaction that year was her election to the Fellowship of the British Academy, a rare distinction and rarer still at that date for a woman. A few years later the patience of Cambridge women was at last rewarded by their uncontested admission, on the eve of Helen's departure for Harvard but just in time for her to enjoy the first-fruits, to full membership of the University. Clothed now by right in scarlet, Helen Cam walked with the women professors, doctors and heads of houses in the ceremonial procession which in June 1948 welcomed Field Marshal Smuts on his installation as Chancellor.

The announcement of Helen Cam's appointment to a Harvard chair caused a great stir in Cambridge and she was inundated with letters of congratulation: 'Stupendous news, the Americans have much to teach us!'; 'You are just the right woman to promote understanding between the two countries'; 'Being a fundamentally humble person in spite of all your great gifts, you probably won't realise how much you will be missed'; and from the Vice-Chancellor, E. A. Benians, 'The appointment brings honour to our History school as well as to yourself'. Adventurous by nature, still bursting with energy (Professor David Knowles, consulted by a Harvard scout, instanced her energetic progress up Castle Hill on a bicycle as evidence of sound health), she rejoiced at the prospect of 'at least five more years of active life with the most marvellous leisure to write'.

This second, much longer taste of 'the American experience' proved as exhilarating at the first, but leisure remained elusive. As a celebrity Professor Cam received invitations from far and near to deliver special lectures; honorary degrees were heaped upon her; students beat a path to her door. In Cambridge, Massachusetts, she even enjoyed shopping, with the result that her wardrobe took on a hitherto unaccustomed elegance. She revived old friendships from her Bryn Mawr days and made many new friends and disciples: her achievement in helping to close 'a wide gap of age and culture' was singled out for special mention in a campus profile written shortly before her retirement in 1954. Paradoxical as it may sound, Helen Cam was both rejuvenated and mellowed by her six years as Zemurray Professor; but her return to England, to a settled home life with her sister Norah in Sevenoaks, still did not signify 'retirement'.

For one thing, much of her time was occupied until she was well into her seventies with high-level work for the International Commission for the History of Assemblies of Estates, of which she had become President in 1949. The manner in which Helen Cam conducted the Commission's affairs is well summed up by the comment of a colleague: 'We had come under the rule of a great abbess!' Businesslike, hospitable, urbane, practical in her approach to the historical questions under investigation by the Commission, she set the organisation on its feet again after the war, widened its scope, drew its needs to the attention of potential sponsors and by her evangelistic efforts attracted new members. On her retirement in 1960 she received as a seventh-fifth birthday present the two-volume *Festschrift* prepared in her honour by scholars of thirteen countries, which was published with the blessing of the Commission under the title *Album Helen Cam.*

Her pamphlet *Historical Novels*, issued just a year later by the Historical Association, was the result of a lifetime's fascination with the genre. Scrupulous as ever, Helen did not fail to provide a 'select bibliography of historical novels', arranged in chronological order of subject and annotated in the style that came naturally to an ex-Tripos examiner: each item is awarded a class mark, alpha, or very exceptionally a starred alpha to indicate outstanding quality, beta, sometimes beta plus but never minus, or even gamma, 'for some novels are included as covering unusual periods or topics'. Of still greater interest is the preceding essay in which Helen tells how she was led from her childhood enchantment with the historical fictions of Charles Kingsley, Charlotte M. Yonge, Bulwer Lytton and many other authors who are now forgotten to the exploration of 'grown-up history books'. The intervening stages each made a contribution to the sharpening of her critical faculties. Confronted with Kingsley's *Hereward* and Lytton's *Harold*, each of them heroes but deadly enemies, how could one contrive to worship both? Next came the shock of discovering that the authors of historical romances were not bothered by dates. The disillusionment was fleeting, made up for by 'the vindictive delight of catching out a printed book in flagrant inaccuracies'. But this was still a game, 'the savage game of criticism', and it might have palled but for the realisation that 'romantic escape from the tame routine of daily life had somehow involved one in a new game, the pursuit of reality'. Arguing in favour of historical novels, Helen added the caveat that they should be both good history and good literature. Her own appreciation of the latter grew from an early and unforced love of the English classics – yet another legacy from her parents – but she was in no sense a literary snob, or for that matter a snob of any kind. She enjoyed detective stories and nearly always carried one or two in her luggage. Above all, she was a devotee of unpretentious 'family novels', whether English (Charlotte M. Yonge's *Daisy Chain* sequence for example) or American; 'their charms', as she had noted in a pamphlet she wrote for the YWCA many years earlier, 'consist very largely in their familiarity'.

First and last, the life of Helen's own family revolved around their mother, who lived to be over ninety. Kate Cam's personality, astringent but wholly benign, pervades the account Helen gave of her childhood in the talk 'Eating and Drinking Greek' she broadcast in 1964, and the enquiring edge of her mind was clearly not blunted by old age. Kate Cam was in her eighties when she remarked to Helen, 'Isn't it nice how many things there are still to find out?' To the end of her life, Helen's appetite for new knowledge remained equally unjaded. So, while she accepted with gratification the honours bestowed on her in recognition of past achievements and services, becoming in 1957 a Commander of the British Empire, in 1962 a Doctor of Letters *honoris Causa* of Oxford University and in 1964 an Honorary Fellow of Somerville College, she was continually moving forward. There were visits to new places, Budapest for example, from which she would return with fresh examples of the artistic talent, mainly for sketching, which was yet another string to her bow. She kept abreast with the affairs of Hillcroft College. When she was invited back to Girton in 1956 to deliver the Founders' Memorial Lecture, the subject she chose, 'Law as it Looks to a Historian', gave her the opportunity, as she said, 'to justify a long-standing devotion'. And it is true that law had captured her interest well before she embarked on the historical studies which turned very largely on the analysis of legal institutions. Intending lawyers among her

Girton students always met with especial encouragement, perhaps not untinged by envy. In effect, however, the Lecture can be seen as a prelude to the major undertaking which occupied Helen for the remaining twelve years of her life and which she left virtually complete when she died: the edition for the Selden Society of an important legal source, the records of the London Eyre of 1321. It is obvious why the task appealed to her. Human nature, of which Helen Cam was a keener and more sympathetic historian than some of her more austere writings might suggest, was the very stuff of the court cases paraded before the Justices. No less appealing was the chase after variant readings, the puzzling out of meanings, in short all the textual and contextual complexities which it gave Helen such delight to unravel. Above all, there was the enjoyable sensation of breaking new ground: 'After all these years I feel I'm only now beginning to discover what fun law is.'

Helen worked on the *Eyre of London* at home, which since 1954 was the little house in Sevenoaks she shared with Norah. Their youngest sister, Marjorie, lived close by and this partial reconstruction of the family circle, from which Helen had never in any serious sense departed, was a source of great contentment. Life in a residential college had relieved her of household responsibilities, as was the case with many women dons of her generation. At Harvard the Zemurray Professor had successfully fended for herself; but Norah was the better cook, and in Sevenoaks the Professor Emerita was proud to assume the humbler duties, 'sweeping and suchlike', which fell to her share. The steeply sloping garden, last of the many gardens Helen had made or tended, was their joint responsibility, proudly displayed to a stream of visitors. For Helen's friendships lasted; she valued people for their own qualities, stood by them, but refrained from meddling, even with the best intentions, in their lives. Entire families, on either side of the Atlantic, were the objects of her affection and, it must be said, of her approval, inasmuch as marriage and the rearing of children counted in her eyes as 'the greatest enrichments to life a woman could have'. She felt, she shyly confessed to one special confidante, that 'as a spinster she had only made the best of the second best'. The best, in Helen Cam's case, needed no qualification. On her last visit to America she stayed with a former graduate student, Patricia Labalme, who was lamenting the poor showing of her garden when compared with the flourishing flower beds to be seen in Sevenoaks. 'Never mind,' said Helen, 'it makes land yours to work it. Locke said somewhere that property is that with which one has mixed one's labour.' Patricia Labalme's thought, 'Then how many places, how many people, how much of the past must belong to this woman', remained unspoken; in one form or another, it must surely have sprung to the minds of the many people, both learned and simple, who six months later, in February 1968, mourned Helen Cam's departure.

NOTES

The author is grateful to the Mistress and Fellows of Girton College for their permission to consult and quote from papers deposited in the Helen Cam Archive, and to the College Archivist, Kate Perry, for her generous assistance.

C. R. Cheney's description of Helen Cam at work in the Bodleian is quoted from his memoir, 'Helen Maud Cam 1885–1968', published in the *Proceedings of the British Academy* 55 (1969), to which this present account is heavily indebted.

The text of Helen Cam's broadcast, 'Eating and Drinking Greek', appeared originally in *The Listener*, 21 May 1964, and was reprinted with the editor's kind permission in the *Girton Review* (1969).

Chapter 5

MARJORY STEPHENSON
1885–1948

Joan Mason

A monograph by MS
Would do much to relieve the distress
Caused by all these inferior
Books on bacteria.

MWA

Margaret Whetham Anderson's clerihew appeared in 1929 in *Brighter Biochemistry*, the 'better than *Punch*' magazine that flourished in the 1920s in Frederick Gowland Hopkins's department in Cambridge.[1] It was an advance notice of Marjory Stephenson's book *Bacterial Metabolism*, which came out in 1930, establishing the new field of bacterial biochemistry. The second edition in 1939 was almost a new book, as was the third, posthumous, edition in 1949, as the field grew.[2] *Bacterial Metabolism* became a standard work, being translated into Japanese in the 1940s.

Marjory Stephenson was known to her friends, colleagues and students as MS, and Margaret Whetham was her first research student, from 1920.[3] MS worked for most of her life on external funding, from the Beit Foundation and then the Medical Research Council, the MRC. She had kindly gatekeepers in Hopkins, who built up Biochemistry in Cambridge, and Walter Morley Fletcher, Secretary of the MRC. She made her way in science by pioneering her own field, and her life was her work and her friends. She helped to found the Society for General

Microbiology in 1944, and became its second President in 1947, following Alexander Fleming, discoverer of penicillin. She died in office, and the Society instituted a biennial Marjory Stephenson Memorial Lecture, which was published in its *Journal*.

Her formal recognition came late in life, in part because she was of the generation that went to war, and in part because the University, unlike Hopkins, was so slow to let women in. From 1926, forty-five years after women's formal admission to University examinations, women could be appointed to University offices. But few women were appointed, very few indeed in science. Women did not become members of the University until 1948.

MS worked in the Biochemistry Department for thirty years. In 1936 she was one of the first women in Cambridge to receive the title to the degree of Sc.D. She lectured to Part II students from 1925, when Biochemistry separated off from Physiology, and ran practical classes. She was given her own MRC Unit for Chemical Microbiology in 1945, and her course in Microbiological Biochemistry became a Part II course in 1947. She was the first woman biologist to be elected to the Fellowship of the Royal Society, in 1945, with Kathleen Lonsdale as the first woman physical scientist. She was appointed University lecturer only in 1943, at the age of 58, and Reader[4] in Chemical Microbiology in 1947, the year before she died. Her biographer commented: 'It is a curious reflection on the difficulties in the path of women scientists and perhaps also a sign of the distrust of a somewhat new subject that so original a worker should have been an annual grantee for so many years.'[5]

Marjory Stephenson grew up in Burwell in the fenland, between Cambridge, Ely and Newmarket, where her great-grandfather had trained race-horses in the eighteenth century. Her father was an enterprising and successful farmer, 'extremely interested in scientific agriculture', which he read up for himself. Her mother felt she had suffered from the lack of education available to girls of her day, and made better provision for her daughters.

There was a nine-year gap between Marjory and her older siblings. She wrote:

Owing to position in my family, almost an 'only child' and somewhat of a little prig. Acquired a childish interest in science from my beloved governess and later from my father. Also a sceptical attitude towards orthodox religion from the same sources. I remember being told by my governess that the first chapter of Genesis was not literally true (age about 7) and hearing the facts of symbiotic nitrogen fixation from my father as we crossed a clover field (age about 10).[6]

Robert Stephenson pioneered fruit orchards in the fen country, and the cold storage of fruits. He mustered the farmers' support for the University to set up a School of Agriculture, against opposition in the Senate, and helped to found the Cambridge and County High School for boys. Elizabeth Stephenson ensured that her eldest and youngest daughters went to Newnham College.

Marjory's ambition was to go into medicine, so she read chemistry, physiology and zoology for Part I of the Natural Sciences Tripos. Women were excluded from the University's practical classes in chemistry and zoology, but chemistry was well taught by Ida Freund in the Newnham College Laboratory, and biology in the women's Balfour Laboratory.

In 1906 she 'was obliged to teach as no funds were available to proceed to medicine'.[7] She studied domestic science at Gloucester Training College, taught there for a while, then moved to King's College (of Household Science) for Women, in London. She was rescued in 1911 by R. H. A. Plimmer, at University College London, to teach advanced classes in the biochemistry of nutrition. University College has a good record in the higher education of women, but Plimmer was no feminist. When the Biochemical Club, forerunner of the Biochemical Society, was founded in 1911 he carried the motion that only men should be eligible for membership, this decision being reversed the next year by George Barger and Henry Dale. The Chemical Society admitted women only in 1920, after a campaign spanning forty years.

In Plimmer's department she soon began research in the biochemistry of nutrition, publishing metabolic studies of fats, and of experimental diabetes. She was awarded a research grant by Newnham, and a Beit Memorial Fellowship for medical research, in 1913. When war broke out a strong sense of duty led her to volunteer for the British Red Cross. She ran hospital kitchens in France, then served as VAD Commandant in Salonika, where she was mentioned in dispatches, and was awarded the MBE, in the military division. In later life she seldom spoke of her early days in domestic science, or of her war service.

In 1919 she moved to Hopkins's laboratory in Cambridge, with the freedom of her Beit Fellowship. When this ran out she received annual grants from the MRC, and in 1929 became a member of the MRC's external staff. In Cambridge she was once again in the Balfour Laboratory, which Newnham leased to the University from 1914, when all the University practical classes were opened to women. In 1924 the biochemists moved into the fine new Dunn Institute in Tennis Court Road, and Margaret Whetham wrote a Triumphal Ode for *Brighter Biochemistry* for the occasion.[8]

The 1920s became a golden age in the Biochemistry Department, with Hopkins's breadth of vision, and gentle but inspired leadership. J. B. S. Haldane was appointed Reader in 1923, working on the mathematical theory of enzyme processes, genetics, heredity, the causes of evolution, and the origin of life. Another polymath was Joseph Needham, a philosophical bio-chemist, working on chemical embryology with his wife-to-be Dorothy Moyle, before moving into comparative biochemistry, and later, the history of science and civilisation in China. Needham succeeded to the Readership in 1932 when Haldane moved to London.

Hopkins encouraged all his people, women and men, young and old, to develop their own ideas, in these growing fields. His laboratory was a talking-shop, a ferment of new ideas, with members from around the world. MS inspired her students by her own example, by her thorough and well-controlled experimental work, by her enthusiasm and her generosity. She would pioneer a line of research, then leave it to a younger co-worker to develop. Her Certificate for the Royal Society in 1944 mentioned her personal originality, and the number of her pupils who 'continued to distinguish themselves in the subject', filling chairs of chemical microbiology around the country. Hopkins's biographer Ernest Baldwin wrote of the bacterial studies 'so brilliantly pioneered' by Marjory Stephenson.[9]

RESTING CELLS

MS's first work was on fat-soluble vitamins, combining her interests with those of Hopkins. With Margaret Whetham she studied the fat metabolism of the Timothy grass bacillus, this being 'more susceptible of laboratory control' than higher organisms. A major contribution to microbiology during the 1920s was their refinement of Louis Pasteur's technique of 'washed cell suspensions', which they called 'resting cells'. The cells were cultured, separated by centrifuge, and suspended in a medium containing no nutrients. This technique allowed them to construct a metabolic balance sheet for the cell, in the absence of growth, or cell division.[10]

Her first preface to *Bacterial Metabolism*, in 1930, explained her choice of organism: 'Perhaps bacteria may tentatively be regarded as biochemical experimenters; owing to their relatively small size and rapid growth variations must arise very much more frequently than in more differentiated forms of life, and they can in addition afford to occupy more precarious positions in natural economy than larger organisms with more exacting requirements.'

Marrying biological and chemical techniques, she investigated oxidation–reduction reactions of anaerobic bacteria (living in the absence of oxygen), with Margaret Whetham and Juda Quastel. The gut bacterium *E. coli* which they used in their early studies was to become the workhorse of bacteriology. Their work on resting cells was published in the *Biochemical Journal*, and noticed also in *Brighter Biochemistry*. Haldane's *Report to the Sir William Trustees for the Year 1924–1925* included the lines:

> Attached hereto there is a pastel
> Portraying Dr J. H. Quastel
> Surrounded by his bugs protesting
> Against the work they're given while resting.
> Wooldridge and Woolf (who will not rhyme)
> Assisted in this sordid crime.
> Still harder were the problems set 'em
> by Misses Stephenson and Whetham.

The pastel by Barnet Woolf showed Quastel resting in bed, and protesting bugs marching across the coverlet carrying banners, 'B. Coli Communist Party of Great Britain'. 'No More Birth Control for Bacteria', 'An Eight Hour Day', 'Our Dumb Friends' League', and 'Back up Bacteria, our Baby Brothers'.[11]

She described limitations of the technique in her first Preface:

[W]e are in much the same position as an observer trying to gain an idea of the life of a household by a careful scrutiny of the persons and material arriving at or leaving the house; we keep accurate record of the foods and commodities left at the door, patiently examine the contents of the dustbin, and endeavour to deduce from such data the events occurring within the closed doors.

They followed up their work on intact cells by studies of biochemical compounds extracted from them, and rebutted the suggestion that the cells were not 'resting' but moribund, by showing that they could grow again if nutrients were supplied.

ENZYMES

Hopkins's vision was of a living cell composed of ordered and *comprehensible* chemical reactions, in space-time, as against the vitalism, the inscrutable 'protoplasm', 'biogen' or 'proteid' of his earlier contemporaries.[12] He pointed to revolutionary new concepts and techniques moving into chemistry from physics, and into biology from chemistry. Biologists and chemists must learn a common language, that of biochemistry. He turned his attention, by 1920, to enzymes,[13] the proteins which catalyse the processes of life. The enzyme fits the substrate as the key fits the lock, in Emil Fischer's phrase. The first pure crystalline enzyme, urease, was isolated in 1926, and the complete structures of many enzymes have now been determined by X-ray crystallography.

Marjory Stephenson was the first to separate a bacterial enzyme from the cell, in 1928, when she extracted lactic dehydrogenase from *E. coli*. She characterised the enzyme hydrogenase with Leonard Stickland in 1931 in bacteria from the mud of the river Ouse, which was particularly smelly, due to fermentation of waste material from a sugar-beet factory. They showed that gut and other bacteria were using hydrogenase to produce hydrogen sulphide and methane.

The 1930s saw her classical work on 'adaptive enzymes' in micro-organisms, in response to chemical changes in the medium, with Stickland, John Yudkin and Ernest Gale. Louis Pasteur, seventy years before, had observed 'chemical adaptation' in yeast. In 1930 the discussion of 'adaptation' was clarified by Henning Karström, in Finland, who distinguished between 'constitutive enzymes', in the functioning cell, and 'adaptive enzymes' produced as a response to changes in the medium, the addition of particular substrate material, for example.[14] She demonstrated the unambiguous production of such adaptive enzymes by *E. coli* in 1933 and by a yeast in 1936. Since the cells were not replicating there was no question of 'natural selection' of mutant individuals, genetic variants. The 'adaptation' was not inherited. The organism reverts to 'normal' on removal of the stimulus, 'if indeed a "normal" bacterial cell exists', she remarked.

Terms such as adaptation, variation, induction, feedback, or 'induced biosynthesis' came and went as the field developed. 'Adaptation' raised fundamental questions of the regulation of physiological processes, and of differentiation or evolution of the organism. In her first Preface she had written of bacteria as biochemical experimenters, opportunists, using the example of bacteria living in especial niches on outlandish materials: 'No large animal or plant . . . could hope to survive if obliged to depend solely on the oxidation of ammonia or sulphur for its energy. Autotrophic bacteria are of intense interest as suggesting courses which physiological evolution might have taken had a slightly different equilibrium established itself in the inorganic world.' In her third Preface she wrote: 'but with bacteria, constant evolutionary changes occur under our eyes and can be controlled and imitated in the laboratory'. Nowadays, in genetic engineering, bacteria can be given precisely coded DNA so as to produce new forms of enzymes and hormones.

She worked on enzyme adaptation in the 1930s with Ernest Galen, then began metabolic studies of nucleic acids, the material of the genes, with A. R. Trim. Work on bacterial nutrition in Paul Fildes's MRC Unit in London supported her view of the importance of microbial chemistry to biochemistry as a whole. Thus, B. C. G. (Gabe) Knight showed that vitamins important for animals were needed by particular bacteria, and Donald Woods, that the new sulpha drugs inhibited the growth of sensitive bacteria by competing successfully with the B vitamins they required.[15]

When the Second World War came, Paul Fildes's unit moved to Porton to develop techniques for bacterial warfare. MS was fiercely anti-war, following her experiences in France and the Balkans in the First World War. During the 1930s she was active in the Cambridge Scientists Anti-war Group, with Dorothy Needham, Tony (Antoinette) Pirie, Dorothy Hodgkin and others.[16] Her first 'war work' was on pathways of anaerobic fermentation, as used to make industrial solvents in the First World War. Her major activity, however, was as Secretary of the MRC's Committee on Chemical Microbiology, contributing her biochemical approach to medical bacteriology. She played an active part in the Toxin Committee, which was concerned with the development of toxoids and antitoxins for active and passive immunisation against bacteria carrying disease, particularly gas gangrene.

THE ELECTION OF THE FIRST WOMEN TO THE ROYAL SOCIETY OF LONDON

Quastel was elected to the Fellowship of the Royal Society at the age of 40, in 1940, Gale at the age of 39 in 1953. Academies of Science are self-replicating bodies, and women had to wait much longer for admission. The US National Academy of Sciences elected its first woman in 1925, but elected only four by mid-century. The French Académie des Sciences elected its first woman in 1962, from the Institut Curie, having rejected Marie Curie and Irène Joliot-Curie.

At the Royal Society, Hertha Ayrton was proposed for the Fellowship in 1902, but the Society's lawyers held her candidature to be unacceptable since she was a woman, worse, a married woman. Under the Common Law a woman's *person* was covered by that of her father, or husband if she was married. It could be argued that a woman could not, therefore, be a Fellow of a body incorporated by Charter. In 1906 the Royal Society awarded Hertha Ayrton its Hughes Medal, given annually for original discovery in the physical sciences, and she is the only woman to have received it.[17]

In 1919 the Sex Disqualification (Removal) Act disallowed

legalistic arguments discriminating against women, and in 1929 the Privy Council ruled that women are 'persons' in law. But no woman was then proposed for the Fellowship. It was J. B. S. Haldane who raised the flag, in the *Daily Worker* in 1943. He was strongly involved in the anti-Fascist movement in the 1930s, joining the Communist Party and the editorial board of the *Daily Worker* in 1940.

Haldane described the twenty newly elected Fellows in an article in April 1943.[18] Complimenting the Royal Society on having elected six Indians among 470 Fellows, he moved from racial to sex discrimination, declaring: 'The most striking omission is the name of any woman. There are probably not 50 British women worthy of the FRS. There are certainly half a dozen. The Society has no colour bar; it cannot exclude women indefinitely.' A. V. Hill, the Society's Biological Secretary, wrote to him immediately:

I read with much interest this morning your article in the Daily Worker on the new FRSs . . . The Society . . . does not exclude women . . . Personally, I should be very glad to see a woman elected, provided, of course, that she was elected purely on merit and not as a consolation prize for being a woman . . .

That the Society will ultimately elect women on their merits, I have no doubt, but I can't think they will ever make up a large fraction of the Fellowship . . . Anyhow, it is up to you . . . to see that they are proposed . . . Otherwise you are neglecting your duty![19]

Haldane replied on 12 April:

I am aware that there is nothing to prevent the election of women to the Royal Society. Nevertheless when I have brought the question of the candidature of certain women up, I have met with opposition on the grounds of their sex . . . I am pretty fully occupied with war work, but if I have a little spare time it will be easier to do so after the war.

With regard to possible candidates, I should name Marjorie Stephenson, and I think I could mention more than four others . . . I could certainly think of biochemists and bacteriologists elected in recent years who seemed to me to have a weaker claim than hers.

I think that the attitude of the Royal Society to women in the past is exemplified by the fact that Madame Curie did not receive any of its medals (you will correct me if I am wrong).[20] This attitude still persists among certain of the Fellows, not all of them senior ones either.

I am glad that you at any rate are not unsympathetic to the suggestion.[21]

Lancelot Hogben wrote to JBS on 30 July that the Society's Council were very sympathetic to the election of suitable women, asking him to ask Haldane for names of suitable biologists. Haldane replied on 18 August:

I think the strongest claim is that of Dr Marjorie Stephenson who was the first person in the world to do work on bacterial metabolism as exact as that on mammalian metabolism, and who has continued to do good work in this field, discovering, for example, a number of new enzymes, in particular those dealing with the production and consumption of hydrogen . . . I do not know if Miss Elles, the palaeontologist, is still alive. I believe she did pretty good work on graptolites . . . I do not know much about female botanists, but I do not think any of them are absolutely first-rate, though Agnes Arber has done some good work.[22]

A. V. Hill as an Officer could not propose candidates, and Haldane was too busy. Hopkins, in his eighties, was in failing health. The prime mover was Charles Harington, who developed clinical biochemistry at University College Hospital in the 1930s, following Henry Dale as director of the National Institute for Medical Research in 1942. Harington wrote to several Fellows to canvass support for Marjory Stephenson, and asked Lawrence Bragg to suggest a woman on the physical side. Bragg proposed Kathleen Lonsdale, who had worked in the laboratory of his father William Bragg, who died in 1942.

The President, Henry Dale, could not act publicly, but wrote several strictly Private and Confidential letters, on 15 November.[23] To Fildes:

I have confidential information that a Certificate is to be presented this year for a woman candidate on the Physical side. The candidate is a strong one, but I regard it as on all grounds undesirable that there should be only one woman on the first List of Candidates containing any. You have shown your interest in Miss Stephenson's claims, and there is still time, if you hustle, to get a Certificate signed and presented before November 30th.

To Haldane:

Hill showed me some correspondence he had with you, when you made public allusion to the absence of women from the Royal Society Fellowship nominations last year . . . [A] Certificate is to be presented for a woman Candidate on the Physical side . . . Perhaps I may hint to you that Fildes had some interest in the claims of Miss Marjorie Stephenson, and . . . you might . . . communicate with him.[24]

Fildes replied on 17 November: 'This is quite interesting. The situation about Miss S is that, without discussing it with me, Harington as biochemist decided to pursue her and asked me to second . . . and I agreed . . . Her certificate is in Harington's hands and I have obtained the support of the bacteriologists . . . I imagine H has (?)contact with the Cambridge Fellows.'[25] Fildes enjoyed a reputation as a misogynist, but was 'devoted to the memory of his great-grandmother Mary Fildes who, as President of the Female Radical Reformers of Manchester, took a leading part in the meeting on 16 August 1819 which ended in the Peterloo massacre by the Manchester and Cheshire Yeomanry'.[26] Haldane replied on 22 November: 'I have already signed Dr. Stephenson's certificate . . . I have no doubt at all that had [she] been a man she would have been elected to the Fellowship some time ago. I was particularly impressed with the accuracy of her work, and the very large amount of research which it has directly inspired.'[27]

Eighteen Fellows signed Marjory Stephenson's certificate. When the certificates were presented the Society took legal advice, which pointed to the force of the 1919 Act. The Treasurer Thomas Merton, however, was concerned with the break in the traditions of the Society, and (he said) with democratic principles. He proposed a postal ballot of the Fellows, which the War Emergency Powers made possible. Henry Dale objected:

Do you or do you not wish the Council to continue a discrimination against women candidates which the Law has removed? If the matter is left to Council, I myself regard it as quite unlikely that any woman will be elected while the war lasts. If we try to force the issue, we may find ourselves faced with a political campaign, which is on all accounts to be deprecated.

[I]f we took the suggested poll on this matter, it would be very difficult to resist a future claim by any disaffected body of Fellows, that any other matter submitted for Council decision must be made the matter of some kind of unofficial advisory referendum. I believe that we shall be imperilling the whole structure of government of the R.S., which I regard as a matter of as long, and much more important tradition, than the question of whether a few women shall at any time be admitted to the Fellowship.

Dale then decided that a ballot on amendments to the Statutes would be a useful tactic, so that

'any Fellow who wished that women should not . . . be nominated could . . . vote against the amendments', even though their object was 'obviously nothing more than to make the accepted legal position clear' . . . Altogether, I believe that we could in this way do what we wish to do without any suspicion of illegality, or danger to our traditions of indifference to any but scientific merits or demerits, which I regard as far more important to the Society than that of its purely male Fellowship.

Dale wrote to Hopkins, a former President of the Society (1930–5):

I can tell you, when I see you, what I know of the way in which the project of presenting a Certificate for Miss Stephenson probably originated. My . . . view is, that the proper attitude for the Society is one of strict observance of the law . . . [I]n 1922 . . . a clear opinion [was] obtained, that the Sex Disqualification (Removal) Act of 1919 had made women beyond doubt eligible for election to the RS . . . Counsel . . . advised . . . alterations in the Statutes to make this position explicit . . . Nothing was done . . . in that direction . . . Now that Certificates have actually been presented . . . I have no doubt myself that, whether the Statutes are altered or not, the Certificates are admissible.[28]

Hopkins replied on 3 December:

I wondered just what had happened when I received Harington's letter concerning Marjory Stephenson. Their election would be revolutionary, of course, but I do think the time has come for justification of the policy. We have heard much of equal pay for equal work, and we may well feel that this should apply to intellectual work and the honours accorded to it.[29]

The ballot was held, and the Council reported: 'When the poll was closed at 30 June 1944, it was found that 336 Fellows had voted in favour of the proposals, 3 in favour but with qualifications, and 37 Fellows against them.'[30] Kathleen Lonsdale and Marjory Stephenson were elected in March 1945.

It is interesting that the initiative in proposing Marjory Stephenson was taken in London, not in Cambridge. Harold Himsworth, MRC Secretary, 1949–68, and one of Harington's biographers,[31] wrote:

I think that what motivated him . . . was that he had an exceptionally well developed sense of justice. If he saw anybody, man or woman, being denied their rights for what he regarded as an irrational reason he would be moved to take the matter up. He had not several judges in his family background for nothing! Thus when he saw women who had done work which, had it been done by a man, would have entitled him to be considered for election to the Society, being debarred from that body, he was moved to do something about it . . . What motivated him was the fact that an injustice was being done to an individual and, in that connection, the sex of the individual was to him a total irrelevancy.[32]

Marjory Stephenson fled to the country to avoid publicity when her election was announced, leaving her friend and colleague Sidney Elsden to look after her Khaki Campbell ducks. But not even *Nature* remarked that the Royal Society had elected its first women.

HER LAST YEARS

After the war, MS moved into her own building, the 'Bug Hut', behind the Institute on the Downing Site, funded by the Rockefeller Foundation. A Parliamentary Committee had considered why the commercial production of penicillin, discovered in this country, had been developed much faster in the USA. It was decided that one factor was the dearth of British chemical microbiologists, and recommended that these should be trained by Marjory Stephenson in her MRC Unit.[33] She also ran a successful summer school.

MS returned to her work on bacterial nucleic acids and their breakdown by enzymes, and wrote not long before she died, 'I have got onto the most interesting piece of research I have ever done and where it's going to turn next I just don't know.'[34] The structures of the nucleic acids DNA (the double helix) and RNA were established a few years later. She should have lived longer, to continue to run her own Unit, and to see the fruition of her work as Gale, Monod and others, working with bacteria, began to demonstrate the genetic control of enzyme synthesis.

A month before her death she wrote to Sidney Elsden:

I am terribly sorry to disappoint myself and you (note order) but I shall not be able to visit you and Erica as planned. Recently such marked symptoms of secondaries have appeared mainly dizziness and mental confusion that I must just stay at home. You can't cheat cancer forever . . .

I hope this nomenclature tangle will be resolved before British bacteriology makes a complete ass of itself; do not let the medical diehards force the Society into premature action . . . I wonder if these birds have the slightest conception of the work involved in producing a 'system' of any kind and of the *insuperable* difficulty of producing anything but a *provisional* system . . .

Marjory Stephenson, the person

Marjory Stephenson looks stern in the portraits that were taken in later life when she was ill. Plate 5 shows her outside the laboratory with her Springer spaniel who came to work with her. Dorothy Needham's comment on an earlier dog was that her contribution to biochemistry was that, like all Dalmatians, but unlike human members of the laboratory, she excreted uric acid.

Marjory Stephenson was quiet in public, disliking public speaking and publicity. Her colleagues and friends described her 'infectious gaiety'. She enjoyed entertaining, and loved gossip 'because she liked to know how things worked'. Her personality was described as 'striking' by the Needhams, and 'vivid and arresting' by Donald Woods, who was inspired to read biochemistry at Cambridge after hearing a talk she gave on BBC radio in 1930. Margaret Whetham Anderson described her as 'formidable . . . because she was so able'. In the department she became 'a dominant force, Hoppy's confidant' in the 1930s. Her biographer wrote that 'she had a slight tendency indeed to include dynamite among her reforming measures'.[35]

The Needhams wrote of her as 'a liberating influence, whose scorn of cant and humbug still lived in their minds'.[36] She teased her male colleagues, 'fussing about their reputations . . . as if they were ageing virgins in a Victorian novel'.[37] She was scornful of fancy words cloaking a lack of understanding. Gale called his Memorial Lecture, with new evidence of transport across bacterial membranes, 'Don't talk to me about permeability', which she had declared to be 'the last resort of the biochemist who cannot find any better explanation'. He continued:

MS was forthright and believed in striking while the temper was hot. There were days when we tiptoed around the lab, hoping that lightning really did not strike twice in the same place. Then the storm would pass, enthusiasm bubbled out of her room and we all joined in argument and riotous assembly while MS's laughter rang through the building . . .

When she had an idea she acted on it forthwith. At the time of the abdication of Edward VIII, while the rest of us were holding indignation meetings of one sort of another, MS was down in the telephone booth dictating a telegram of support to Buckingham Palace.[38]

Gale took charge of her MRC Unit when she died, and became Professor of Chemical Microbiology in 1960.

Bacterial Metabolism was strongly grounded in the history of the field, and she had intended to write lives of Pasteur and of Hopkins. In her first Preface she thanked Hopkins, 'at whose suggestion the book was written and to whose influence alone I owe the incentive to think on biochemical matters'. Her second Preface concludes: 'It has been the peculiar happiness of this department to work with a Professor who shares his own unique inspiration with his colleagues, and fosters in them the same spirit of co-operation.' The article in which she took most pride was her description of Hopkins and his scientific influence.[39]

She was scornful of some kinds of theoretical biology. Her second Preface remarks: 'Happily this subject [bacterial growth] now attracts mathematicians and statisticians less than formerly but has passed into the hands of biochemists.' Haldane was not in her mind. Her fable 'The Biochemists and the Mathematician'[40] told of a Stork Mathematician holding a tea-party for animals tired of their fare of mussels, eggs, and tissues in culture. But his food is in a very tall jar, in which the contents are far too deep for any of them, even for the good-natured Reeder [Haldane], 'a bird with a very long beak, and good natured withal, and would often fish up for the other animals out of pools and holes morsels which they were unable to reach for themselves'. When the jar is broken the contents are found to be hard tack. The Wise Serpent [FGH] 'who presided over their destinies, and was often accustomed, at tea-parties, by a little skilful rearrangement of the provender, to turn unpromising material into an appetising meal' was not surprised. He said, 'I have always heard that you only get out of those jars what you put in to them . . . but one day we will catch a stork very young, and teach him to prepare dishes for *us* out of mussels and eggs and bugs in jelly.'

The 'tea-parties' referred to the celebrated weekly colloquia, the Tea Club Meetings, over which Hopkins presided with 'subtle sagacity' (Norman Pirie's phrase).

She celebrated her bacteria, of course, in *Brighter Biochemistry*. In 'Down the Microscope and What Alice Found There'[41] Alice is escorted by Pyo (*B. pyocyaneus*), who admires her pretty arrangement of flagella. They go to a lecture by an active little coccus on Housing Conditions in the Human Body. They observe the great life ceremony, multiplication by division, 'the final Sublimation of Family Life: the mother one with the daughters, and fathers and brothers nowhere'. They go to a dance, and Alice recognises the Bacterial Origin of the Charleston, in pitiable efforts of non-motile forms. By chance, she attributes a surface (a heinous accusation of superficiality) to a coli bacillus. She is arrested, tried, and found guilty of treason to the Bacterial State, and to members of a proud and ancient race. The perpetrators of the outrage, the Human Race, were declared pathogenic, and she was sentenced to be autoclaved at 20 lb pressure.

Marjory Stephenson enjoyed Jane Austen, music, painting and travel. She noted: 'From my Mother I derived a taste for English literature and an interest in painting, especially the Dutch and Flemish Schools.'[42] In politics, with most of her colleagues, she belonged to the intellectual, anti-fascist left. She toured the USSR with Dorothy Needham, known as Dophi, and Kits van Heyningen in 1936, and was both impressed and disappointed. She served as Vice-President of the Association of Scientific Workers, of which Hopkins was President in 1938. She also enjoyed giving hospitality to colleagues, friends and students.

She worked for women's suffrage in her youth, and remained a feminist, taking a practical interest in the affairs of her College, Newnham, and in the founding of the Women Graduates' Club in Mill Lane. Myra Curtis, a friend and contemporary from their student days, with whom she shared a flat in London, became Principal of Newnham in 1942.

WOMEN IN SCIENCE IN CAMBRIDGE

Hopkins's laboratory was unusual in its high proportion of women, about 15 per cent.[43] Walter Fletcher remarked in 1927: 'His place bristles with clever young Jews and talkative women.'[44] Dorothy Needham wrote in later life:

Women research workers were very rare in Cambridge at that time [1920] ... [Hopkins] welcomed them, and there were perhaps nine of us ... Hoppy as we called him affectionately, was a very accessible head of department ... would come frequently to our bench to hear the latest state of play ...

Looking back over my 45 years in research I find it remarkable ... that although a fully qualified and full-time investigator ... I simply existed on one research grant after another, devoid of position, rank, or assured emolument ... [I]t was calmly assumed that married women would be supported financially by their husbands, and if they chose to work in the laboratory all day and half the night, it was their own concern. Moral support I also received consistently from Joseph, but it was never in his power to give me the self-respect which comes from a recognised and established position.[45]

Dorothy Needham was elected to the Royal Society in 1948 for her work on muscle chemistry.

Biochemists have formed the largest single category in the female Fellowship of the Royal Society, and this is not unconnected with Hopkins's acceptance of women in this new field. Most women dropped out of research, for family reasons. Margaret Whetham, who married a fellow biochemist Bruce Anderson and left the laboratory when their first child was born, is an example of the loss to science. Hopkins's laboratory was unusual in the number of women 'survivors' in research, but most were childless.

CONCLUSION

Marjory Stephenson's ingenuity of approach allowed her to make sense of cell chemistry, while handling intact cells as quasi-living tissues. Her 'feeling for the organism', to borrow Evelyn Fox Keller's description of Barbara McClintock,[46] included a feeling for the molecule. Thus she wrote of 'enzymes . . . organised to serve growth . . . while others are . . . mere "free lances"'.[47] She was interested in the universality of a chemical process, in animal, plant, or microbe, as well as its selectivity in a particular organism.

Her first Preface acknowledges 'valuable criticism throughout the book' from Margaret Whetham Anderson, whose contribution to science continued through her family.

NOTES

I thank Margaret Whetham Anderson, Patricia Clarke and Sidney Elsden for their help.

1 Margaret Whetham was founder-editor with Juda Quastel of *Brighter Biochemistry*, known as *BB*, which appeared quasi-annually in the Dunn Institute from 1923 until May 1931. Her clerihew appeared in volume 6, p. 47.

2 *Bacterial Metabolism* (London: Longmans, Green, 1949). This book contains the sources of the biochemistry described here.

3 Muriel Robertson, *Obituary Notices of the Fellows of the Royal Society* 6 (1949), 563.

4 Gertrude Elles was appointed Reader in Geology in 1936.

5 Robertson, *Obituary Notices*.

6 M. Stephenson, *Personal Records*, Royal Society.

7 Ibid.

8 *BB* 1 (1923), 51.

TRIUMPHAL ODE
to be sung on the Occasion of the Removal of the Biochemists to their New Building

Bang the Brasses;
Break the glasses;
Blow the bagpipes, beat the drum.
Lo! Professor Hopkins passes;
Lo! the Biochemists come.
And following after are driven their flocks and herds,
Hypoglycaemic rabbits, polyneuritic birds,
Goats, ducks, performing dogs
Deadly bacilli, frogs,
Rats in a teeming shoal
Bound for a gleaming goal,
A far-off promised land
. . .

See how the windows in the sun are shining,
See how the roof is red,
And how symmetrical the whole designing;

Note the neat cycle shed (*soon*).
O, there in dreaming marble halls
Always the Central Sucker calls,
And soup and superheated steam,
Gas coffee and electric power,
Flow each in never-ending stream,
In every biochemist's bower.
There tea,
A feast unparalleled shall be,
Of sugared cakes and crumpets.
(Sound ye trumpets!)
And in the library, carved in gold,
Empanelled heroes shall behold
The biochemist's literary labours
(Ring out, ye tabors!)
When to this refuge biochemists win
(Soft, soft, O violin!)
Then there shall be
Yet one more crowning glory
(O strange enchanting story!)
For each a store-room key.*
(*I don't think.*)
etc.

*On the contrary, Charles will wear uniform and carry a gun.

FGH

9 *Dictionary of Scientific Biography* (1972), 498.
10 D. D. Woods, *Biochemical Journal* 46 (1950), 377.
11 *BB* 3 (1925), 11.
12 Joseph Needham, *Notes and Records of the Royal Society of London* 17 (1962), 117.
13 The word enzyme derives from the Greek word for yeast, which ferments sugars.
14 *Bacterial Metabolism*, pp. 296ff.; P. H. Clarke, 15th Marjory Stephenson Memorial Lecture, *Journal of General Microbiology* 126 (1981), 5.
15 Robert E. Kohler, 'Marjory Stephenson', *Dictionary of Scientific Biography* 18 (1990), 857; 'Innovation in Normal Science: Bacterial Physiology', *Isis* 76 (1985), 162; 'Bacterial Physiology: the Medical Context', *Bulletin of the History of Medicine* 59 (1985), 54; *From Medical Chemistry to Biochemistry: the Making of a Biomedical Discipline* (Cambridge: Cambridge University Press, 1982).

16 Gary Werskey, *The Visible College* (London: Allen Lane, 1978).
17 Joan Mason, 'Hertha Ayrton (1854–1923) and the Admission of Women to the Royal Society of London', *Notes and Records* 45 (1991), 201.
18 Joan Mason, 'The Admission of the First Women to the Royal Society of London', *Notes and Records* 46 (1992), 279.
19 Haldane papers (Burdon Sanderson Archive), University College London.
20 Marie and Pierre Curie received the Davy Medal jointly in 1903, following their Nobel prize with Henri Becquerel. Following Pierre Curie's death in 1906 only Becquerel was elected to Foreign Membership of the Society.
21 Mason, 'Admission of the First Women'.
22 Ibid.; Gertrude Elles (1872–1960) was not elected to the Fellowship. Agnes Arber was elected in 1946.
23 Dale Archive (93 HD), the Royal Society.
24 Mason, 'Admission of the First Women'.
25 Dale Archive.
26 G. P. Gladstone, B. C. J. G. Knight and G. Wilson, *Biographical Memoirs of Fellows of the Royal Society* 19 (1973), 316–47.
27 Mason, 'Admission of the First Women'.
28 Ibid.
29 Ibid.
30 *Year Book of the Royal Society* (1945), 92.
31 *Biographical Memoirs* 18 (1972), 267.
32 I thank Sir Harold Himsworth for these comments, in a letter to me dated 29 August 1991.
33 Mark Weatherall and Harmke Kamminga, *Dynamic Biochemistry* (Cambridge: Wellcome Unit for the History of Medicine, 1992).
34 S. R. Elsden and N. W. Pirie, 'Marjory Stephenson (1885–1948)', *J. Gen. Microbiol.* 3 (1949), 329.
35 Robertson, *Obituary Notices*.
36 Henry Holorenshaw [J. Needham], 'The Making of an Honorary Taoist', in *Changing Perspectives in the History of Science*, ed. M. Teich and R. Young (London: Heinemann, 1973).
37 Weatherall and Kamminga, *Dynamic Biochemistry*.
38 *J. Gen. Microbiol.* 68 (1971), 1.
39 J. Needham and E. Baldwin (eds.), *Hopkins and Biochemistry 1861–1947* (Cambridge: Heffer, 1949).
40 *BB* 6 (1929), 38.
41 *BB* 5 (1927), 36.

42 M. Stephenson, Personal Records.
43 Roster of Hopkins's collaborators and colleagues, in *Hopkins and Biochemistry*, p. 333.
44 Clarke, Memorial Lecture.
45 In Derek Richter (ed.), *Women Scientists: the Road to Liberation* (London: Macmillan, 1982).
46 Evelyn Fox Keller, *A Feeling for the Organism: the Life and Work of Barbara McClintock* (New York: Freeman, 1983).
47 M. Stephenson, 'The Economy of the Bacterial Cell', in *Perspectives in Biochemistry*, ed. J. Needham and D. E. Green (Cambridge: Cambridge University Press, 1937).

Chapter 6

FRANCES CORNFORD
1886–1960

Helen Fowler

Stone, serious familiar colleges,
Cambridge, my home . . .
The same since I was born, the same to be
When all my children's children grow old men . . .

So wrote Frances Cornford in the 1920s. Her grandson, Adam, in California, echoes the poem seventy years on:

'Address to my Famous Forebears'

There you all stand like a row of saints above a cathedral door . . .
like saints recognizable by your trappings . . .
your names flaring and guttering in the black chandelier of the family tree
eight hours of the sun's turning from Cambridge where most of us grew up
the changeless university town that has changed so much since I was born
not quite *the same to be*
when all my children's children grow old men
as you Grandmamma once asserted so confidently.[1]

Confidence, of the special paradoxical Cambridge understated sort, was not lacking in Charles Darwin's granddaughter. In Frances's case it was the family confidence that gave her a quality of assured and enlightened common sense which informed all her relationships and friendships with a variety of people from Rupert Brooke onwards.

Rooted in one of the great 'network' families, Frances had the inborn stability which enabled her to juggle with ideas and convictions, to pursue self-awareness and self-knowledge and to behave with unselfconscious unconventionality. Being part of that charming mob of quirky Darwins, portrayed by her cousin Gwen Raverat in *Period Piece*, Frances imbibed a heady spirit of independence together with affectionate dependence on people, which characterised them all.

She was born in 1886, the only daughter of Sir Frank Darwin, third son of Charles and closest to him, and of his second wife Ellen Crofts, Lecturer in English at Newnham and a great-niece of Wordsworth. With Bernard Darwin, son of a first marriage, they made up a fond, small family. Gwen Raverat considered them as the most sophisticated of her Darwin tribe. Frank was an untypical Victorian paterfamilias, musical, gentle, devoted, involved; Ellen, a clever Renaissance scholar with short hair, 'parrot-tailed Cockatoo-tufted Ellen' as her stepson described her,[2] given to long gossip-sessions smoking on the verandah at Wychfield amongst Persian pots and rugs with her great friend Jane Harrison. Like all the Darwin girls, Frances did not go to school, was educated at home by governesses and taught no science. 'Highly cultivated but quite uneducated', she later described herself. Some aspects of her upbringing were unconventional enough. As Gwen Raverat has recorded, Frances was once keen to persuade her that Christian baptism and belief were not at all the thing and rather provincial.

Photographs of her as a child and adolescent show a girl with a look of resolute containment and a certain wary pride, lots of unruly wavy hair controlled into a bun in later teenage, family close about her, a book never far away. Geoffrey Keynes described her in the *Dictionary of National Biography* as of medium height with dark hair and eyes. Her gypsy look and colouring has also been remembered and a recollection of an ivory complexion and dark 'pitchball' eyes, warm, intent and lively.

What she unhappily also inherited from the Darwins was their disposition to melancholia and depression. In Frank, his depressions began with his first wife's death but the family's 'black dog' may have given him a predisposition to expect the worst. Unfortunately for Frances, her mother too suffered from fits of depression. Such periods, of an intense and exiling kind, from which Frances suffered for years on end, removing her from family and the world outside, can possibly be explained by what she inherited; there may be other and more modern explanations of hormonal causes. Her first breakdown came after her mother's death in 1903, when Frances was 17, and lasted four years.

Frances emerged suddenly and unscathed with painting and drawing as her mainstay and lessons with Sir William Rothenstein, an old family friend. It was he who read her early poems and persuaded her father to have them printed. This world of art which she shared with her cousin Gwen led them into designing the costumes for a production of *Comus* in Christ's Fellows' Garden in 1908. Rupert Brooke, their friend, was producer and Comus was played by Francis Cornford, a young Trinity classics don. He was Jane Harrison's star pupil and companion who shared her missionary zeal for a new approach to classical philosophy. Not only *Comus* but Frances's 'Aunt Jane' brought Frances and Francis together. Jane Harrison failed to foresee the consequences; they fell in love; she herself had a serious breakdown. In later life Frances acknowledged that her adopted aunt had been deeply in love with Francis, who had shared not only work but many holidays and expeditions and a closed world of private jokes and pet names, but that he had been oblivious of this. And indeed the letters Frances had from Jane, asking that she be no longer 'Aunt Jane' gave her no clue either at the time.[3]

F. M. Cornford was a figure in Cambridge not only for his brilliant classical scholarship, but because of his lively and unorthodox opinions: he challenged compulsory chapel and became a member of the Fabian Society. He was a founder member of the Marlowe Society and in 1908 for the delight of the more liberal elements of Cambridge then and every subsequent generation, he wrote a brilliant satire on academic politicking, *Microcosmographia Academica*. A. C. Benson described him in his diary in 1905 as 'the great agnostic, with a fine sturdy pale face and crimped black hair – like a king or Prophet'.[4] Virginia Woolf said he looked like something carved in green marble on a tomb and was as silent.[5]

The Cornfords' marriage took place in the Registry Office in 1909. Jane Harrison wrote that this was hideous but right, 'and one has to do right – still I wish you could have been married under a tree by the old snake'.

Rupert Brooke and his coterie thought of themselves as neo-pagans. The new pair were more honorary than paid-up members. As married people they were comfortably outside the occasionally frenzied ins and outs of emotional and physical entanglements and yet Frances in particular was sympathetically involved in most of what happened and remained Brooke's confidante for all of his short life. Indeed, it is on their letters to each other and other written records of hers that biographies of Brooke have been so dependent. But Brooke was critical of her poetry and malicious about it in letters to great comic effect; as a person he loved, admired and envied her as he did no one else. Frances's famous epigram called 'Youth', but undoubtedly about Brooke, she lived to regret. She was clear-eyed about Brooke and his problems, but deeply fond of him.

> A young Apollo, golden-haired,
> Stands dreaming on the verge of strife
> Magnificently unprepared
> For the long littleness of life.

She was at the beginning of their friendship when that was written. It demonstrates perfectly her shrewd, witty and compassionate grasp of people and her capacity for producing polished and lapidary verse at a very young age. It has all the force and surprise of the true epigram.

Rupert Brooke, we have come to realise, was a complicated young man, enormously talented, endowed with charm, humour and good will, unsure of his affections and of his true sexual nature, longing for the simplicities of a *grande passion* and given to dissipating his capacity for love amongst various women with equal sincerity. Most of his circle were similarly given to uncertainties in their affections; accounts of the various summer camps and reading parties with their pleasures, disasters and emotional intrigues make astonishing reading, for the young especially, eighty years on. It was Frances's role to listen, comfort and advise. One sees her as a swift rescue ship steering a sure course amongst the battered sails and smashed masts of a hopeful little fleet struck by storms and tempests, which had, of course, ignored every weather warning.

Brooke derived great pleasure from contemplating her happiness. When he was in self-imposed exile in Germany in 1911, he wrote to express particular homesick pleasure at a letter from her.

It made me shake with joy to know that Cambridge and England (as I know it) was all as fine as ever . . . Oh I sometimes make up a picture of Conduit Head, with Jacques in a corner and Gwen on the other cushions and Justin [Brooke] on his back and Ka [Cox] on a footstool and Francis smoking and Frances in the chair to the right (facing the fire) . . . It stands out against the marble of the Luitpold Café and then fades . . . But say it's true![6]

His difficulties over his relationship with Ka Cox, not to mention his love for Noel Olivier, he found could only be perfectly understood by Frances. 'She's good and not being a virgin, she understands things. She wants me to go abroad for a year – to Australia or somewhere and work manually. It'd be better for Ka she thinks – It'd be better for me, because I might get well again, she thinks.'[7]

Brooke followed this advice eventually and went to America and the South Seas in 1913. He responded to news of her pregnancy: 'O Frances you seem to have lived very successfully.

Did you square the gods or anything? It must be wonderful to have perfected life.'[8]

In their newly built house, Conduit Head, off the Madingley Road, with the spring of the ancient University water supply bubbling in the garden, Frances must have wondered about the old gods. A sentence later in the same letter must have also made her feel a propitiary libation might be in order: 'I still flirt with the idea of a European war.'

To her poetry, Brooke had this ambivalent attitude. Frances always, though, found him helpful and constructive. His unsentimental jargon-free attitude to writing poetry 'made it feel like carpentering'.[9] He made fun of their versifying attempts, imagining a critic muddling a review: 'Mr Cornford has some pretty thoughts but Miss Brooke is always intolerable' and 'Major Cornford and the widow Brooke are both bad, but Major Cornford is the worst'.

Decidedly when writing to others he thought her the 'worst', describing her and her like as the 'heart criers': 'Women aren't meant to write, I suppose' and inventing a splendid triolet version of a Shakespeare sonnet as by her:

> If you would only have a son,
> William, the day would be a glad one.

Frances was probably aware that Brooke wrote and said different things to different people. That was part of his trouble.

Brooke was staying with the Cornfords at their Norfolk house when the First World War broke out. (The writer was with them at the beginning of the Second.) None of them, perhaps surprisingly, was a pacifist although Frances developed pacifist convictions later in life. Francis became a Sergeant Instructor of Musketry almost at once. Brooke was commissioned into the RNVR and took part in a raid on Antwerp in which his sleeping bag, a parting gift from Frances, perished. 'We all pay our little bit these days,' he wrote to her when safely back.

In little over six months' time, Brooke was a casualty of war and a legend – the young dead heroic poet – a legend which has obscured the importance and value of his poetry and the particular quality of his personality and ideas. The Old Vicarage and Grantchester were to become legendary too. For Frances he was not a legend, but a deeply mourned friend. A sense of her anguish is conveyed in 'Contemporaries', which she wrote that autumn. Those who find the poem a little headily romantic should reflect on her reaction to the statue erected to Brooke on Skyros fifteen years later: 'I daresay I ought to think about the compliment to English poetry and not that it looks like an advertisement for Elliman's embrocation.'

The Cornfords called their next child Rupert John but the first name was later dropped by them as being too romantic. Its bearer was to become as much a heroic legend to his contemporaries as his namesake was to his.

In that same year, 1915, her second volume of poetry was published and one of the liveliest and most loved of the charmed circle, Ferenc Bekassy, was killed on the Eastern front in the Hungarian Army. A scholar of King's, he was one of a number of Bekassys who were at Bedales. Frances wrote a poem about him which is haunting and deeply felt. The impact of romantic sensibility reflected in some of the lines is modified by the economy of her evocation of him.

> Burning brain, and ardent word,
> You the lovely and absurd,
> Say, on that Galician plain
> Are you arguing again?
> Does a trench or ruined tree
> Hear your – O, I don't agree!

Frances was tangled in Brooke's legacy for many years: she consoled Ka Cox and Kathleen Nesbitt by letters and visits. She was also the intermediary between Brooke's difficult mother and Edward Marsh over the latter's memoir and forty years on was involved in objections to the publication of his letters. 'These Darwins are, at heart, dreadful Victorian moralists', wrote Justin Brooke, another old friend of Rupert.

But life for Frances was now to be bounded by being a don's wife, Conduit Head and the children and the writing of poetry. The enlightened upbringing she had enjoyed with her parents was reflected in the easy and close terms between her, Francis and their children. Frances was expected to be interested in what interested them and indeed her son Christopher always claimed that everything was immediately enhanced by her presence. The children ran about the garden barefooted, fresh air and healthy food were insisted upon. Cricket and war games on the beach near their Norfolk mill were *de rigueur* later. They were all sent to fairly conventional schools however, but where some attention was paid to modern ideas.

Frances, far from being a conventional atheist, became a good Anglican. 'They got her in the end,' as Gwen Raverat said. The unorthodox Francis went with the family to services in Madingley Church. Tolerance was the keyword of his life. The younger children always had prayers after breakfast and at bedtime.

Frances had moved easily through Rupert's neo-pagan world, shedding on it her benign common sense and understanding. Now she was to become the same fount of wisdom for her children.

> They must go free
> Like fishes in the sea . . .
> But when there falls the stalking shade of fear
> You must be suddenly near,
> You, the unstable, must become a tree . . .

'You, the unstable': after Christopher's birth in 1917 Frances disappeared into despairing limbo for two years. 'All the Darwins incline that way,' Virginia Woolf wrote in relating the Cambridge gossip. 'The poor woman . . . has now spent two years going from rest cure to rest cure.'[10]

FMC (as he was always known to his growing children) was left to manage a large house and three children, but with servants, nannies, relatives and the ease given by Frances's private income. He was a man of calm intelligence and infinite forbearance, who only panicked sometimes over their clothes.

But Frances's exile ended and she came back, though Christopher remembered her as a little invalidish and retreating often to her summer-house in the garden to write endless letters. Two more children, were born, Hugh and Clare. It was a free and loving life, with stories at bedtime with Frances lying on the floor, an unselfconscious idiosyncrasy, and Sunday evenings reading aloud.

Her husband was now a senior Fellow of Trinity, later to be a professor. Frances was that almost extinct species, a Cambridge lady and academic wife, knowing her place in the College hierarchy, doing her duty by her husband's pupils. There is a rumour that in Trinity they were known as the Duke and Duchess of Madingley. They would have been puzzled to know this. FMC had a daunting silent manner (not unknown in Cambridge) and Frances a consciousness of family prestige but too interested in people to be conventional. Conduit Head was a window on the literary world, with diverse people like Eric Gill and Edward Marsh coming to stay. It was an unstuffy family life, suffused with Cambridge doubt, partially 'parlour-pink', but rooted in old traditions and good manners.

Stowe was chosen for John because it was not an entirely conventional school; but to him it seemed entirely too conventional; he rapidly thought it all a waste of time. He could learn as much at home.

Christopher's reminiscences show the depth of affection and commitment he felt towards John. He was no colourful 'sport' but very much one of the five children who all mattered to each other.

But Frances's close relations with all her children faltered a little with him. John was often brusque and rude to her; one senses that he would not have been at ease with anyone of her faintly sibylline presence. However, Frances was not a wise woman for nothing: she found mutual territory with John in poetry. He had begun to be as passionate in writing poetry as in studying Marxism. Both parents tried hard to understand John's politics, but he despaired of converting his mother. He realised that for her, 'what matters is the inner spiritual freedom', and that devotion to truth characterised the family approach. Frances recognised as part of the Darwin inheritance 'an inalienable right to be doing what is most interesting to oneself and most important all the time', and also 'an unselfconscious demanding too muchness of all of us'.[11]

The search for perfection was characteristic of Frances in all her dealings. One is struck, reading her correspondence with John, by how seriously and intently they took each other, with bravery and candour. Frances sent him her 'Tapestry Song'. John's view was unabashed: he did not like it. For a 15-year-old he was acute in his appraisal of his mother: 'It always seems to me that you have a great deal that needs to be said more urgently but can't because of your view of poetry . . . thanks to Eliot and Graves I am able to tackle a far wider range of subjects in a more direct way.'[12]

Because of this correspondence one necessarily knows more of her relations with her eldest son than with the others, but it reflects that general family intimacy and involvement: the cosy 'Mumma' and 'Dadda' terms by which the Cornford parents, when they were not FCC and FMC, suggest this: they were old-fashioned and slightly childish names.

John left school early and after a year at LSE came up to Trinity at 17: he was remembered even thirty years later by those who taught him for his remarkable mind and brilliance. The poetry he wrote had energy, passion and wit. The all-absorbing political convictions which took him to his death deprived England not only of a thinker but a poet. His unconventional life had already led him into two intense relationships: he had a son by the time he was in his second year at Trinity. To many of his Cambridge contemporaries, he was the most important figure of his day.

Before this happened, Frances fell into one of her worst depressions, which lasted from 1934 to 1940. She left her family to face without her involvement, whether away or at home, John's departure for the Spanish Civil War and his death in 1936. Her illness spared her having to face this terrible fact in all its bleak intensity. By 1940 when she came back to life with a suddenness which startled her family, four years had passed with their veiling shadows. The Second World War had developed from its phoney period to horrible reality. The children had grown up. She was only to have three more years of her husband's life to share. Christopher commented later that despite 'the most awful mental suffering . . . her breakdowns were a kind of psychological strategy of withdrawal and responsibility sharing'. There are of course other views of this, but at the time, her elected absence must have seemed an intolerable strain to the family.

The renaissance of life at Conduit Head after 1940 was 'extraordinary', according to the family. The house was shared with friends, refugees and evacuees; amongst them was Edward Marsh, who relished the unaccustomed family life. There were the sounds of children in the garden again, including now John's son James. Christopher remembers his mother's lively salon consisting of all the literary and artistic world who came to rest in Cambridge, including the First World War poet, Robert Nichols.

It was during the war that Frances began to be interested in translating poetry, from the Russian at first and later from the French. But she continued to write poetry herself. Even when her children were grown up, Frances would be, by choice, the last to bed. As the house grew silent, she would work at a poem and then show it to the family and friends at breakfast for comment and emendation. Her poems were never private or sacred: they were meant to be published and talked about.

FMC's death in 1943 (he was only 69) brought to an end a singularly felicitous marriage. The long periods of depression and breakdown which punctuated this partnership placed on him enormous burdens but did not weaken their attachment. As Professor of Classical Philosophy he had achieved a considerable reputation and is remembered for his teaching and sympathetic understanding by his pupils. His particular gifts brought him close to his wife. The pride he had in John, whom he wryly realised from his schooldays had a mind finer than his own, had given place to unassuaged sorrow at the extinction of so blazing a spirit. At their last parting he had given John his old revolver: a practical symbol; weapons were scarce. Frances would have been appalled but she would have understood.

In the years after her husband's death, Frances's life was active, serene and productive. She was a concerned friend, a shedder of wisdom and blessings and now had a new role to enjoy as mother-in-law and grandmother. Never a sentimentalist, she visited Christopher's wife and child in hospital and observed that babies were brought to their mothers on a trolley, 'like joints of meat at Simpsons', and had first thought they were their mothers' luncheons.[13]

In 1954 her *Collected Poems* was the choice of the Poetry Book Society and she did some readings of her poems on the radio, 'horrified' by the sound of her voice. The year before she died she was awarded the Queen's Gold Medal for Poetry. Deprecatingly, she made a joke of it, remarking that it was originally intended to encourage young poets. Her award, she claimed, was an old boy's prize.

Cambridge and its surrounding landscape, the houses she had lived in, the children she had borne, and her grandchildren, steeped FCC in beloved familiarity. They were all the soil from which her poems sprang. She went on writing to the end of her life when illness brought about a final darkness and detachment. She died in 1960 aged 74.

Frances Cornford has been a neglected poet for many reasons. She herself was humble about her gifts: 'for a woman wanting to lead a usual domestic life, there is no form of creation so feasible as scribbling spontaneously on the backs of envelopes, and then struggling hard with the scribbles during the quiet interludes of time'.[14] One cause of her neglect lies in her exclusion from all the volumes of Georgian verse edited by her friend Edward Marsh, but paradoxically having to share the obloquy heaped on them when fashion in poetry changed. Nor is she mentioned in any of the various books on Georgian poetry. Robert Graves unkindly wrote to James Reeve who was editing a collection of Georgian poetry in 1959, 'Consider Frances Cornford. Then omit?' Various of her poems do appear in many other anthologies: she has the distinction of being included in both Q's *Oxford Book of Victorian Verse* and Yeats's *Oxford Book of Modern Verse*.

What the Georgian poets were trying to recapture was simplicity and joy. FCC herself remarked on the heavy cargo of affectations and half-dead poeticisms from which any minor poet had to get free: a determination to be simple and sincere could lead to trouble. Brooke had lumped her in with the 'heart criers'. A recent book describes her in a footnote as a 'poetess': what more damning?

She seems to have been blamed for the sort of poetry which, in the main, she did not write. What she did write was to be totally uninfluenced by any other poet: there is no evidence that she read Pound or Eliot or Auden or Yeats and if she did, they had no bearing on her kind of creativity. Beauty was a dirty word for John Cornford, according to Christopher. He loathed the escapism, false lyricism and romanticism of the Georgian poets, but in his letters to his mother John managed not to say outright that he classed her poetry with them. Beauty as such, in inverted commas, is not what strikes the reader first, however, about Frances's poetry and this comes perhaps as a surprise. Initially she had wanted to be a painter. Her artist's training gave her a clear eye, an acute sense of an image seen, a feeling for the context of what she was looking at. The family propensity for word games, particularly those played with her half-brother Bernard Darwin, gave her an early feeling for words. Her mother read Elizabethan and seventeenth-century poetry to her. It might be noted that her view of the latter, including Donne, was totally dismissive: 'the poetry of decadence animated not by real originality but by a desire to run in subtle and obscure currents of thought'. Was there some inherited distaste for the subtle and obscure in her daughter? In an early poem, Frances anticipates a new day, 'Whole as an apple'. That image gives a clue to the flavour of her best poetry.

Apart from 'Youth', the most anthologised poem of hers is 'To a Fat Lady Seen from a Train'. Including this triolet in the 1910 volume was an act of rebellion against her father, who opposed its inclusion, perhaps because he recognised the lady as the wife of the Professor of Astronomy. A recent *Oxford Companion to English Literature* dismisses it as 'curiously memorable though undistinguished'. Possibly 'O fat white woman whom nobody loves' is as haunting a phrase as Stevie Smith's 'Not waving but drowning', both poets being doomed to be known by many for these few words. But undistinguished? This brief poem has economy of wit and is elegantly contrived; it has an appealing charm from childhood on: quite a distinction.

Autumn Midnight, published in 1923 and dedicated to the Raverats, has a number of poems which it is easy to mock, 'The Princess and the Gypsy' for instance, with its assemblage of poetic decor. Nevertheless, the princess does not go with the raggle-taggle-gypsies-oh, but is put off by stones cutting her bare feet, bones aching with cold, dogs barking in farms. The apparent sentimentality of 'The New Born Baby Song' suddenly ends with the satisfaction of the baby biting its mother's breast. In 'Susan to Diana', youth is aptly described as 'a water-wetted stone / Bright with a beauty that is not its own'. And the volume contains 'Contemporaries': that face of Brooke's so unmemorably mass-produced since, is memorably 'drowned in time'.

Different Days, published in 1928, celebrates landscapes and figures, old farm horses, brisk gallivanting cocks and hens, a Lincolnshire farmhouse with faded paint on the window sills, a scythe hanging in a sycamore tree, the smell of the church aisle, an old aunt's death-bed quieter than 'the bare, ploughed fields that lay outside', Cambridgeshire haystacks 'like blunt impassive temples', 'square, primeval, dung-stained carts', elms on the Backs 'bark-wrinkled, puddled round their roots'. It is these images one remembers, not the embarrassing elves dancing on tippety toes or even the ichthyosaurus padding about in night gardens snuffing at windows. In all the poems there is a line which tugs one back to reality – a blistered washing stand, the washerwoman's blouse the colour of lilac, a dumpling without any apple, children 'fresh as young colts with every field before them'. The poem in memory of Ferenc Bekassy described earlier and written in 1915 is also in this volume. One wonders if the last poem, 'The Sick Queen', reflects her own feeling of invalid inadequacy when confronted with her lively children and if her way of cutting visiting philosophers down to size was to imagine them with their baby toes once in their mouths.

Mountains and Molehills (1934) has 'The Ode on the Whole Duty of Man' in it, reflecting her views on her role *vis-à-vis* her children. The charming picture of that relationship is given in a witty last line: at the end of the day you have to be 'Sir Isaac Newton sitting on the bed'. 'The Trumpet Shall Sound (*Messiah* 1742)' is deliciously comic with its evocation 'crowned with asphodel and moly', echoing the cries of 'Holy, Holy, Holy'.

Her touch was always sure: the old servant in the poem of that name remembered for dealing with the child's torn skirt,

> Stitching all the while,
> Your cottons on the floor, look up and show
> The sudden light perpetual of your smile –
> Then, with your darning finished, being dead
> Go back and lie, like stone, upon your bed.

Mrs Thompson's death is recorded by the maids:

> They will know first, because the fish-boy heard;
> And as they dust, be sorry, glad, and stirred.

The archaism of these poems is now, amusingly, redolent of the poeticised language of *The Tapestry* or of the *Fairy-Tale Idyll*. The elegiac 'Cambridge Autumn' brings us back to the loved familiar landscape; pheasants, circling rooks, asters by the farm labourer's door, all held in a golden glow of light perpetual.

There was a long interval before the next collection came in 1948, *Travelling Home*, with its plea:

> So let me in this Cambridge calm July
> Fruitfully live and undistinguished die.

The train passes through 'our sober, fruitful, unemphatic land', but it is home and loved for its familiar sights, of an old horse squelching down to a pool, a derelict thatch overgrown with rambler roses and of hot white butterflies floating 'over the soft savannahs of the corn': a most hauntingly sibilant and evocative line.

There is a dramatic flavour to most of the poems: waking up in an attic bedroom or greeting the dawn with – yes indeed – a yawn, a child's view of old age, 'veins like small fat snakes on either hand'. There are Norfolk beaches and in a poem called 'Family Likeness', a Darwinian nudge:

> That eager, honouring look
> Through microscope or at a picture-book,
> That quick, responsive, curious delight –

But some of the poems go back to wartime, when on listening to Schubert's *Lieder* one's enjoyment was streaked with the misery of contemplating the 'enemy alien heart', and falling leaves are a gentle comfort after fallen bombs. The robust simplicity and compassion of 'Soldiers on the Platform' make it worthy of inclusion in any anthology of war poetry.

> Look how these young, bare, bullock faces know
> With a simplicity like drawing breath,
> That after happiness we fall on woe
> And in the midst of life we are in death.
> See how in staring sameness each one stands,
> His laden shoulders, and his scoured hands;
> But each behind his wall of flesh and bone
> Thinks with his secret he is armed alone.

'In the Backs' goes back to an older Cambridge, where in another poem

> Soon he will vanish like a summer's midge
> That calm-struck soldier leaning on the bridge,
> And things are always as they always were.

Things as they ever were include the river hauntings of past poets:

> Milton and Chaucer, Herbert, Herrick, Gray,
> Rupert, and you forgotten others . . .
> [who have] seen the boats come softly as in dream . . .

The River Cam runs through many poems, as it does through Gwen Raverat's drawings. In fact the theme of *Travelling Home* seems to be the comforting continuity of place and people, whether in Cambridge or Norfolk or in her mother's northern home.

In 1954 her *Collected Poems* appeared, containing all the poems she wished to preserve, together with a few later unpublished ones, including an epitaph for Charlotte Brontë in Haworth churchyard which is a perfect example of her skill in the creation of short epigrammatic verse:

> The children of my fiery heart and brain
> Endure, created, like the wind and rain
> Imperishably wild.
> But near this stone, and this iron air,
> I died, because my body could not bear
> A mortal child.

On a Calm Shore, poems with designs by Christopher Cornford, appeared posthumously in 1960, but the preface and explanation are by Frances. 'The coloured designs are not intended to be direct illustrations of the text. Partly they are there as invitations to the reader to pause between one short poem and the next but more essentially they are a sort of obbligato of imagery evoked by my verses in the imagination of an artist of another generation.' The book is certainly a successful marriage of words and design. Her consciousness always of the look of things had affected the way most of her books were produced and illustrated. Eric Gill, her old friend, 'decorated' with wood engravings *Autumn Midnight*. Both *Spring Morning* and *Mountains and Molehills* were illustrated with Gwen Raverat's woodcuts. The paper the poems were printed on and their layout on the pages lend a visual and tactile complement to them.

FCC was not a poet who worked in solitude in her own ivory tower in sole contact with her muse. She acknowledged her debt to Edward Marsh, 'who with unfailing and constructive patience, helped me to civilise them [the poems] and guide the obdurate words nearer to my heart's desire'. This predilection for craftsmanship rather than flashing inspiration is a notable quality in her work and it is this aspect which both caused her to be interested in translating poetry and made her so good at it.

She translated, with her friend, Esther Salaman, various Russian poems, published in 1939, and produced with Stephen Spender a translation of *Le Dur Désir* by Paul Elouard and later some poems of Apollinaire in 1950 which were posthumously published in 1976. In her preface to *Poems from the Russian*, she declared that a good translator should perceive at once what is essential in a poem, both in words and meaning, and remain faithful to this at all costs but be permitted to invent when the literal translation is laboured. Obviously making an English version of these poems, like carpentry, was satisfying and she enjoyed working with Esther Salaman, who produced the language expertise.

Stephen Spender, in his introduction to *Le Dur Désir*, wrote of the necessity of reproducing the poetic intensity of the original. He had been dissatisfied with his version and sent it to FCC, 'who is, in my opinion, one of the best translators living'. The result was a collaboration and they were aided by Lucy and Christopher Cornford and Father Dominic de Grunne. The poems, written under the shadow of the German occupation of France, were illustrated by Marc Chagall. His elegant, mannered, sparse drawings reflect in mood the dry mannered images of the poems.

Fifteen Poems from the French were stylishly printed on marbled paper by the Tragara Press in Edinburgh. There are poems by Apollinaire, Heredia, Baudelaire and du Bellay, with translations faithful to the spirit and inspiration. One can imagine the pleasure the exercise gave her.

Pleasure indeed is what writing gave her, the pleasure of turning everyday experiences into 'real poetry in a book' and the pleasure of finding the right word, the right line. When her very first clutch of poetry was published, it was reviewed by Roger Fry and he wrote about it in a letter: 'she has felt things quite for her self and managed to say them. It's strange that should be so rare because when it's done it seems so simple and as though anyone could do it.'

It is this transparent quality which marks out her poetry. It has no opaque density, no ambiguities, no layering of meaning.

Perhaps this is what brought her poems to the common reader in the various periodicals which published them, such as *Encounter*, *The Listener*, *Time and Tide*, *Country Life*, *The Spectator*, *The New Statesman*, etc.

When she died, her obituary in *The Times* suggested that the quiet and distinctive quality of her work, its precision and unpretentiousness had brought about her own minor revolution in poetry: there was nothing new but there was nothing out of date either. Her obituary in the *Cambridge Review* disputes her assertion that she was not a professional poet by placing her in the decent company of many of the so-called leisure poets: Cavalier lyricists, Elizabethan sonneteers, Herbert, Herrick, Marvell, Arnold, etc.[15] She would have been agreeably surprised to find herself in such a troop. Yet scribbling on the backs of envelopes is not so very different from Jane Austen's brushwork on ivory (two inches wide) slid under a blotter at domestic interruptions.

NOTES

Conversations with the late Professor Christopher Cornford, with Dr Hugh Cornford and Dr Tim Rogers have greatly helped in this study. Other references include:

1 Adam Cornford, 'Address to my Famous Forebears'.
2 F. Darwin, *The Story of a Childhood* (privately printed 1920).
3 Letters from Jane Harrison (Newnham College Archives).
4 David Newsome, *On the Edge of Paradise* (London 1980).
5 Virginia Woolf, *Letters*, vol. 1 (London 1975).
6 *The Letters of Rupert Brooke*, ed. Sir Geoffrey Keynes (London 1968).
7 *Song of Love: Letters of Rupert Brooke and Noel Olivier*, ed. Pippa Harris (London 1991).
8 *The Letters of Rupert Brooke*.
9 Rupert Brooke, *Collected Poems, with a Memoir by Edward Marsh* (London 1918).
10 Virginia Woolf, *Letters*, vol. 11 (1976).
11 *Selected Writings of John Cornford with Some Letters of F. C. Cornford*, ed. J. Galassi (Carcanet Press 1976).

Frances Cornford, 1886–1960

12 *John Cornford: a Memoir*, ed. Pat Sloan (London 1979).
13 Edward Marsh, *Ambrosia and Small Beer* (London 1964).
14 Poetry Society, *Bulletin* no. 3 (1954).
15 John Press, *Cambridge Review* 15 October 1960.

Chapter 7

EILEEN POWER
1889–1940

Maxine Berg

When G. M. Trevelyan published his *English Social History* in 1944 he dedicated it to the memory of Eileen Power, Economic and Social Historian. Her story has not been told, yet she brought together high academic honours, an international reputation, and a popular literary following in ways the great male historians did not achieve. For Eileen Power, as part of the academic elite, sought to write the history of the broad spectrum of society, and to take this history out beyond the small world of academic audiences. She brought medieval history into the general culture and made social history a prominent part of the historical disciplines. In doing so she was also a leader in the field, staking out new historical subjects and methods.

Eileen Power was educated in Cambridge and taught there for eight years. She subsequently taught at the London School of Economics for the rest of her career. She remained, however, closely connected to Cambridge through friends and other historians, especially J. H. Clapham and his family and M. G. Jones, and she returned there to work most summers over her life.[1] She turned down the almost certain opportunity to hold the Chair of Economic History in Cambridge in 1938 so that her new husband, M. M. Postan, could apply. She finally spent the last two years of her life there as his wife and as a member of the London School of Economics during the war years when it was evacuated to Peterhouse.

Eileen Power was born into a substantial middle-class family in Altrincham, an exclusive suburb of Manchester. She was the oldest of three sisters. Her father had Irish roots; her mother's family was middle class, and there were close connections with two spinster aunts and her maternal grandfather. This extended family was to be important, for her father was convicted of a massive fraud on the Manchester Stock exchange in 1891, was declared a bankrupt in 1893, and served a five-year prison term, and several others in the years afterwards for subsequent financial crime.[2] Her mother moved with her and her baby sisters to Bournemouth and lived for a time under an assumed name. The family was deeply affected by the scandal; they were financially ruined, and given no support by their father's side of the family. Their mother's family was not well off, but provided what support they could. The scandal also had a deep emotional impact on Eileen; she never saw her father again, and perceived his crime as a dark shadow on her life.

Her mother died of consumption when Eileen was 14. The sisters were then brought up by their spinster aunts and maternal grandfather, moving to Oxford to attend the Oxford High School for Girls, the school their mother had wanted them to attend. The school was a part of the Public Day School Trust, with minimal fees and a high academic reputation. There the sisters were brought up to expect that they would earn their living. All went on to university. The school also fostered in Eileen a deep interest in literature and history, and from her school-days she built up a wide-ranging command of poetry and an ability to write it herself.

Eileen Power went to Girton College, Cambridge, in 1907 on a Clothworkers' Scholarship, and also held the Pioneer's Prize for History during the three years she was there. She took a First in both parts of the Historical Tripos in 1910. There was only one other woman in her year among the history students with these results. She was taught history there by Ellen McArthur, an economic historian, and later by Winifred Mercier, who became better known later as an educationalist.[3] The College, and especially Ellen McArthur, had a close connection with Archdeacon William Cunningham, a Fellow of Trinity and one of the first academic economic historians in England. It was through this connection that Eileen Power was later to follow the path from Girton to the LSE taken before her by Lilian Knowles.

She was also taught by tutors outside the College, though there is now little evidence of who these were. She kept an undergraduate essay set by one tutor on the pedestrian question, 'Describe the chief forces at work which made for change in Europe towards the end of the fifteenth century'. His comments on her essay: 'You show a tendency to deal in the a priori imaginative reconstruction which . . . is somewhat dangerous today.'[4] Eileen's comment back was: 'My good man, how else do you expect me to treat the Renaissance?'

Though the Girton history dons played an important part in Eileen's early career, it is unlikely that they filled the role of mentors in her historical interests. Eileen Power was trained in economic history while an undergraduate, but Ellen McArthur was teaching at Girton only for Eileen's first year. Probably a greater influence on her historical interests was provided by Edward Armstrong (1846–1928), Bursar and history tutor at Queen's College, Oxford. Eileen visited him frequently in Oxford during holidays, and his own interests in the Renaissance, languages and travel attracted her. He offered historical advice, lent her books, and asked her out to plays at Bradfield, where he was Warden.[5] He played the older man, mentor and father figure she longed for at an impressionable age.

During Eileen Power's time at Girton the Mistress was Emily E. C. Jones, famous for the high quality of her final examinations, especially in economics. Her success had challenged the position taken by Alfred Marshall, who had fought the participation of women in teaching and in the wider university life of Cambridge. He conceded after Jones's Tripos that women were good at examinations, but this, he argued, was because they were naturally diligent, and they lacked the ability to go further. Jones in fact later published several major treatises on logic.[6] Miss Jones was known as 'Jonah' to the undergraduates, and was later described by Dora Russell, another old Girtonian, as 'fragile and exceedingly ladylike'.[7] The Vice-Mistress was Katherine Jex-Blake, a classics don. She was seen by the students as a severe character, 'thoroughly robust and rather like a horse', and popularly known as 'Kits'.[8]

There was then a marked difference between the older and younger generation of dons. The older ones belonged to or identified with the pioneers of women's higher education; they were Victorian in dress and hairstyle, feminist and committed to the campaign for women's suffrage, and single-mindedly academic. The younger generation was closer to the students who now looked on their education as part of, not an alternative to, futures which might include marriage and family life. Dances, clothes and love affairs were for them as much a part of university life as they had not been for their elders. Eileen joked about Miss Jex-Blake to her friend Margery Garrett in 1910, 'Miss Jex-Blake's latest: What *is* a camisole?'"[9]

Eileen may not have found the serious bluestocking feminism of the Girton dons particularly appealing, but she certainly became closely involved in feminist and suffragist activities while she was at Girton. Her best friends included Margery Garrett, later Spring-Rice, the niece of Elizabeth Garrett Anderson and Millicent Fawcett and Karin Costelloe, sister of Ray Strachey, daughter of Mary Berenson and niece of Alys Russell. Her other close friend at Girton, and the one with whom she remained in closest touch throughout her life, was Mary Gwladys Jones. She was influenced in her own personal approach to feminism to a large extent by her upbringing in a family of self-reliant women, and by her contemporaries at Girton, but she always maintained a great affection for McArthur and Mercier, who were not only tutors, but leading suffragists of their older generation. She joined the National Union of Women's Suffrage Societies, and was initiated into speaking on platforms by Alys Russell. She later did some organising work for the National Union, and her sister Beryl and several of her close friends became full-time organisers.

This did not divert her from the hard work of preparing for her examinations, and doing enough work in economic history to be hired while still in her final year to coach Newnham students in the subject: 'a great "honnah" for EEP to say nothing of some £25 per annum in her pocket – 18 freshers to coach, and I get 2/6 per paper and 1/6 per hour's coaching once a fortnight'.[10] The First she earned in the Historical Tripos also brought with it the Gilchrist Scholarship.

This took Eileen Power to the Ecole des Chartes in Paris for a year, and there she studied under the supervision of C. V. Langlois, the eminent medieval literary and social historian who also taught Marc Bloch. The time allowed her to range widely over medieval and Renaissance art and literature. She wrote in the autumn of 1910:

I don't believe one can ever do good work on the history of a period without getting soaked in its literature, art and general atmosphere, and that is what I am doing now . . . I love being able to spread myself over what at college had to be irrelevancies – the art and literature and to feel that duty and pleasure coincide.[11]

She also worked seriously on palaeography, and benefited from Langlois's expertise in that area. At Langlois's suggestion she started a thesis there on Isabella of France, wife of Edward II (popularly known as the 'she-wolf'), and described by Eileen Power as 'the most disreputable woman of her day – her young life was a perfect hotch potch of lovers and murders and plots'.[12]

In the summer of 1911 she returned to England, her funds depleted, and expected to seek a teaching position in a school or a college. She was very unhappy at the prospect of teaching, but knew she had to support herself, and for a time her sisters too. She had written to Margery Garrett from Paris,

You don't know how I long to be able to research & write books all the time. I am so infinitely more cut out for that than for stumbling along the dull path of dondom, & I could weep sometimes when I think that sooner or later I shall have to start earning my living & only be able to get in fitful research work, in odd moments . . . I'm dead keen on work at present & I will not hurry Isabella & do her badly . . . O Margie, I don't really think I feel like a don. I want to write books. Oh dear, Oh dear![13]

She then heard about a Fellowship at the LSE; she applied for and was awarded the Shaw Research Fellowship there for two years. This paid her £105 a year, and she also assisted Hubert Hall in his research. On this she kept a set of rooms big enough to accommodate her sisters, Rhoda and Beryl, both now at university, during their vacations. Money was always short in the family; the house in Oxford had been given up after her grandfather's death, and one of her aunts was doing secretarial work in London.

Under the terms of her Fellowship, she had to give up her research on Isabella in favour of broader work on medieval women. The LSE did not initially appear very attractive, and she wrote of her feelings:

I am extremely perturbed because the whole thing has turned out very much more economic than I expected, and I sometimes have doubts whether I am doing the wisest thing . . . I am bound to enter my name for the degree of D.Sc. (Econ) at London. I don't want that degree: I simply detest Economics and always have, and besides I'm a perfect fool at them – the literary and purely historic side is my line.[14]

She was also horrified when the School sent her a list of 'six perfectly disgusting and exclusively narrow economic subjects' to choose from. The topics made her 'weep with boredom'.[15] Despite the topics set her, she did manage a compromise, and pursued research then on medieval English nunneries under the supervision of Hubert Hall at the LSE and G. G. Coulton in

Cambridge. The first four chapters were submitted for a London MA, and Power eventually published her first major book on this work, *Medieval English Nunneries*, in 1922.[16]

As it happened, however, Eileen stayed at the LSE for only two years; by the summer of 1912 she was also back tutoring at Girton. After the constant worries over money while she was in London, she now had free rooms and meals in college, and earned £27 6s over the summer. Despite the rapid descent of 'dondom', she was clearly pleased to be back, and was teased by the dons about her clothes.[17] Over the next two years she combined a Directorship of History at Girton with some lectures at the LSE, and lived between Girton and a flat in London she shared with Karen Costelloe. The flat also provided a place during the vacations for her sisters, her friends and the occasional hunger striker or refugee. She felt particularly responsible for Rhoda: 'her delicacy makes her a great responsibility & as I upheld giving up the Oxford house & am moreover the only monied woman (lord!) of the three, the family looks to me to see after her, naturally'.[18] In the spring of 1915 she applied for and got the Pfeiffer Fellowship at Girton with the backing of Lilian Knowles, but continued to do some teaching at the LSE. The Pfeiffer allowed for a reduction of her tutorial teaching, and gave her more opportunity for writing. In 1917 she was awarded the Gamble Prize for an essay, 'The Enclosure Movement in English Nunneries'.[19]

Eileen Power's closest mentor for her research while she was in Cambridge was G. G. Coulton of St John's. He was the renowned anti-clerical historian of monastic life, with a mission in life to dispel the myth of medieval golden ages in religious life and in the lives of the peasantry. In doing this he wrote not of their ideas or of the laws and customs affecting them, but of their daily lives, with all their peccadilloes and inadequacies. Eileen Power followed Coulton's approach, though with a less polemical tone and more sympathy and wit, applying it to the lives of medieval nuns. The Master's thesis and the book which emerged from it were the first social and economic studies of women's religious communities in the Middle Ages. It broke free of earlier historical traditions in manorial history and medieval religious thought to present a highly readable account of the distribution of wealth among convents, their economic activities and division of labour, and the social backgrounds, daily lives and careers of the nuns. She wrote of her subjects with warmer sympathy than did Coulton of his, for he was much more preoccupied with discrediting the Roman Catholic historians' ideas of the Middle Ages.

Eileen Power also wrote during these years her widely read articles, 'Medieval Ideas about Women', and 'The Position of Women' in Crump and Jacob's *The Legacy of the Middle Ages*. She was dismissive of the latter piece as 'one of those gossips about social life which ought to be bought by the yard at a department store'. Her piece on medieval ideas had originally been rejected by the editors because it was 'not sufficiently respectful of women, the church and the proprieties'.[20] Eileen Power's book and articles, researched and written during these years in Cambridge, established her as an authority on medieval monastic life.[21] When she turned her attention to bourgeois and working women she seemed to enjoy their company more than she had the nuns'.[22] But the novelty of this work, and her ability to comment on women's position across the social spectrum of medieval society reinforced her reputation as a social historian and established her as one of the first major historians of medieval women.

Teaching during these years was dominated by the war and suffrage work. Wartime Cambridge had the reputation of a bleak place of women and old men. But it also opened up some opportunities for women tutors in the University. In practical terms, the early days of the war meant only some disruption to teaching and the presence of soldiers about the place. The war disrupted classes, and by late September 1914 Eileen heard that nearly all the young men at the LSE had enlisted. She wrote to Beveridge offering to postpone her lectures: 'After all it would be horrid to come up weekly for an audience of two or three.'[23] Eileen wrote to Margery in January 1915:

We are having what the Daily News calls Cambridge in the Grip of War. The War Office at one blow struck our light out and our bells silent on the eve of his Imperial Majesty's birthday . . . And there is a picket of soldiers at the bottom of Woodlands & a barricade of carts & a sentry across Huntingdon Rd & any cars going in & out are stopped & searched & the name of the occupant taken. The Director of Studies in History much enjoys being saluted & questioned by romantic young officers on her way back from her Thursday lecture.[24]

But a few months later the killing had affected her own family, and her youngest uncle had died in Egypt.[25]

Eileen found life in Cambridge very tedious by the later stages of the war, and complained after visiting Margery:

I get the most ghastly blues over the contrast between you & this. I don't believe I was ever cut out for this sort of life: I die within month by month . . . the war makes it worse, for Cambridge is an awful place to be in just now – no one under forty! . . . It seems such a short life for all the best years of it to be spent here . . . I really think the deadliness is chiefly due to abnormal war conditions – there *isn't* anyone to talk to even in Cambridge.

By 1918 she was entertaining hopes of a job coming up eventually in London, and in the meantime, wished that she could go half time at Girton, and have the rest of the week in London.[26]

She survived the time, however, by frequent trips to London, doing some work for the National Union, and doing some lecturing for the WEA and the League of Nations. She gave one with Mrs Fawcett in 1915 at a suffrage meeting, and spoke on the Congress of Vienna,[27] and followed the topic up a few years later for the WEA:

I'll do something I'm very keen on & have just lectured on here – to wit the Congress of Vienna & the attempt at government by a confederation of Europe 1815–23. The parallel with the present is simply amazing . . . it is exceedingly important as propaganda because it broke down for reasons which will wreck the League of Nations after the Congress at the end of this war, if its mistakes aren't avoided.[28]

Eileen was also sustained by her friends among the younger tutors at Girton, especially Elizabeth Downs and M. G. Beard, the German tutor, and by teaching. When Dora Russell was a student she often saw Barbula Beard and Eileen together, Beard 'a tall elegant Irish woman with a slight stoop and a lorgnette and a very agreeable brogue' and Eileen: 'we always found it a pleasure to watch her, tall and placid and very much a personality, as she came in to take her place for dinner at high table. She had very beautiful candid blue-grey eyes.'[29]

Eileen's youth made her a popular and favoured tutor and chaperone, and she was well aware of this:

I wish it made no difference to the students to have people like me & Pico [Elizabeth Downs] here. And yet when I look at some of them after I've put three years of my best effort – moral & intellectual – into them I cannot conceal from myself that they've started life better equipped than they would have been without us.[30]

Her students, especially the favoured inner circle, clearly idolised her. She was a good lecturer, bringing all into her confidence, and she provided the style, intelligence and wit they all aspired to. She was their 'princess out of a medieval story book' who 'sat at the edge of her chair, offering chocolates'.[31] She had a room with a black carpet and ran poetry and musical evenings, reading avant-garde poets like Rupert Brooke, Ralph Hodgson and W. H. Davies.

Eileen's Sunday poetry readings were an institution: 'We looked forward to them all week and wore our best white or pink crepe de chine blouses in honour of the occasion.'[32] Mary and Theodora Llewelyn Davies, students at Girton between 1914 and 1920 wrote: 'we were a generation of young women starved at a sensitive age of most of the normal poetry of life. Our imaginations were caught and our affections held by Eileen's dazzling personality, by her brilliance, her beauty and her goodness.'[33] The students found themselves somewhat in awe of an intellectual superiority and a social poise that kept them at a distance. Interspersed with these performances, however, were more down-to-earth confessions to Margery Garrett: 'I am feeling dreadfully depressed owing to dowdiness. My new coat & skirt which I got at the end of the summer (a silly thing to do anyhow) looks hopeless and I cannot see in the whole of London a hat that looks decent. Also I want a coat dress more than words can say.'[34]

The war ended, and with it the old enclosed order of the College. The men returned to the University, and Dora Russell was a Fellow in Girton on the occasion when

> just after the First World War ended a horde of undergraduates stormed out from Cambridge, . . . yelling 'where are the women we have been fighting for?' Hanging out of every window and preparing to descend were, needless to say, the women in question. Miss Jex-Blake, like an abbess, in her plain alpaca bodice and full long skirt, followed by a retinue of senior dons, received the invaders at the doorway under the arch . . . Then she invited them to a dance at the College on the following Saturday. Such a function would not have been thought of only a few years previously.[35]

Dances at Girton were one thing, but integration into the Cambridge academic community was still some way off for the women. Eileen was clearly unhappy with the new 'double standards' of post-war University life. When she was asked to write a women's column for *The Old Cambridge*, she used the space to denounce the idea.

> Let the women of Cambridge speak out in 'The Old Cambridge', but let it be side by side with the men under any of the headings which interest them, and not snugly tucked into their own column, cheek by jowl with the fashions . . . Editors and reviewers are all the same: they think they know a woman's work when they see it . . . But they have no real criterion, because there is no real difference. The difference is between good books and bad books, straight-thinking books and sentimental books, not between male books and female books.[36]

If Cambridge had not yet moved on enough even after the war to accept fully an academic woman like Eileen Power, her own life and those of her friends had. Eileen continued work on her *Nunneries* book, and spent part of the winter and summer of 1917 and 1918 in Coggeshall living in the Paycocke house while she worked on papers there for her *Paycockes of Coggeshall* (1920).[37] She supported Margery Garrett over these years in her pregnancies, the death of a child, and the death of her husband Edward Jones at the Somme. She watched her friends Ruth Dalton, Mary Brinton Stocks and Karin Costelloe Stephen marry,[38] but had herself formed no serious liaisons. The great event of her life was to come with an interview in 1920 for the Kahn Travelling Fellowship.

The Kahn Fellowship was a special prize fellowship providing funding for a year's travel around the world. It had been held in 1912 by Goldsworthy Lowes Dickinson, who used it to travel with E. M. Forster, but it had never before been held by a woman. Eileen Power wrote of her interview with Sir Cooper Perry, the Vice-Chancellor of London University:

> But I rather doubt their giving it to a woman. Sir Cooper Perry obviously did not take women's work very seriously (or perhaps it was me he didn't take seriously!) One of his obiter dicta was 'I have often been amused of women historians; so many of the springs of human action must be hidden from them.' He also suggested that I might defeat the objects of the trust (*sic*) by subsequently committing matrimony, so I suppose he keeps his wife in purdah: anyhow these silly remarks would not be made to male candidates. However he obviously can't help being made like that, so I possessed my soul in patience and without argument.[39]

This trip, at a still formative part of her life, had a major impact on her subsequent historical interests. Her innovative perspectives on writing comparative social and economic history were first formulated during this year, as were her interests in medieval travellers and merchants. And it was on this trip that she acquired the special attachment to China for which she became well known. While she was in China she met Reginald Johnston, the tutor to the young Emperor of China; on a subsequent trip in 1929 she became engaged to him for a time.

Marjory Stephenson, 1885–1948

Frances Cornford, 1886–1960

Eileen Power, 1889–1940

Nora Kershaw Chadwick, 1891–1972

She visited Oscar Browning in Rome, the 'great old boy of Eton and Kings, hero of a hundred stories'. He was then at the age of 83 writing 1,000 words a day of a *History of the World*. In India she joined in debate over reform in the wake of the Amritsar Massacre, attended the Nagpur Congress, and met Gandhi. She found parts of India for 'all the world like the middle ages', something of a relief from the Congress, 'westernised Indians discontented with westernisation'.[40] She spent two months in China, and was profoundly affected by it. She wrote several imaginative pieces and poetry while she was there, and felt herself entering a medieval world. The country touched the romanticised orientalism deeply embedded in her cultural heritage. She was fascinated by its combination of a rationalistic rather than religious outlook with a 'medieval carelessness of all that we mean by progress'.[41] She was to write to Coulton some years afterwards: 'The A.K. fellowship has been my ruin, for my heart will stray outside its clime & period. I think I shall have to compromise by working at the trade between Europe and the East in the middle ages.'[42]

Eileen Power's life was changed even more significantly while she was in China on the Kahn Fellowship journey, for it was there that she received a letter from William Beveridge offering her a job at the London School of Economics. She felt some regrets about leaving friends at Girton, but she was ready to go, her resolve steeled by the vote in Cambridge against giving women University degrees and making them full members of the University. 'I want to be in London for a bit & I'm tired of community life . . . I'm damned tired of being played fast & loose with by Cambridge University.' The compromise of the 'titular degree' 'left women's position in the university exactly where it was. I've never felt so bitter in my life.'[43] 'My idea of life is to have enormous quantities of friends, but to live alone. And I do not know whether Girton or the study of medieval nunneries did more to convince me that I was not born to live in a community.'[44]

After Eileen Power came to the LSE the predominantly literary, cultural and social framework of her history was to change under the influence of the social sciences then being fostered there. When she first came to the LSE she described herself as half-way through a major study of medieval women, from which the book on nunneries was a diversion; but now the larger book was never written. Instead, this work emerged in a number of major lectures on working women, bourgeois women, medicine and midwifery, and in the studies of the menagier's wife and the medieval nun which appeared in *Medieval People*. Her translation and edition of *The Goodman of Paris*, and her work on the family of clothiers, the Paycockes, included extended discussions of courtship, marriage and middle-class women's domestic lives.[45]

One major influence on Eileen Power's work from the time she went to the LSE was her great political commitment to the peace movement, and subsequently, from the mid-1930s, to the anti-appeasement movement. For during and after the war, Eileen Power, like many women who had campaigned for the vote, now joined peace organisations such as the League of Nations Union or the Women's International League for Peace and Freedom. She fostered the study of social and economic history and international and comparative history in the universities and the schools. Eileen Power saw this as her great contribution to the cause of the League of Nations. European and world history, and especially social history, would help to create a community with common historical ideas and with a sense of the likeness between nations. This was the framework for her most famous work, *Medieval People*, for her article 'A Plea for the Middle Ages' and for her research projects afterwards.[46]

When Eileen Power came to the LSE she worked closely with R. H. Tawney. Together they had worked out the courses of study which created the discipline of economic and social history during the 1920s and 1930s. Tawney had a profound influence on her; he was the socialist prophet who gave vision and purpose to her history. Tawney chose a personal engagement with the processes of history to explore fundamental truths. Eileen Power never had his religious sensibility, but she developed a framework of lectures on the medieval economy which focused, like Tawney's own lectures, on the early modern economy, on international connections, trade, merchants and manufacturers and travellers. And Tawney found in Eileen Power the energy, humanism and personal inspiration that made social and economic history as it flourished in Great Britain for half a century their special creation. Together they shifted the focus of economic history away from its former preoccupation with tariffs and the regulation of trade towards social, agrarian and industrial history. Together they compiled *Tudor Economic Documents*, and they pursued common aspirations for changes in economic history towards more sociological, comparative, analytical and international history. Together they founded the Economic History Society in 1926, and Power acted as its Secretary and key organiser until her death in 1940.[47]

The field Eileen Power entered in economic history was a new one, but it was one in which women already played a more than proportionate role in comparison with others. Lilian Knowles herself had supervised a number of women at the LSE whose names became associated with major works: Alice Clark, Joyce Dunlop, Ivy Pinchbeck, Mabel Buer, Dorothy George, Julia de Lacy Mann and Vera Anstey. Women comprised 20 per cent of the 500 people who joined the Economic History Society in 1927.[48]

Eileen Power developed the international aspects of medieval history – medieval trade, comparative economic history and world history – but she kept this history immediate and human by combining it with literary references and personal portraits. Her chapter in 1932 for the *Cambridge Medieval History*, 'Peasant Life and Rural Conditions (*c.* 1100 to 1500)',[49] succeeded in combining a large-scale comparative history of the peasantry across Europe with descriptions of village life, women's work and witches. Her work, within the framework of the social sciences at the LSE and of the international peace movement, thus turned from social and cultural history to comparative economic history and to international trade and industry.

During the 1920s and 1930s Eileen Power's research and her supervision of students focused increasingly on medieval trade and industry. During this time she also worked closely with M. M. Postan, her student, then research assistant, and later a lecturer at the LSE. Postan, a Russian émigré, arrived in England with a background of study in economics, sociology and methodology at the Universities of St Petersburg, Odessa and Kiev, and came to study economic history at the LSE. Eileen Power taught him, and after his disappointment in achieving only a second-class degree in 1924, she hired him as her research assistant, supervised his MA, then found posts for him at University College London and subsequently at the LSE. By the early 1930s they were working closely together developing new courses at the LSE, running the medieval economic history seminar, and pursuing research on the wool trade. They were both also actively seeking, through papers and working groups, to stimulate close connections between economic and social history and the social sciences. Postan was a historian with a great comparative knowledge and a middle European training in sociology and economics.

Eileen Power's own research and the Medieval Economic History Seminar she ran with Postan now traversed the terrain of merchants and clothiers, trade routes, wool farming, taxation, the staple system and politics. The great *Cambridge Economic History of Europe* which she initiated, and the first volume of which she edited with J. H. Clapham and which was published in 1941 just after her death, was perhaps the greatest testimony to the analytical, comparative and international history she fostered at the LSE. It was a far cry from the early social history which she had learned and written at Cambridge. Her own research was to result in a full-scale study of the medieval wool trade. The outlines of this were delivered in her Oxford Ford Lectures in 1939; but her sudden death in 1940 prevented completion of her book.[50]

The Medieval Economic History Seminar which she conducted with Munia Postan trained a generation of medieval economic historians; among these were a number of women including Marjorie Chibnall, Eleanora Carus-Wilson, Sylvia Thrupp, Alwyn Ruddock and Dorothy Oshinsky. It was one of the first such seminars which co-ordinated research on a single topic – medieval trade – making use of the customs accounts as a source. One of the results was her and Postan's *Studies in English Trade in the Fifteenth Century* (1933).[51]

Eileen Power's years at the LSE were marked by close friend-ships, and sociability. She liked the progressive views prevailing there, and the informal and friendly atmosphere. In comparison she described Oxford's academics as 'flies in amber (or are they more like prawns in aspic?)'[52] She exchanged clerihews in the *Clare Market Review* with A. L. Bowley, the statistician: 'Holy Holy Holy, Arthur Lionel Bowley, Decomposing slowly.' His reply was: 'Eileen Power, Fair as a flower, Things will come to a pretty pass, When she withers like grass.' Her friends and close colleagues, Harold Laski, Charles Webster, Tawney and Postan, Sir Mathew Nathan, Humbert Wolfe, the Clapham family and others, gravitated to her house in Mecklenburgh Square where there were frequent dances in the large kitchen in the basement. She held many dinner parties managed by her capable house-keeper, Mrs Saville. These brought together some students, young lecturers and political figures such as Hugh Gaitskell and Evan Durbin with writers, including H. G. Wells, publishers, and visitors from the USA, China and many other countries. She frequented the Gargoyle Club, the Soho nightclub favoured by London's bohemian intellectuals, until she resigned after the Club refused to allow her to take in Paul Robeson when he was visiting London. She was a part of literary London, publishing often in the weeklies, and was loosely connected to Bloomsbury. Neither did she give up her friends in Cambridge. She spent most summer vacations working in Cambridge, staying either in Girton or with the Claphams, and she took many holidays with her old friend M. G. Jones.

She stood out among contemporary academic women as a tall, slim figure, between 5 foot 6 and 5 foot 7 with classic good looks. She was described by John K. Fairbank, the Harvard Professor and historian of China, as 'a remarkable phenomenon . . . she had a Meryl Streep kind of startling good looks, except perhaps a firmer jaw. But her primary characteristic was that she had an LSE mind (I mean this as high praise in the 1920s). She was incisive and intellectually well organized and rather made a point of being well dressed.'[53] Eileen Power fostered a reputation for a taste in exotic and designer clothes. On the publication of an article, she was said to reward herself with a flight on Imperial Airways from Croydon Airport to Paris to buy a new outfit.[54] J. H. Clapham recalled commenting to her at some learned gathering: 'Eileen, you look like Semiramis.' She had replied, 'I thought I looked like a Professor of Economic History.'[55]

In 1937 Eileen Power married Michael ('Munia') Postan, who was by then a lecturer in economic history in Cambridge and a Fellow of Peterhouse. She was then aged 47, and he approximately ten years younger. The marriage was a shock to many because of the difference in their ages, their positions and their physical appearance. Eileen's housekeeper, Mrs Saville, on hearing of the marriage, said, 'I don't like to think of Miss Eileen being walked over at her age, but these foreigners are rather good at it.'[56] A few months later Clapham's Chair in Economic History at the LSE was advertised. Eileen Power was urged to apply and Clapham expected she would be appointed.[57] But this was the chair she had long considered a suitable one for Postan, and she stepped aside in favour of him.

Eileen Power had fostered his career, and long prepared him for this post. She wrote to him in 1932:

Clapham's chair will be vacant in about 7 years' time. You can't get a chair in London or Oxford, because you are blocked by myself and Clark; but I have for some time had my eye on Cambridge for you. It is a snag that you are not a Cambridge man; but as far as I can see there aren't going to be any Cambridge men available, for Clapham has failed to train up any successor of the right calibre . . . It depends entirely on how big a reputation you can amass in the next 7 years, & on how we manage Clapham.[58]

When the time came Eileen Power stepped aside, with the excuse that she preferred living in London.

I do find the LSE a much more stimulating place to work in and London a more congenial place to live in than Cambridge . . . I'm not sure how I should settle down in the much more formal society of Cambridge . . . It would be an honour to hold Clapham's chair (tho' not more of an honour than to hold Mrs Knowles's) – and I know that it would be a good thing from the point of view of the position of women for one of us to get it.[59]

After their marriage they commuted between the house in Mecklenburgh Square Eileen Power had lived in since 1922, and a new architect-designed house they had built at 2 Sylvester Road in Cambridge. But the commuting was soon to go into reverse after the beginning of the war, for Postan was appointed to the Ministry of Economic Warfare and went to London, and the LSE was evacuated to Cambridge. Eileen took two LSE students into her house as evacuees. The dinner parties and dances once held in Mecklenburgh Square were now replaced in Cambridge by Sunday afternoon 'at homes' for economic historians and a mixture of others from Cambridge and London.

Eileen Power gathered many honours over the course of her career. She was given an Honorary D.Litt. in 1933 by Manchester University and by Mount Holyoke College in 1937. She gave the Founder's Memorial Lecture in Girton in 1936 with a paper on 'Pastoral England in the Middle Ages'. She became a corresponding member of the Medieval Academy of America in

1936, and was the first woman to give the Ford Lectures in Oxford in 1939. These lectures were published after her death as *The Wool Trade in English Medieval History*.

Eileen Power died suddenly in London of a heart attack in August 1940. Her death was a great blow to her friends, colleagues and students, for as a personality, a teacher and an initiator of research, she had been so much more than the books and articles she wrote. She left much unfinished, but by the time of her death she held a central place in the creation of the new discipline of economic and social history, and in making this history a major part of the national culture during the inter-war years.

NOTES

1 J. H. Clapham, 'Eileen Power, 1889–1940', *Economica* 20 (1940), 355–9; M. G. Jones, 'Memories of Eileen Power', *Girton Review* 114 (1940), 3–13.
2 *The Times*, Criminal Courts, 29 April 1905.
3 Ellen McArthur (1862–1927) was educated at St Leonard's School under Louisa Lumsden, and lectured in economic history in Cambridge between 1902 and 1912. She was Director of Studies in History when Eileen Power came up to Girton, but left in that year to supervise the History Department at Westfield College. See M. B. Curran, 'Ellen Annette McArthur, 1862–1927', *Girton Review* 75 (1927), 83–103.

   Winifred Mercier (1875–1925) was trained for school-teaching and taught for five years in Scotland. From here she went to Somerville in 1904, and completed a degree in Modern History. She returned to teaching at Manchester High School, and in 1909 went to Girton as Director of Studies in History. She stayed at Girton until 1913, then went into teacher training at Leeds City Training College. She became Principle of Whitelands Training College in 1916, and pursued educational reform until she died in 1925. See Lynda Grier, *The Life of Winifred Mercier* (Oxford 1937), and 'Winifred Mercier', *Time and Tide* (17 July 1925), 695–6.
4 Power Papers, Cambridge University Library.
5 See letters from Eileen Power to Margery Garrett, and the diary Eileen Power kept during her year in Paris in 1910–11. Both are in the Power

Papers held by Lady Cynthia Postan. These are hereafter referred to as Postan Papers to distinguish them from papers in the Cambridge University Library and in Girton College.

6 Alon Kadish, *Historians, Economists and Economic History* (London 1989), p. 149; Rita McWilliams-Tullberg, *Women at Cambridge* (London 1975), p. 88; E. E. C. Jones, *As I Remember: an Autobiographical Ramble* (London 1922), p. 55.

7 Dora Russell, *The Tamarisk Tree: My Quest for Liberty and Love* (London 1975), p. 35.

8 Russell, *The Tamarisk Tree*, p. 35.

9 Eileen Power to Margery Garrett, n.d., 1910, Postan Papers.

10 Eileen Power to Margery Garrett, n.d., 1910, Postan Papers; Newnham College, Education Committee Minutes, 28 April 1910, Newnham College Archives.

11 Power to Margery Garrett, 6 November 1910, Power Papers held by Lady Cynthia Postan.

12 Power to Garrett, 26 March 1911.

13 Eileen Power to Margery Garrett, 17 May 1911, Power Papers.

14 Power to Margery Garrett, 22 July 1911, Postan Papers in possession of Lady Cynthia Postan.

15 Ibid. Eileen Power was interviewed for the Fellowship by Hubert Hall. Charlotte Shaw, a Fabian and wife of G. B. Shaw, provided the funding for the Fellowship, and set the topics. See Shaw, Research Studentship file, BLPES. I owe this point to Carol Dyhouse.

16 Eileen Power, *Medieval English Nunneries, c. 1275–1535* (Cambridge 1922).

17 Power to MLG, 9 July 1912; Power to MLG, August 1912.

18 Power to MLG, 13 September 1912, 17 November 1913, 21 July 1914, 16 March 1915.

19 Power Papers, Girton College Archives.

20 Eileen Power to G. G. Coulton, 5 September 1920, Power Papers, Girton College Archives.

21 'A Melancholy Chronicle', *New Statesman* 20 (27 January 1923), p. 412; 'Medieval People', *Times Literary Supplement* (11 September 1924), p. 551; Bertha H. Putnam, 'Medieval English Nunneries', *American Historical Review* 29 (1924), pp. 538–9.

22 Power, 'The Menagier's Wife, a Paris Housewife in the Fourteenth Century', in Power, *Medieval People* (1924), London 1986, pp. 96–120; Power, 'The Working Woman', in Power, *Medieval Women*, ed. M. M. Postan (Cambridge 1975), pp. 62–70. Power has since been criticised for her failure adequately to set out the extent of these

women's subordination in spite of their contributions. See J. M. Bennett, '"History that Stands Still": Women's Work in the European Past', *Feminist Studies* 14 (1988), p. 270; Olwen Hufton, 'Women in History: Early Modern Europe', *Past and Present* 101 (1983), pp. 38–41.

23 Power to MLG, 25 September 1914.

24 Power to MLG, 21 January 1915.

25 Power to MLG, 16 March 1915.

26 Power to MLG, 25 September 1918.

27 Power to MLG, 16 March 1915.

28 Power to MLG, 7 July 1917.

29 Dora Russell, *The Tamarisk Tree*, p. 36.

30 Power to MLG, 10 June 1917.

31 Dorothy Marshall, Diaries. Dorothy Marshall (1900–1994) was taught by Power at Girton as an undergraduate from 1918 to 1920, and was supervised by her later at the LSE. She did research on the Poor Law, then lectured at Bedford College for four years, followed by a two-year appointment at Durham. She went to a History appointment at the University of Cardiff in 1936, and stayed there until her retirement in 1967. She was the author of several books, among them, *The English Poor in the Eighteenth Century: a Study in Social and Administrative History* (London 1926); *The Rise of George Canning* (London 1938); and *English People in the Eighteenth Century* (London 1956).

32 'Memories of Eileen Power at Girton' by Mary Llewelyn Davies and Theodora Calvert, Girton College Archives.

33 Ibid.

34 Power to MLG, 22 September 1916.

35 Dora Russell, *The Tamarisk Tree*, pp. 35–6.

36 Eileen Power, 'Women of Cambridge', *The Old Cambridge* (14 February 1920), p. 11.

37 Power to MLG, 26 February 1917, 25 September 1918.

38 Power to MLG, 24 September 1914, August 1912.

39 Power to Coulton, 27 April 1920.

40 Eileen Power, Travel Diary, 'Tour du monde', 1, 21 December 1920, Postan Papers.

41 Eileen Power, *Alfred Kahn Travelling Fellowships. Report to the Trustees September 1920–September 1921* (London 1921), pp. 49–55. Cf. G. L. Dickinson, *Letters from John Chinaman* (London 1901).

42 Eileen Power to Coulton, 5 September 1925, Power Papers, Girton College.

43 Eileen Power to Margery Garrett, 21 July 1921, Postan Papers; Eileen

Power to Bertrand Russell, 20 October 1921, Russell Papers, McMaster University.

44 Power to Coulton, 30 January 1922, Power Papers, Girton College.

45 Power, *Medieval People*, pp. 73–95, 152–73; Power, *The Paycockes of Coggeshall* (London 1920); Power, *The Goodman of Paris: a Treatise on Moral and Domestic Economy by a Citizen of Paris c. 1393* (London 1928).

46 Power, *A Bibliography for Teachers of History* (London 1919), published by the Women's International League; Power, 'A Plea for the Middle Ages', *Economica* 5 (1922), pp. 173–80; Power, 'An Introduction to World History', unpublished typescript of book, Postan Papers held by Lady Cynthia Postan.

47 R. H. Tawney and Eileen Power, *Tudor Economic Documents* (London 1924); D. Ormrod, 'R. H. Tawney and the Origins of Capitalism', *History Workshop* 18 (1984), 138–59; J. M. Winter, 'Introduction', in Winter (ed.), *History and Society: Essays by R. H. Tawney* (1978), pp. 1–35; Tawney, 'Eileen Power', address delivered at Golders Green Crematorium, 12 August 1940 (1940).

48 See Maxine Berg, 'The First Women Economic Historians', *Economic History Review* 45 (1992), pp. 314–15.

49 Power, 'Peasant Life and Rural Conditions *c.* 1100–1500', in *Cambridge Medieval History* VII (Cambridge 1932), pp. 716–50.

50 Power with J. H. Clapham, *Cambridge Economic History of Europe*, 1 (published posthumously, Cambridge 1941); correspondence between J. H. Clapham and Eileen Power about the *Cambridge Economic History*, Postan Papers; Power, *The Wool Trade in English Medieval History* (Ford Lectures, published in Oxford posthumously, 1941).

51 The studies eventually emerging from the group of students who attended the Power–Postan seminar include Sylvia Thrupp, *The Merchant Class of Medieval London* (Ann Arbor 1948); Alwyn Ruddock, *Italian Merchants in Southampton* (London 1951); E. M. Carus-Wilson and O. Coleman, *England's Export Trade, 1275–1547* (Oxford 1963); E. M. Carus-Wilson, *Medieval Merchant Venturers* (London 1967); M. K. James, *Studies in the Medieval Wine Trade* (Oxford 1971).

52 Power to Postan, 26 February 1932, Postan Papers.

53 Cited in W. H. McNeill, *Arnold Toynbee a Life* (Oxford 1989), p. 310.

54 Interview with Sir Michael and Miss Barbara Clapham, 21 July 1993.

55 J. H. Clapham, 'Eileen Power, 1889–1940', *Economica* 20 (1940), 355–9.

56 Interview with Sir Michael Clapham and Miss Barbara Clapham, 21 July 1993.

57 Power to Helen Cam, 6 January 1938, Power Papers, Girton College Archives; interview with Miss Barbara Clapham, 21 July 1993.
58 Power to M. M. Postan, 29 January [1932], Postan Papers.
59 Power to Helen Cam, 6 January 1938, Power Papers, Girton College Archives.

Chapter 8

NORA KERSHAW CHADWICK
1891–1972

Hilda Ellis Davidson

Nora Kershaw came up to Newnham College in 1910, to read English in the Medieval and Modern Languages Tripos, when she was 19. She is said to have fallen in love with both town and University, deciding that this was the place where she most wanted to live. Her wish was granted, for after spending the war years lecturing at the University of St Andrews, a legacy enabled her to come back to Cambridge as a private individual, sharing a house in Owlstone Road with Enid Welsford and continuing her researches into Anglo-Saxon and Old Norse until her marriage with Professor Chadwick in 1922. She remained in Cambridge all her life, devoting her time and energies unsparingly to the study of early literature and traditional wisdom, and inspired many generations of students with her rare enthusiasm, originality and breadth of knowledge.

She travelled comparatively little outside the British Isles, although many remote parts of Wales, Scotland and Ireland were familiar ground to her. But she was never a cloistered and sedentary student. From her fixed centre in the flat fenlands her mind voyaged adventurously into the far corners of the world, becoming absorbed in the early turbulent history of Russia, in the Tatar peoples and the Sea Dyaks of Borneo, and the poetry and legends of the islands of the South Pacific. She was an adventurer all her life, driving her little car at great speed out from Cambridge to the Celtic West, and learning to manage a coracle on Welsh rivers; one of her last desires, which horrified her friends and remained sadly unfulfilled, was to travel across Asia on the Trans-Siberian Railway.

Moreover, for all her devotion to Cambridge, she steadfastly refused to accept the constricting social conventions of University life for the wife of a professor between the wars. The Chadwicks ensconced themselves in an old house called Papermills, on the Newmarket Road, where the only means of entry was a small door in a high wall, or through the yard of the Globe Inn to the back of the house, where Nora allowed a family of friendly gypsies space for their caravan in winter. While friends and fellow scholars and students past or present could always find admittance, and the Professor did most of his lecturing there, the door was locked against chance callers and the bell was broken. Nora had no intention of letting her husband's valuable work be interrupted by trivial chit-chat, and she herself steadfastly refused to be distracted from what she believed to be of major importance. Along with her intense devotion to Hector, she had a single-minded dedication to learning and unceasing desire to search for keys to the many problems of the past. 'First things first,' Enid Welsford remembered her saying firmly near the end of her life, when she refused to be tempted from her desk for a drive into the country, although she no longer had a car and relied on such offers to escape from her flat in Fen Causeway. It was this utter commitment which led Elsie Duncan-Jones to describe her as 'a saint of scholarship'.

Not that this meant that she led a grim, austere life devoted to the grey heights of obscure learning. On the contrary, she and Hector had enormous fun together. There were constant expeditions around Cambridge and further afield, with Nora driving, often accompanied by a few students, and ending up at some favourite cottage for a delectable tea. Nora carried a tiny recorder in her handbag and would sit under a tree playing it after a picnic lunch, while at home she had a series of harps, large and small. In the summer she might bathe in the mill-stream which ran past their front door, and both of them derived much pleasure from a succession of dogs with mythological names like Grendel and Loki, together with cats and kittens, and geese, ducks and junglefowl wandering in the garden, to the delight and occasionally the apprehension of the students. 'Excuse me, the goose has got one of the ducks,' I remember the Professor exclaiming suddenly in the midst of a learned exposition on an early Icelandic poem, as he lumbered out to restore harmony. It was said that he wanted to install a little bear as part of the menagerie, but was ultimately dissuaded. Delicious and ample meals, superbly cooked by the devoted sisters, Vera Steven and Nelly Plumb, who spent some forty years in Nora's service, were provided for favoured visitors, together with good wine. Hector, supported and encouraged by Nora, was a superb raconteur, and I can remember sitting helpless with laughter at some of his stories of College life. He was an unexpectedly keen observer of the foibles of human nature, and took a mischievous delight in fantastic situations. One morning when we arrived for a lecture it was to find him entranced by a new problem, a set of false teeth discovered in a tree just inside the garden wall; he was busy concocting possible explanations with the same happy concentration which he showed when discussing the nature of the Anglo-Saxon invasion of Britain, or the origin of the cult of Odin in the North.

For a long time Nora had no official standing in the University, and her unusual subjects of work, well outside any normal University syllabus, might have been expected to cut her off from colleagues and students alike. On the contrary, she made lasting friendships with some of the liveliest minds in the University, establishing contacts with all interested in the Dark Ages in the British Isles, or in the remote peoples of Asia or Africa. As a research student in the 1930s I can remember being first bewildered and very rapidly enthralled by this surprising person, neither a don nor a lecturer, with deep blue eyes and an enchanting smile, who possessed such a wealth of information on unfamiliar topics, and whose approach to early literature was new and unsettling. She continued to open windows for me on to a new world, and busy though she was, she seemed always willing and eager to make time for long discussions in the pleasant tea-room of the University Library or the little summerhouse in the Papermills garden which revolved to catch the sun, where she worked whenever possible.

Nora was strikingly attractive in her youth, and something of her serene beauty remained with her into old age. 'I have a vivid recollection of a strikingly beautiful woman with golden hair in a long blue dress – rather Edwardian style – playing a harp at Papermills in December 1939,' wrote Michael Dewar, one of the Professor's last pupils. 'To describe her appearance can only be done in clichés,' wrote Kenneth Jackson; 'her large, quiet eyes really *were* a cornflower blue, her piled hair which she wore Edwardian fashion really *was* the colour of ripe corn'. Someone who remembered her in the early days told me that when she attended the Professor's classes there was a certain tension among the young men sitting around her, causing them to glare at one another, something of which Nora seemed totally unaware. She herself took little care over her appearance; she never used make-up or had her hair styled in the prevailing fashion, and wore her good, sensible clothes for years, while she seemed unperturbed by the fact that she put on weight considerably after her marriage. But the warmth, animation and sincerity in her face, and the impression which she gave, as long as her husband lived, of an intensely happy and fulfilled woman, gave her irresistible charm. She had also the quality of repose, relaxed but not passive. When her husband lectured on archaeology at Papermills in the 1930s, she used to work the epidiascope for him, showing numerous pictures from his vast collection of postcards and photographs. 'I wonder what she thinks about,' one student said, somewhat concerned at what seemed to him a boring occupation for someone so distinguished in her own right. 'I think she just dreams,' said someone else, remembering her serene face. Dreams certainly meant a great deal to Nora, who often commented on the part which they played in early literature. Someone who was up at Newnham with her told me that a talk on dreams was once given there by a visiting speaker, who asked his audience if any of them found it difficult to distinguish clearly between their dreams and their experiences in waking life, and Nora put up her hand.

Nora was born on 28 January 1891 at Great Lever, near Bolton in Lancashire. Her father, James Kershaw, whom she loved dearly, was a cotton manufacturer and mill owner; when war began in 1914 he was too old to be called up, but he volunteered to go to France with a YWCA canteen, and was killed in an accident. Her mother was Emma Clare Booth, and she had one younger sister, Mabel, whom she described as the lively, outgoing member of the family, enjoying parties and entertainments while Nora preferred a more retiring life, absorbed in books and music and the countryside. Their parents were both keen naturalists, and Nora retained all her life a knowledge and love of birds and plants. Their childhood appears to have been a free and happy one; Nora did not go to school until she was 9, and is said not to have known her five times table at 10. 'Rumour says she was an unmanageable and an unruly child,' we are told in an article about her in the *College Echoes* of St Andrews, and certainly she never lost that strong sense of independence which some of her friends described as stubbornness. Her lifelong friend Nan Ure, who was with her at Stoneycroft, a small private school near Southport where Nora was finally Head Girl, remembered a long tussle with her mother over a dress allowance. It was at last agreed that she should be responsible for her own clothes, and she arrived at school in a state of great excitement: 'That afternoon she went down town and came back jubilant with a Chaucer, a Spenser and I don't know how many other books that she had bought with her dress allowance – no clothes of course.' Nora thought it surprising that it was the lively Mabel who afterwards became a Roman Catholic and entered the enclosed Carmelite Order, but it seems evident that both girls, different in temperament though they were, possessed the capacity to give themselves fully to a demanding ideal.

At St Andrews Nora was described as 'one of those comfortable people who delight especially in non-competitive athletics', although she had played golf, tennis and hockey when younger, and even won a medal at school for climbing a rope. She must have spent much time on music, as she once told me she found it difficult to decide between music and the study of literature as a career, and she was also qualified to teach drawing. In her four years at Cambridge she gained a Class II in 1913 in English (Section A) and Old English (Section B), and a Class I in English (Section A2) in 1914. It was when working on Old English that she encountered Hector Munro Chadwick, who became Elkington and Bosworth Professor of Anglo-Saxon in 1912, and was to be the dominant influence in her life.

She must have considered school-teaching after her time at Cambridge, and I was amazed to hear that she had once been interviewed for a post at my own school in Birkenhead, but the opportunity of an Assistant Lectureship in English Literature with additional lecturing in Old English came up at St Andrews, and she went there in 1914. She is said not to have been wholly happy there, but was clearly popular with the students. One of them described her as 'extremely keen on work for its own sake, she loathes working for set examinations – a point of view which is very welcome in our examination-ridden little University', and goes on to say: 'It is no small tribute to her enthusiasm and keenness that many of her classes have awakened to the fascination of Anglo-Saxon, who erstwhile regarded it as the dullest of all things dull.'

Her return to Cambridge in 1919 brought her back into

contact with Professor Chadwick, at a crucial time when he was working to introduce a radical change in the teaching of Old English and Old Norse as part of English studies. These languages had previously been studied purely from a linguistic standpoint, but Chadwick, who began as a classicist, realised the importance of bringing together poetry, history, art and archaeology as well as language for a fruitful understanding of the literature of the past. He had introduced papers on Anglo-Saxon, Teutonic and Viking Age history into Section B in 1907, and when Nora came back to Cambridge she was able to attend his new course on Anglo-Saxon and Kindred Studies. She threw herself wholeheartedly into the crusade, and her first two books, *Stories and Ballads of the Far Past* and *Anglo-Saxon and Norse Poems*, were evidently produced with the needs of his students in mind.

The first, published in 1921 by the Cambridge University Press, is a collection of translations from the Icelandic 'Sagas of Old Time', tales of early heroes, magic and the Otherworld very different from the more realistic Family Sagas of Iceland. She selected tales which were not easy to obtain outside university libraries, only one of which had previously been translated into English. They dealt with subjects which continued to interest her all her life, such as the journeys of heroes into the Otherworld, the visit of a girl to her father's burial mound to confront the dead and obtain a wonderful sword, and a riddle contest between a northern king and the god Odin in disguise. It was characteristic of her that she did not limit herself to translation and notes; she added an extract from the later Icelandic *Rímur*, and several Faroese ballads sung to accompany dances, since she had discovered that these contained later versions of some of the medieval tales. All this, together with some of the Faroese tunes and information about the music and dancing, was presented unpretentiously, with plenty of information about sources and manuscripts. Indeed to some extent the richness and originality of her approach is obscured by lack of good presentation, since it is not easy to find a clear way through the various sections and to see the book as a whole; this was to remain an occasional weakness in Nora's later work.

The second book appeared in 1922, again published by the Cambridge University Press. It was a collection of texts and translations from Anglo-Saxon and Old Norse of some important and in some cases very difficult poems, with helpful notes and a short introduction to each. There is no glossary, but with the help of a good dictionary and the fairly free translations, the material was now available to students, and could be set as texts for special study.

In 1922, the year this book appeared, Hector and Nora were married. During the previous year they had travelled to Italy with Enid Welsford as chaperon, and there had been many other expeditions together, explained by Hector to the Master of Clare as 'Archaeologising, ye see, Master, archaeologising'. According to Nora, it was on one of these outings that he proposed to her on the Leys at Barton. It was due to Nora's influence that he began to enjoy visiting interesting sites and encouraging his students to do so. Although never an intrepid explorer like Nora – 'I've no head for heights,' I remember him saying apologetically on the extremely limited slopes of Devil's Dyke – he could make a map come to life and bring out the significance of the geological position of some ancient earthwork or fortification to an unusual degree. Nora persuaded him to use a car, a means of transport he had hitherto regarded with profound mistrust, and with her as driver they were able to embark on many exciting quests, such as tracing the various journeys described in the *Mabinogion* across the hills and valleys of Wales.

Their marriage must have astounded academic circles and been a great shock to Hector's devoted elder sister, who had assumed that he was a confirmed bachelor. Hector was twenty years older than Nora, a scholarly recluse and much set in his ways. For instance, he refused to consider for a moment buying new clothes, and when one of his shaggy green tweed suits became impossible to wear any longer, Nora would have an identical substitute made to leave in place of the old one one night, trusting that he would not notice the difference. But such problems bothered Nora not at all. She remembered the new inspiration and happiness which came to her about this time, which she attributed to her discovery of Polynesian literature, but which others thought more likely to be due to her new relationship with Hector.

The wedding itself produced some notable Chadwickian folklore, passed on to later generations of students. It took place very quietly, with only her mother, now remarried to a Dr Martin and living at St Ives not far away, her stepfather and Enid Welsford present for the two ceremonies. There was a service at St Bene't's Church, drastically rewritten, it was said, by the couple, followed an hour later by a second ceremony in the Registry Office, in case the truncated service was not fully legal. Enid thought the choice of St Bene't's was on account of its Anglo-Saxon tower. The hour's gap was occupied by the purchase of a mackintosh by Hector, and a visit to the Archaeological Museum in Downing Street, where he discoursed on the burial urns. Then after a pleasant tea in Clare College the Chadwicks began their new life at Papermills, but took Enid with them to spend what she describes as an 'unforgettable term' – with, alas, no details – in their company.

Although many must have shaken their heads over such a marriage, both were to benefit greatly from the alliance. In 1912 Chadwick had published a major work, *The Heroic Age*, in which he broke away from his earlier work on Anglo-Saxon history and law to introduce a new approach to early literature. He compared the way of life and the ideals found in the Homeric poems with those in *Beowulf* and other heroic poems in Anglo-Saxon and Norse literature. He set out to show how great heroic poetry developed out of an unsettled period before the establishment of powerful kingdoms, when there were many kings and chiefs with small bands of loyal followers seeking lands and wealth, engaged in warfare and feuds, invasions and deeds of daring, memories of which were recalled by later generations and resulted in a rich crop of poems and sagas. These at first would form part of an oral tradition, recited at the courts of kings and great men, but ultimately inspired written literature in a more settled age. This idea of a close link between certain types of literature and the societies in which they were produced seems a commonplace now, but at that time was new and startling. The book also included material from Slavonic and Celtic literature, and Chadwick had intended to develop this further, but had for years been occupied in teaching and in schemes for broadening the study of Anglo-Saxon in the University, so that no more books had appeared. Nora now urged him to return to his theme, and he agreed on condition that she would collaborate with him. The three huge volumes making up *The Growth of Literature*, published in 1932, 1936 and 1940, were thus a joint achievement.

The Preface to the first volume makes their objectives clear. They selected a number of literatures, some ancient, some modern, which appeared 'at least partly independent', their choice depending on the accessibility of the material and 'the limitations of our own knowledge'. They would work mostly on the 'unwritten' literature of isolated and remote peoples, as recorded both in the past and in recent times, although they would not be concerned with the origins of literature, since the collected material gave every indication of a long period of development. The contents of the work were certainly impressive. The first volume dealt with the ancient literatures of Europe: Ancient Greek, Anglo-Saxon, Old Norse, Old Irish and Old Welsh, Nora being responsible for the section on Old Irish literature. In 1927 she had published *An Early Irish Reader* as an aid to students, with the text of 'The Story of Mac Datho's Pig' in Old Irish, together with translation, notes and glossary. She was venturing here on to new ground, and the book received some adverse criticism from

Irish scholars, but it filled a gap and helped to establish the study of Old Irish in Cambridge.

The second volume of *The Growth*, as Chadwick was accustomed to refer to it in a somewhat sinister manner, had sections by him on Yugo-Slav oral poetry, early Indian and Hebrew literature, while Nora was responsible for that on early Russian literature. She had already produced a book on *Russian Heroic Poetry* in 1932, which was well received. The bulk of the third volume was her work, with sections on the oral literature of the Tatars and of Polynesia, together with short ones on that of the Sea Dyaks of Borneo and some African peoples. This was followed by a general summing-up, presumably largely Hector's work. Not surprisingly, so original and daring an enterprise shocked some reviewers, and the Hebrew section in particular met with some hostile criticism, but on the whole scholars from many countries paid tribute to the greatness of the achievement. It is hard for us now to realise the impact it made when it first appeared. Kenneth Jackson as a young research student found it 'one of the most exciting books I had ever read', while José de Navarro wrote in his Obituary of Hector Munro Chadwick: 'If the term epoch-making may be applied to so large a synthesis, and one which broke so much new ground, *The Growth of Literature* may well be so described, and it should take its place in English scholarship with such works as Frazer's *Golden Bough.*'

For the most part the authors worked on original sources, and were not limited to translations, with the exception of the Indian and Hebrew sections and those on the Sea Dyaks, Polynesians and African peoples. Nora shared with her husband what de Navarro called 'an almost Pentecostal gift of tongues'. Beginning with a knowledge of Latin and Greek, French and German, Anglo-Saxon and Old Norse by the time she was at St Andrews, she afterwards acquired a good reading knowledge of Russian, Old Irish and Turkish, with partial knowledge of many others. Both of them could gain understanding of a new language with remarkable rapidity. Hector's favourite method was to obtain a relevant copy of the Bible from the British and Foreign Bible Society, while I remember Nora displaying with delight a children's reader with coloured pictures when exploring the language of the Lapps.

While the ideas behind this impressive work were basically Chadwick's, the wide range and scope of the material seems likely to be due to Nora's influence. Kenneth Jackson refers with justice to her 'wide range, breadth of interests, enthusiasm, imaginative awareness of different *types* of evidence, and ability to see significant likenesses'. He admits that she was not a specialist in accordance with the demands of modern scholarship, and that her enthusiasm and impatience to put her discoveries into words sometimes led her to ignore small errors on the way and to indulge a trifle rashly in speculation; for instance, she clung obstinately to the belief that the Druids were noble-minded scholars and not priests capable of cruel sacrifices, in the face of much contradictory evidence. Her claim was that time would winnow out the bad and leave the good grain behind. As long as she had her husband to correct and control the work, however, such tendencies were kept in check, and the two made an almost perfect combination. As a reviewer in the *TLS* put it in 1940: 'It is not often that a life's work *à deux* reaches such a height of achievement.'

Nora produced a number of additional works in the course of her labours on *The Growth*. One of the most readable, and typical of her approach to the past, is a small book on *Poetry and Prophecy*, based on three papers given at meetings of the British Association in 1937, 1938 and 1939. It is dedicated to 'The Prophets and Poets of other Continents, whose Spiritual Vision and Art has been perfected without the aid of writing'. The Preface contains some of the articles of faith which governed Nora's approach to the study of literature:

Comparative work is essential, and the wider the field of comparison the better. The experience of exclusively literate communities is too narrow . . . The first qualification for such a study must be a wholesome humility . . . Lack of respect and sympathy for the leaders of native thought, and ignorance of the language in which it is expressed, have allowed much of the past and present mental culture of unlettered communities to perish unrecorded.

She emphasises the urgent need to investigate the medium of transmission of thought over long periods of time, one of the dominating inspirations behind *The Growth of Literature*. One of her main discoveries was that of the importance of the shaman at a time before Eliade's book on shamanism appeared, and when there was little general interest in the phenomenon. She had been influenced in this direction by her friendship with Ethel John Lindgren, the Swedish anthropologist, who had spent some time in Mongolia, lived for a while with a Tungus female shaman, and witnessed Tungus and Mongol shamanic ceremonies.

When I was a research student at Cambridge, I was working on religious beliefs about the dead in pre-Christian Scandinavia, and can well remember reading two articles by Nora published in the *Journal of the Anthropological Institute* in 1936 dealing with shamanism among the Tatars. These had an immediate effect on my own work, far removed as it was from the Tatar peoples; it was as if a new light had suddenly illuminated the northern material which I had been studying. This must have been the experience of many scholars and students who came into contact with Nora's writings or teaching. Her work on the Tatars appeared in volume III of the *Growth of Literature* and was reprinted in 1969 together with new work by Professor Zhirmunsky of the USSR, under the title *Oral Epics of Central Asia*.

The Second World War brought to an end the idyllic, creative life at Papermills. The Chadwicks had recently bought an old house at Vowchurch, in the Golden Valley in Herefordshire, and looked forward to enjoyable visits there, while Hector worked on a book on Early Wales, but these plans had to be abandoned. They regretfully left Papermills for a house on the corner of Adams Road, since pulled down when Robinson College was built. This was conveniently close to the University Library, and work and teaching went on, but some of the magic had faded. Hector was haunted by the war, and found it hard to sleep, sometimes staying up all night. He felt forced to reconsider the value of the studies to which he had given his life, and his later writings, *The Study of Anglo-Saxon* (1941) and *The Nationalities of Europe* (1945) were concerned with such themes. He was particularly distressed by the dangerous arguments for the Germans as a master race, and sought to prove their falsity. During the war the Chadwicks provided a home for a Turkish professor with his temperamental Armenian wife – who painted fantastic animals all over Nora's summerhouse – and their four children, which must have added to the strain.

In 1946 Hector became seriously ill, but apparently recovered during the summer and was able to sit out in the garden and work on a new book on Early Scotland. At the end of the year, however, he had a sudden relapse, and was rushed into the Evelyn Hospital. He had managed to avoid medical treatment for most of his life, and now his one desire was to escape and return home to finish his book, but on the morning of the day when he was to be moved, 2 January 1947, he died in his sleep.

The effect of his death on Nora was very great; it was as if a jagged hole had been torn in her life, and at first she seemed inconsolable. However, she had many years left to live and write, and she derived strength and courage from a firm resolve to finish what Hector had left undone, and to establish a Celtic lectureship at Cambridge in his memory. At one time her friends were alarmed at the possibility that she would pour all her money into this and leave herself penniless, but fortunately the University delayed matters for a while, and she was able to live on in her house in Adams Road, working as untiringly as ever, providing a wonderful home for a number of fortunate research students, whom she encouraged, helped and inspired, and treated with the utmost generosity. Her capacity for making friends continued unabated, and now her interests turned increasingly towards Celtic studies, not only in the British Isles but also in Brittany, a much neglected field.

First she finished Hector's book on *Early Scotland*, which was published in 1949, and then she took on a new University Lectureship in the Early History and Culture of the British Isles, while also acting as Director of Studies in Anglo-Saxon and Celtic in Newnham and Girton. This took up much of her time, for she devoted herself unsparingly to her pupils, even taking them to conferences and summer schools in remote parts of the country. Yet at the same time she managed to produce an amazing number of books, papers, broadcasts and public lectures. One outstanding book which some consider her best was her *Poetry and Letters of Early Christian Gaul*, published in 1955. It was another exploratory move into virtually unmapped territory, and when she embarked on the rich Latin material available, this was intended merely as a step towards the fuller understanding of British history. However, she confessed in her Preface that 'while reading what was written in Gaul at that momentous period, I have fallen in love with my subject'. This was very typical of Nora, and in the pages of her book pagans and saints, bishops, poets and scholars come to life under her touch.

Between 1957 and 1963 she made three visits to Brittany with Edith Whetham. She visited for the first time such remote places as the part of the coast where it was once believed the souls of the dead embarked for the Otherworld, and the magic fountain in the forest of Broceliande. Edith, who was driving, soon discovered that Nora was no map-reader. After they had lost themselves many times and found they were travelling in circles, she learned to recognise 'the signs of enchantment which fell upon her at intervals; whenever we met an oxcart, I ignored her directions, and got to our destination by guess and the sun'. Her book on *Early Brittany* appeared in 1969.

Another enterprise which kept Nora occupied was the bringing together of Celtic scholars to contribute articles on the period following the Roman occupation of Britain, particularly on the Celtic church, Latin learning and intellectual life. David Walker in a review in *Cambridge Medieval Studies* in 1987 mentions the important contribution made by Nora and her circle 'in bringing the study of Wales in the Dark Ages much closer to the groundstream of medieval scholarship in English universities . . . no mean achievement'. Nora's many books and articles on Celtic subjects have been ably reviewed by Kenneth Jackson in the Obituary he wrote for the *Proceedings of the British Academy*. Some of her work was semi-popular, and as time went on, more inaccuracies crept in, but this was hardly surprising, in view of the amount she produced; moreover after she was 70 she appears to have suffered a series of minor strokes, as her mother and sister had done previously. But even the less successful writings convey something of her originality in interpreting the past, and her power to convey to new explorers the fascination and demanding discipline of the way she had chosen to follow; this power remained with her until at last her memory and concentration could no longer be relied upon.

Before she retired many honours were bestowed upon her. She became an Honorary Fellow of Newnham College, a mark of distinction for outstanding scholars which did not involve them in the work of the Governing Body, and a Fellow of the British Academy in 1958. She received Honorary Doctorates from the University of Wales in 1958, the National University of Ireland in the year following, and the University of St Andrews, where her teaching career began, in 1963. She was invited to give the O'Donnell Lectures at Edinburgh, Cardiff and Oxford, and the Riddell Memorial Lecture at Durham in 1960; her last public appearance was to give the Sir John Rhys Memorial

Lecture at the British Academy in 1965. She became a Commander of the British Empire in 1961, and characteristically derived great pleasure from the fact that one of the older staff on duty at the desk at the University Library met her with delighted congratulations on the morning that the Honours were announced. In spite of her long teaching experience and distinguished career, she was excessively nervous before giving a lecture. I remember travelling up to London with her when she was to give a talk to the Viking Society, not a particularly alarming assignment, when she was in a sorry state of near panic. It was part of Nora's modesty to distrust her powers and anticipate hostile criticism; she did not share Hector's robust reaction to critics which led him to remain unperturbed and indeed to chuckle with appreciation when a review of the first volume of the *Growth of Literature* appeared under the heading: 'Ten Wasted Years'.

Finally Nora gave up the house in Adams Road and her car, and retired to a small flat, 7 Causewayside, where she lived surrounded by books – they blocked out the noise of traffic, she claimed – and some of the fine old furniture which had fitted so well into Papermills. The faithful sisters who had worked for her there continued to cycle into Cambridge on weekdays and Sundays, so that for a time she could remain independent.

After a fall, Nora went for a while into the Hope Nursing Home in 1970, but was able in a wheelchair to attend a luncheon at St John's College in celebration of the centenary of Hector's birth. Out of those present, forty-five were past pupils of either Hector or Nora, and this was an occasion she was able to enjoy to the full. The next year for her eightieth birthday Isabel Henderson produced a delightful booklet for Nora with a full list of the Chadwicks' published work, as well as some of the commendations they had received on various occasions, and two drawings by Brian Hope Taylor; this was presented to her at a small party in the little nursing home to which she had then retired. The saddest aspect of her last days was the final loss of the independence which she valued so highly, and of the intellectual activity which had filled her life; after she was finally moved into the Hope Nursing Home, she told Morfydd Owen that she hated being a prisoner. But it was rare to hear her complain, and she died peacefully on 24 April 1972. In one last determined gesture she had bequeathed her body to Addenbrooke's Hospital and left instructions that no memorial service of any kind should be held after her death.

Those who knew Nora remember above all her stimulating company, her warmth and generosity, her gracious dignity, and her pursuit of learning with undiminished faith and resolution until her mind failed. Her lack of personal ambition or resentment against other scholars was something rare in the too often embittered academic world. Her attitude to the past was an unusual mixture of refreshing, earthy common sense, which often led to a simple solution of problems presented by early records, and a keen appreciation of spiritual values. Nora's attitude to the Christian religion was a puzzling one. Enid Welsford, a dedicated Anglican, was once heard to ask in some exasperation why Nora spent so much time pursuing mystical beliefs and symbolic rituals in remote corners of the world, which she might find in the English church if she only looked. Nora only attended church services in Welsh or Gaelic; it was as if she felt that all inspiration had departed from the English church long ago, although she was a whole-hearted admirer of the early Christian saints and scholars in Celtic lands. Part of her objections may have sprung from her dislike of set ceremonial, whether secular or sacred, and to quote Enid again: 'She was an incurable optimist with a robust faith in the validity of reason, and the power of education to make men follow its directions. She had little or no belief in a life after death but she never doubted the value of life in this world . . . and of the vast possibilities open to the adventurous human mind.' Yet, Enid went on to say, she seemed drawn sympathetically towards those who accepted religious belief, and was once heard to remark at a College dinner table, 'I never have been able to understand how anyone with a brain greater than that of a flea could be an atheist.'

At the close of her book on *The Age of the Saints*, published in 1961, Nora refers to the beauty of the 'simple disciplined life' of early Celtic scholars, their lofty ideals and retreat from the world of material values in what was no selfish withdrawal, as well as 'the singular purity of their inspiration'. Such an epitaph is surely not unfitting for Nora herself.

NOTES

I am most grateful to Dr Isabel Henderson for putting me in touch with material on the Chadwicks in the Cambridge University Library. Her own excellent publication, *A List of the Published Writings of Hector Munro Chadwick and of Nora Kershaw Chadwick* (Cambridge 1971), has been an invaluable source of reference. I have drawn also on my own memories, and, as is appropriate in any account of the Chadwicks, on oral tradition.

I have also derived information from the following:

Anon., 'Miss Nora Kershaw', *College Echoes* (University of St Andrews 1915).

J. M. de Navarro, 'Hector Munro Chadwick, 1870–1947', *Proceedings of the British Academy* 33 (1947), 307–30.

Kenneth Jackson, 'Nora Kershaw Chadwick, 1891–1972', *Proceedings of the British Academy* 58 (1972), 537–49.

Enid E. H. Welsford, 'In Memoriam: Nora K. Chadwick 1891–1972' (published privately, Cambridge 1973).

Morfydd E. Owen, 'Nora Kershaw Chadwick, 1891–1972', *Necrologie* 8/9 (1973–4), 319–24.

Edith H. Whetham, *Gone Away* (1981) (chapter 2: 'Celtic Brittany').

Chapter 9

ENID WELSFORD
1892–1981

Elsie Duncan-Jones

'HER MIRTH THE WORLD REQUIRED'

The very appreciative obituary of Enid in *The Times* left to the last the fact that her 'vast humanity' and 'vast scholarship' were lodged in 'a very tiny body': a civilised way of proceeding. None the less, it seems to me that in the present instance there is something to be said for reversing it. Enid was well-proportioned, nimble, indeed athletic, fond of skiing, skating, and at one time fencing. Her little face wore an engaging expression of eagerness and good humour. Her pleasant voice carried well. But she was so small that in any assembly of grown-up people she seemed at first sight a child. Clothes had to be specially made and objects in common use were difficult for her to handle. Altogether enough of a nuisance to furnish a grievance against life, in any one so inclined. Enid was markedly not so inclined.

She was born in 1892. Like another notable woman writer, Sylvia Townsend Warner, almost her exact contemporary, she was the daughter of a master at Harrow. Her parents had complementary gifts. J. W. W. Welsford was an accomplished mathematician who had for seven years been a Fellow of Caius. Her mother, Mildred Hancock, was an artist, some of whose delicate Alpine water-colours adorned the rooms where Enid taught in Clough Hall and, later, 7 Grange Road. I guess that the lavender bags hanging over the backs of chairs and sofas also came from Harrow. Enid's surroundings were always spacious, fragrant, bright with Venetian glass and flowers. Occasionally she marvelled at her friend Nora Chadwick's relative indifference to comfort.

Enid had one brother, Geoffrey, a little younger than herself. Of him, as of all her family, she was deeply fond. He was killed in the Great War. By the time I first met her, in 1926, the scars of her great loss had healed. Though she then still often spoke of 'Geoff', what she dwelt on were his jokes, his pranks, his innocent breaches of the oppressive chaperonage rules when he came to visit his sister at Newnham. Enid loved to tell stories of the young man's encounters with 'the grim old dons'.

In 1927 when Enid published her first book, *The Court Masque*, on which she had worked so hard and so long, the dedication was 'To My Brother'. In 1935 she dedicated *The Fool* to her mother, then lately dead. Enid is buried, as she directed, in her mother's grave at Harrow.

Although the greater part of her life was spent as a member of the Fellowship of Newnham College, then ordinarily and almost necessarily unmarried, I do not think Enid at all endorsed her admired Jane Harrison's dismissal of the attractions of family life. I have, as it happens, preserved a kind letter from Enid on the birth of my first child, in 1937. 'I long to see the young man,' she writes, 'and when I do I shall have a hard work to suppress my spinsterish envy.' Not, of course, to be taken literally – nobody but herself could have thought of Enid as spinsterish or envious – but Jane Harrison and perhaps most Newnham dons of the time would not have written thus. Enid delighted in the company of children. My daughter remembers Enid's bringing out a clock-work toy, battered but still working, a furry monkey banging a drum: a relic of her own childhood at Harrow.

Of this we have several glimpses. First, appropriately for one who was to concern herself so much with revels, comes the little Enid at the pantomime.

Enid Welsford, 1892–1981

I remember in my childhood being much disappointed when the glories of the transformation scene faded into the prose of the Sausage shop, burgled by Clown and protected by the Policeman. But I was pleased with the spangles of Harlequin and very ready to believe my elders when they told me every gesture had a meaning and that his black mask made him invisible.

Already the child sees the possibility of rewarding investigation.

Her parents evidently appreciated and fostered their daughter's literary promise. It is not, I think, generally known that there is in the Cambridge University Library a book of poems composed by Enid as a child, published in 1904. *The Seagulls and Other Poems* has as a frontispiece an enchanting picture of a pensive little girl with a ribbon round her long brown hair. Newnham has no copy and Enid never spoke of it. It would be a mistake to dwell on this little production; it was not as a poet that Enid was to make her mark. Still, there are points of interest as showing a child in many respects mother of the woman.

The seagulls of the title poem, the best in the book, are the souls of Vikings:

> Your voices shall blend with the wild winds
> Ye shall float on the waves that roar
> Ye shall fly round the grey rocks screaming
> And cry for evermore.

Evidently Enid has already a strong feeling for what C. S. Lewis has called 'Northernness', foreshadowing perhaps her later devotion to the Anglo-Saxon and Norse studies she was to pursue with such success under Professor Chadwick.

The child has a strong sense of the mystery and power of poetry.

> Like a mist before my eyes
> Dreamy, dreamy poetry lies.
> It won't obey or honour my word
> It always comes of its own accord.

Poetry never lost its power over Enid. In the sometimes troubled hours of extreme old age she would always compose herself to complete the recitation of a favourite poem.

What there is no hint of in this little book is that the young author would grow up to be thought of by many as almost an embodiment of cheerfulness. A group of poems on the death of a playmate are uncomfortably naked expressions of pain. Cheerfulness for Enid was never the whole story. As she says in *The Fool*, 'the facts of life are tragic and the human heart is proof against the comic spirit'.

Another glimpse: Enid once related to me a strange little story belonging to her schooldays at Sandgate in Kent. It is so odd that I could almost think I had invented it – but no. Enid and one of her friends discovered that by merely laying their hands lightly on a certain table they could cause it to move, apparently at its own volition. Puzzled and honest, they told this to the headmistress, who didn't believe them. Poor woman, she was rash enough to arrange a demonstration before the whole school, intended to expose the fraud. But the table moved. All that I remember further is that Enid said indignantly: 'As if we would have lied!'

I have no reason to believe that in later life Enid was much concerned with the occult, though I remember her reading with interest Rosamund Lehmann's book on the survival of her daughter Sally. And she did once make me feel that I myself had been nearer to an occult experience than I at all liked. In 1930–1 I was given a room in a house belonging to the College, in Grange Road. When the house belonged to Professor and Mrs Sidgwick it had been the master bedroom: now it was divided by curtains. A pleasant room and I was glad to have it. However, when I went across to breakfast at High Table in Clough Hall I did sometimes mention that there had been moments of panic in the night, enough to make me get up and reach for the electric light switch. Not until I had moved elsewhere did the considerate Enid tell me that my tales at breakfast had been heard with particular interest.

It was believed that mine was a room in which as a widow Mrs Sidgwick had made efforts to communicate with the spirit world. Enid also told me that a previous occupant had heard a voice exclaiming: 'What a lot of curtains!' Enid loved a good story, and the occult adds spice. But, as she had said to her headmistress, she did not tell lies.

When Enid was only 17 she began her long career of scholarship, at University College London, under the 'ubiquitarian' W. P. Ker. 'Nobody liked more things than Ker,' it is said. In meeting him Enid must have entered the atmosphere of wideranging, large-minded, generous scholarship in which she lived for the rest of her life. The untroubled good humour with which her subsequent and principal mentor, H. M. Chadwick, received hostile criticism is gloriously exemplified at the end of Dr Davidson's essay in this volume. Enid herself, though vigorous and tenacious in argument, was never touchy, niggling or merely contentious.

When Enid came to Newnham she found there a student in her second year called Nora Kershaw. So began a friendship that each found one of the greatest blessings of her life. In 1914 Enid was given a First with distinction in Old English in the Medieval and Modern Languages Tripos. Then came what she herself has called the 'long and delightful initiation into research' with Professor Chadwick. For several years before Nora became Mrs Chadwick Enid and Nora set up house together in Owlstone Road. Enid lived for a term that she has called 'memorable' with the newly married Chadwicks in the house called Papermills; if only she had left an account of it! In 1916 she began to teach for Newnham, as she was to do for nearly half a century, and in 1918 she became a Fellow. In 1919, with Maud Haviland, she founded a surely much-needed Research Club for Cambridge women.

It was probably in 1917 or 1918 that Enid made the important decision to work on a later period of literature; the four articles she published in Hastings's *Encyclopaedia of Religion and Ethics* are evidently fruits of the research she had done in Teutonic and Old Russian Religion. Her next published work was an article, 'Italian Influence on the Court Masque' (1923). Something she wrote much later in *The Fool* may a little help to explain the transition. 'The masque', she writes, 'is strangely like the pantomimic ritual dances of which we hear so much from students of comparative religion.'

It must, one would think, have been something of a disappointment to the Chadwicks when Enid made the change; but the friendship and the discipleship continued. 'This book would hardly have been written had it not been for the unfailing interest and encouragement of both Professor and Mrs Chadwick,' Enid writes in her Preface to *The Court Masque*.

The range of Enid's scholarship is well illustrated by the fact that at Newnham she was able to act as Director not only of Studies in English but also of Archaeology and Anthropology; and for eleven years of Moral Sciences. She shared with the Chadwicks an easy mastery of foreign tongues.

My personal knowledge of Enid began in October 1926. Like no doubt many other of Enid's pupils, I can say that meeting her was the beginning of a friendship that was to be lifelong, although in my case it was often at a distance. For many years I taught at a university that was not Cambridge. I had come to Newnham from a school at Torquay where I was fortunate in having an excellent English mistress who had been at Newnham with Nora Kershaw. They were still great friends; she was Elsie Carey, later Mrs Breach. As soon as I arrived in Cambridge I was kindly noticed by the Chadwicks and so saw something of their friend Enid even before she became Newnham's Director of Studies in English. Lately I was admiring the aptness of the quotation from Sir Thomas Browne that ends *The Court Masque*: 'The world to me is but a dream or mock-show, and we all therein but Pantalones and Anticks to my severer contemplations.' It came back to me that one of the undergraduate essays I had written for Miss Welsford

Enid Welsford, 1892–1981

c. 1928 had been on Sir Thomas Browne. It might have been hoped that memory would offer some characteristic remark of Enid's on a favourite author. All it affords is that she rightly disliked my calling Browne a 'medic'.

I dimly recall morning coffees with Enid and Nora in Matthews Café in Trinity Street. But my earliest visual impression of Enid is of her lecturing on Barclay's *Ship of Fools*. This cannot be earlier than 1928, when women were at last brought in to lecture to University audiences. They could not of course wear the gown of members of the University. 'Newnham and Girton decided that the appropriate wear was a hat . . . not large, turned up in the brim,' writes Margaret Grimshaw. What I remember of the occasion is not Enid's hat – that would not have been remarkable, for of course all female members of her audience wore hats too – but the total impression of the small figure, perfectly equal to the occasion, in mind and voice.

In 1928 the lectures that attracted most admiration from undergraduates studying English were the highly unorthodox ones given by Manny Forbes at Clare (eight lectures on a single sonnet of Wordsworth's), and those in which I. A. Richards commented, sometimes devastatingly, on the 'protocols' we had written on unfamiliar poems. Enid's lectures were impressive in a more traditional style. To quote the comment of one visitor: 'There was this little woman, firing off witticisms and paradoxes and full of deep learning. In the States she would have been cheered.'

A brilliant Newnham student much junior to myself had recorded that Enid's lecture on George Chapman had made her read not only Chapman's Homer but Homer himself. I am ashamed to think that I have still not read Barclay's *Ship of Fools*.

It was as a teacher of individuals and small groups that Enid is generally held to have been most influential. The well-known literary critic Dorothea (Doris) Krook found in Enid, by her own account, the Platonic ideal of the Cambridge supervisor, with her 'beautiful selfless availability'. Sita Narasimhan writes of Enid's 'uncommon powers of adapting herself to a pupil's needs'. When Sita came up, aged 18, she was, she says, 'attracted to dogmatic Marxism and deeply influenced by Gandhi'. To Enid both lines of thought were deeply uncongenial. 'But', says Sita, 'she settled down to read not only Marx but Lenin and the English Marxists of the thirties.'

There are still many who recall with gratitude Enid's classes, and the meetings of the Informal Club that she founded. I remember the great glass bottles of sweets and boxes of cigarettes scattered about her room on such occasions. The novelist and biographer Elizabeth Jenkins recalled lately how excitingly Miss Welsford made her pupils understand the literary issues of the day: with these Enid, for all her mastery of the recondite, was always invigoratingly concerned. (And not only in her teaching. Reading again both *The Court Masque* and *The Fool*, I am struck by the degree to which they reflect the time and place in which they were composed.)

Although, of course, Enid was prepared to investigate a text with all the minuteness required by contemporary criticism, she had great respect for what Dr Johnson has called 'the common reader'. She delighted to recall how a cousin of hers, a farmer, after reading aloud a passage from Shakespeare would say, closing the book, 'that's what I call *language*'.

Enid's pupils would, I guess, agree that her teaching fostered creativity. She did not tell her pupils what not to read. She set high standards but did not paralyse. In Leavisian times, when some held that life was too short to bother with Fielding, Enid was prepared in leisure hours to enjoy herself from time to time with works figuring in nobody's concept of the Great Tradition. She had, for instance, one of the best collections to be found in Cambridge of the works of Wilkie Collins. She particularly rejoiced in *Poor Miss Finch*, the story of a young woman who has the misfortune to turn blue. However, I should guess that she read more poetry than fiction. Certainly when it came to writing she wrote of Jonson, Spenser, Wordsworth, rather than the great novelists. At the time I saw most of her it seemed to me that her friends were always discussing the novels of Henry James. The only recorded remark of Enid herself on this great author is characteristic. She wished there were more low life in his novels: and more of Nature.

To revert to my own experience. In June 1928, when the English Tripos results came out, I found that in Part I I had been given a star. As if this was not enough, Enid on this occasion, knowing I was poor, gave me a cheque, with the stipulation that I was to spend it entirely on myself. It was for twenty pounds. It embarrasses me to think how much that would be in today's money. At the same time she invited me to come on a festive drive to Lavenham in her little car. Enid was always adventurous. I doubt whether any other of the Fellows of Newnham at that time had a car. Miss Chrystal came too. It was amusing to see Enid and Edith Chrystal together. Edith, full of respect for Enid as a scholar, chose to consider her as none the less sadly lacking in practical good sense, and needing a good deal of more or less motherly counsel. Enid played along.

When I look back on Enid's dealings with me in my third year I see a degree of tolerance and wisdom that at the time I perhaps did not fully realise. I had found that the star already mentioned dissolved barriers and that I was all at once adopted into the literary world of undergraduates, till then exclusively male. I wrote regularly for the *Granta*, contributed to the anthology of *Cambridge Poets*, was one of what Bronowski, then at Jesus, called the 'conclave' of the very avant-garde undergraduate magazine *Experiment*. All this made Newnham seem to me a little tame. I do not think Enid shared my enthusiasm for the poetry of William Empson, but I remember her once humbly asking me to expound that difficult poem of his called 'The Scales'. This I was prepared to do, the poet's own exposition being much more firmly in my mind than it is now. There was a faintly satirical story that Enid sometimes related about my membership of what she (rightly) called a 'coterie'. One afternoon when she had asked me to bring some of my literary friends to tea with her, I entered with, she said, 'a train' of Cambridge poets from the men's colleges. Silence, then a voice enquired, 'Elsie, what *is* metaphor?' I do not recall the occasion and the question does not sound like Empson or Bronowski or James Reeves: but as I have said, Enid was veracious and there was no unkindness in her laughter. There is a hit at the obscurity of modern poetry in a passage of *The Fool*, linking it in that respect with the Skaldic literature of Iceland.

From 1930 to 1931 I had the opportunity of seeing Enid daily as, though not a Fellow, I was living as a don. Later, when Dorothy Sayers brought out her *Gaudy Night*, a nightmare picture of neurotic ill-will in a community of academic women, I thought 'How very different from Newnham!' Enid as usual was hard-working, perhaps already busy on *The Fool*: happy-seeming and happy-making. Among many congenial companions I remember the enigmatic, fascinating Edith Chrystal; Dorothy Hoare, later Mrs de Navarro, like Enid a disciple and close friend of the Chadwicks, who had chosen to devote herself to more modern literature. There was Jocelyn Toynbee, whose rather severe exterior disguised a captivating fund of merriment; Josie Pybus, full of good humour and good sense. There was also at that time Frau Sommer, a warm-hearted German lady, who once told me that her great-great grandmother had been that brilliant Lady Diana Beauclerk of whom Dr Johnson was so brutally dismissive.

Enid seemed, as I say, much at home in this community. But I dare say that she was no less happy when in later life she moved to 7 Grange Road. Clearly she enjoyed having her own domain and her own little world of non-academic people; she liked to have in her life 'ordinary' people as well as academics. Though she adapted well to community life, there was in her something almost Puck-like which resisted unimportant demands for order and punctuality, however dutifully she strove to fulfil them. This might have been a cause of irritation perhaps particularly to the Principal of the College, then Miss J. Pernel Strachey. But as it happened Enid and Miss Strachey got on particularly well. Enid liked to tell the story of Miss Strachey's silently presenting Enid with an unlabelled bunch of keys she had picked up in the passage. Enid asked, 'But Miss Strachey, how did you know they were mine?' 'Elementary psychology.' There were important matters on which they disagreed, for instance, religion. Miss Strachey's attitude to religion was what one would expect in a Strachey, more or less anthropological. Enid was a devout member of the congregation at St Benet's Church. Yet it was with peals of laughter that Enid told how much Miss Strachey regretted that a theologian they had both been listening to had said nothing of the Trinity. 'The Holy Ghost,' said Miss Strachey, 'so *amusing*, I always think.'

Virginia Woolf's *Diaries* contain good material for a sketch of Miss Strachey: Mrs Woolf finds that the key words for describing her are 'unbuttonedness' and above all 'integrity'. Of Enid, alas, there is no description, though Mrs Woolf does recount a strange tale of Enid walking somewhere on the sands at evening with a companion and finding a man's corpse.

Not the least benefit, perhaps, that Enid conferred on her College was that of providing a store of anecdotes, usually, though not always, showing herself in a ludicrous light. This sounds as though they might be painful. In her telling they almost never were: Enid, locked out of College, crouching in a long evening dress on top of the railings then outside the Kennedy Building causing talk of a gibbering ghost in Sidgwick Avenue; Enid walking out of her lodgings with the bathwater rushing down the stairs after her; Enid buying herself in haste a new bathing-dress to take on a visit to some rather grand friends who had a swimming pool and finding when she arrives and spreads it out that it bears the legend 'Meet me at Margate'. The scene of another story that I remember must be 7 Grange Road. Enid, using a newspaper to draw the fire, finds the paper in flames. She rushes to the window and throws it out. It lands in the lodger's bicycle basket just beneath.

A slightly unseemly one belongs to her days as a research student. Enid is travelling by train to stay with a formidable friend who sets great store by punctuality. The train has no corridor and Enid has to get out at a stop to use the station lavatory. The door sticks, the train is about to leave, the only window is closed and high up. Enid swarms up the pipe and breaks the glass. The station-master, about to blow his whistle, is appalled by the sight of a small bleeding hand. I can vouch for the formidableness of the lady at the other end – who was my husband's aunt.

The most satisfying of Enid's merry tales is perhaps the story of Miss Strachey's infringement of the blackout. The Principal then lived in a flat over the Pfeiffer arch. (Virginia Woolf writes of 'Pernel's high ceremonial rooms all polished and spectatorial'.) One night there was a chink of light between the curtains. (These, historians may like to know, had been made in a hurry, probably by Miss Strachey herself, an unpractised needlewoman, at the time of Munich.) Enid was one of the air-raid wardens for the College. No uniform was prescribed; wardens followed their fancy. One has left it on record that she had a buttercup-yellow siren suit made out of a blanket. Enid sensibly made use of her warm, close-fitting skiing outfit with visored cap. Miss Strachey opened the door and started back. 'Good Heavens!' she exclaimed. 'The Police!' Enid loved to conjure up this moment. It would not be a sufficient analysis of this situation that said only that Miss Strachey was amused at seeing the strange little figure in front of her as an embodiment of authority and that Enid was amused by Miss Strachey's amusement.

Enid in *The Fool* entertains the possibility that, 'in the medieval air of our schools and universities', a scholar with some peculiarities might still 'attain to the legendary proportions of the heroes of the jest-books'. Time will show.

Enid Welsford, 1892–1981

I do not know whether, like her friend Nora Chadwick, Enid felt that 'teaching was less noble than research'. With Enid and with Nora, teaching and all that for them went with it, in the way of 'selfless availability', took much time and energy. Given that all her life Enid felt the impulse to write, the number of her books might seem small. The first two, it might be said, in other hands might have made several volumes. They are alike in being very copious and very learned. *The Times* obituary was not, after all, exaggerating when it spoke of 'vast scholarship'. *The Court Masque* (1927) not surprisingly received a prize from the British Academy and was reissued in 1962. There is evidence that it is still much read. It is a very ambitious book, its declared aim being to deal in the first part with the origin and history of the masque, in the second to show the influence of the masque on art and poetry, in the third to discuss aspects of the masque that throw light upon the nature of art and its social value. The eminent Ben Jonson scholar, Percy Simpson, though giving much of it high praise, wished the book were shorter. 'What the heathen origin of the May Day festival or the uses of imitative magic have to do with Renaissance Italy or Tudor and Stuart England it is hard to see.' 'But surely Enid has shown us,' might be the response. If the austere Oxford scholar had his way we should have lost material of much interest and value that is also, incidentally, highly characteristic of the author and of Cambridge in 1927. One of the many passages whose loss I myself should particularly regret is the description of the merrymaking of the Wisbech fruit-pickers, as no doubt Enid had witnessed it. (In the 1920s the Cambridge churches conducted missions among the large parties from the slums who came annually to work for the local fruit-growers. Cambridge ladies such as Enid did much for the comfort and well-being of the visitors.)

In the middle of one of the fruit farms near Wisbech there is an encampment
. . . a London slum planted in a dirty waste, there is a large marquee tent,
partly open to the evening sun and air, and inside it a crowd of noisy dirty
pickers . . . Some one is singing one of Chevalier's songs . . . which has a
pronounced and haunting rhythm.

> Fair Flo, to watch 'er's a treat
> Can't keep my eyes off your feet,
> And you're nice as you're neat
> I'm dead nuts on your dancing.

Here Enid discerns 'the very essence of poetry, rising up from
squalid London streets, the primal, instinctive unquenchable love
of rhythm'. After I had transcribed these lines I was delighted to
learn from Helen Fowler that at one time in her life Enid was
often taken to the music-hall.

Enid's robustness and lack of squeamishness appear amusingly
in a very different context earlier in the book, in her discussion of
Comus. She is unaccustomedly severe in her remarks on the lady's
alarm (*Comus* 170–6) at the possibility of meeting 'unletter'd
hinds', uneducated farm-workers, that is to say, under the
influence of drink. Enid calls the speech 'tart'.

Very revealing of Enid's own theology is the well-known
description, in the same chapter of 'Milton's harsh creed in which
goodness is identified with power rather than with love, and evil
is identified with sensuality rather than with cruelty or selfishness;
and in which the Universe rests not upon self-expressive love but
upon an everlasting antagonism, an ultimately insoluble dualism'.
Whether it is fair to Milton is another question.

The Court Masque deserves the epithets that Enid somewhere
gives to a book of Jane Harrison's, 'lucid and beautiful'. Many
passages of delicate and subtle discrimination are to be found, as
well as passages of lusty argument.

Enid's energy and enthusiasm, her passion for thoroughness,
the uncommonly wide range of her studies – from archaeology
and anthropology to philosophy, with literature as it were in the

middle – her need to investigate, all asked a large canvas. Certainly this was necessary for a study of the Fool. Part of the fascination of this book is its comprehensiveness. Here are not only Gabba, the buffoon of Augustus, and the Irish Clairvoyant fool, but Charlie Chaplin and the fool still (1935) in employment at the Court of the Emir of Katsina. As always, Enid is concerned not merely to present fact but to interpret it. The arrangement of the book is planned with a view to the asking, if not the answering, of certain questions: 'What are the actual facts as to the historical origin of the Fool as comic entertainer? How far do these facts help us to understand comedy?' And, most ambitious of all, 'What light do they throw on the relationship between life and art and the nature of the social conditions most favourable to the creative imagination?' *The Fool*, like *The Court Masque*, is very much the work of a disciple of Professor Chadwick who acknowledges a great debt to *The Growth of Literature*.

Enid liked to tell, with peals of laughter, how the publisher had said, 'We wanted a book on the Fool and we thought you would be the one to write it', implying, what is certainly not the case, that the Fool is best treated of by a fool. In fact, the publishers probably knew that there is a great deal about the Fool in *The Court Masque*. The second book was very well received. The anonymous reviewer in the *TLS* congratulates Miss Welsford on the way in which she had held the main thread of interpretation through her collection of miscellaneous facts from all ages and on her skill in lighting up the narrative with 'really illuminating' criticism. The *New York Times* rightly observes that, while the book will give unusual delight to scholars and antiquarians, it also provides delightful entertainment for the general reader. The book is still in print and has been widely influential, not least in the theatre. Perhaps the fact – not of course known at the time – that in Russia in the same decade the admired Mikhail Bakhtin was writing of the same subject may add yet more of interest.[1]

Enid's two remaining books are on a smaller scale. That she

should as her last work have provided an edition of Spenser's *Four Hymnes and Epithalamion* is not surprising, for this draws on a kind of learning of which she was thoroughly mistress, and particularly enjoyed. The appendix, in which she argues with Professor Hieatt on the consequences of his discovery of the elaborate numerological structure of *Epithalamion*, is a rewarding specimen of Enid in debate.

But why, in her seventies, did Enid choose, in the volume called *Salisbury Plain*, to concentrate her attention on the gloomiest products of Wordsworth's immaturity, poems which, as she says, have excited more interest as expressions of opinion than as works of art? Part of the answer is, I guess, that they presented a challenge to Enid's strong sense of form. (I used to think that Enid's most frequent criticism of a student's work was 'Of course, it *does* need pulling together'.) She finds that when studied as a group the poems that sprang from Wordsworth's three days of solitary wandering near Stonehenge throw light not only on the poet's thought but on his artistry, and 'particularly on the care he expended on architectonics'. Wordsworth's play *The Borderers* is also considered, a work that Enid allows to be perhaps even gloomier than *Salisbury Plain*. She concludes that 'this particular failure may prove that Wordsworth could not write a great tragedy, but it also proves how honestly he could confront the tragic aspect of human life'. In writing this book Enid was not only exercising her powers of close criticism but herself, I think, confronting the tragic aspect of human things. She had in her own life, as others have said, an uncommon power of making people feel life was worth while, of communicating a sense of what can only be called joy. This power was not cheaply bought. Enid says in her last paragraph that 'Wordsworth never recovered the Utopian hopes of his youth: for a while he seems even to have doubted the goodness of the created universe'. I am reminded of Dorothea Krook's lively account of a partly jesting controversy she had had with Enid in, I suppose, the 1950s:

Enid Welsford, 1892–1981

Doris (Dorothea) 'Yes, dear Enid, I don't suppose I do take the created universe very seriously . . . don't, really, care very much for it.' At this Enid, already standing up, seemed suddenly to square herself . . . she thrust one foot slightly forward as if in a fencing posture . . . 'I must tell you that I for my part . . . I am a passionate partisan of the created universe.'

I was lately presented with a book from Enid's shelves, a collection, as it happened, of essays by Lytton Strachey. The bookplate she was using in 1927 was a simple woodcut of a shepherd boy sitting under a tree, with the inscription, from a medieval lyric, 'Ut Hoy For in his pipe he made so much joy'. It is difficult to enlarge on this subject without falling into what Henry James has called the Key of Pink. It does appear that Enid struck many people as not merely cheerful, but a bringer of joy, or as Sita has it, 'glee'; and that that was her distinctive note. Of course not always, nor for everyone. A nonagenarian survivor from the days when Enid was examining for the English Tripos, asked for his recollections, said: 'Miss Welsford once prolonged a meeting for three hours by her objections to one question. Of course she won.'

NOTE

1 In 1979 Derek Brewer Ltd published *The Fool and the Trickster: Studies in Honour of Enid Welsford*. The dedication of this book celebrates the way in which her outstanding book, *The Fool*, has advanced research in this field of study since its appearance in 1935.

Chapter 10

AUDREY RICHARDS
1899–1984

Adam Kuper

A LADY OF THE INTELLECTUAL ARISTOCRACY

Unprejudiced, unshockable, in many ways unconventional, Audrey Richards nevertheless operated unselfconsciously by the standards of her parents and their class. Her family belonged to the strikingly endogamous and coherent community Noel Annan (1955) called the intellectual aristocracy. This was a very English intelligentsia, 'wedded to gradual reform of accepted institutions and able to move between the worlds of speculation and government'.[1] Its charter was the reform of the Indian and English civil services on meritocratic principles in the mid-nineteenth century. 'No formal obstacle remained to prevent the man of brains from becoming a gentleman.'[2]

Influenced by the Utilitarians, these public-spirited intellectuals were fascinated by the new social sciences. Some became great international figures in history, political science and economics, the most notable examples being Macaulay and George Otto Trevelyan in the nineteenth century and G. M. Trevelyan and Keynes in the twentieth. 'They were agreed on one characteristic doctrine; that the world could be improved by analysing the needs of society and calculating the possible course of its development.'[3] Their theoretical work addressed practical concerns, and their official reports – perhaps their most characteristic genre – sometimes made pioneering intellectual contributions.

In Bloomsbury – the artistic and raffish wing of the intelligentsia that flourished in the first decades of the twentieth century – women enjoyed equal status with men, but in the more respectable circles a woman was expected either to marry or to make a career: it was not expected that she could do both, certainly if she had children. If she did choose a career, she could rise to an important position, but probably not to the very top, more likely achieving maximum influence as the executive assistant of proconsuls, domestic or colonial. Audrey Richards knew, sometimes befriended, often worked with women of similar backgrounds who were making comparable careers; Margery Perham, Lucy Mair, Polly Hill, E. M. Chilver and Camilla Wedgwood among others. (Two of these women did, however, combine family and career.)

Born in London on 8 July 1899, Audrey was the second of four daughters of Henry Erle (later Sir Erle) Richards and Isabel, the daughter of Spencer Perceval Butler. The Butler side of the family was prototypical of the intellectual aristocracy – Annan took them for one of his case-studies.[4] Spencer Perceval Butler, a double First in classics and mathematics, was a barrister and public servant. Two brothers were headmasters, respectively of Haileybury and Harrow. Among his children were Sir Spencer Harcourt Butler, a Governor of Burma, and Sir Montagu Butler, Governor of Central Provinces, India, and later Master of Pembroke College, Cambridge, and the father of R. A. Butler, Chancellor of the Exchequer and Master of Trinity College, Cambridge.

H. E. Richards, younger son of a Welsh lawyer who married a local heiress and became Lord Chief Baron, was educated at Eton and qualified as a barrister. He served as legal member of the Indian Vice-Regal Council from 1904 to 1909, and returned to England in 1911 as Chichele Professor of International Law at Oxford University and Fellow of All Souls. Audrey once told me that this had been a difficult choice – her father could have expected a glittering career in India – and that it was her mother who insisted that the girls should not be sent alone to England, to boarding-school, while the parents remained in India, as was customary. (She also said her father regretted that his four children were all daughters.)

Audrey later recalled that in her younger days her mother

did much entertaining for the clever, popular, amusing husband. There were large, formal parties at Simla and Calcutta . . . Those were the days when the children were pulled up and down on rugs by Indian servants to polish the floors; when the father became more and more exuberant; and the mother, the last flower placed, stood at the top of the stairs to receive her guests with that very charming, almost regal, carriage of the head and opened the ball with the Viceroy to the strains of the 'Blue Danube'.

Her mother she recalled as not only a solicitous and kindly hostess but as a selfless woman and 'one of the sincerest characters I ever met'. And, like Audrey herself, she was very amusing: 'she had all the family's quick sense of the ridiculous, a dry humour and that piercing judgment of character on which so much English fun depends. Her comments on people were a delight.' Her father, by contrast, 'was brilliant, witty, and a born raconteur . . . In his intimate circle he bubbled over with an irresistible flow of pure nonsense and fantasy.'[5]

Audrey attended Downe House School near Newbury, and developed intellectual interests that her parents did not encourage (rebelliously, she read books during meals, holding them below the table). Her parents were against her going to a university, and they insisted that if she did so, she should study science. She attended Newnham College, Cambridge, from 1918 to 1921, and read for the Natural Sciences Tripos.

Coming down from Cambridge she taught for a year at her old school, then worked as assistant to Gilbert Murray, the classicist, who remained a friend and who was to read and criticise her doctoral thesis. (In a spoof reference in 1924 he wrote, 'As for papers, she will hide them so as no inspector could find them.')[6] For eighteen months she did relief work in Frankfurt, at a Friends' Ambulance Unit Family Welfare Settlement, and began to take a practical interest in problems of nutrition. Between 1924 and 1928 she was secretary to the Labour Department of the League of Nations Union in London: 'I was one of the idealists who thought war could be prevented by the League of Nations. We used to speak in its favour on Hampstead Heath, in Methodist chapels, and in schools etc.'[7]

Her two younger sisters married, both to Fellows of All Souls, but her elder sister Gwynedd, who also remained unmarried, embarked on a career as a social worker. Audrey was always close to Gwynedd (who spent some months with her in the field among the Bemba), and it must have seemed that she was drifting into a similar career; yet given her background she could hardly have doubted that academic research might contribute to welfare. Certainly neither she nor her relatives had any doubt that she would have to earn a living.

Influenced by the socialist political scientist Graham Wallas, father of a Newnham friend, she decided to begin postgraduate study at the London School of Economics. According to a letter from Wallas to the anthropologist, Bronislaw Malinowski, asking Malinowski to supervise her work, she intended to treat the history of European ideas about 'nature' and 'freedom' 'in relation to the permanent facts of human biology'.[8] Malinowski took her on but persuaded her to change her topic, and between 1928 and 1930 she worked under his supervision on a doctorate, based on published sources, teaching anthropology at the same time at Bedford College.

MALINOWSKI AND THE LSE

Bronislaw Malinowski, himself a transplanted member of the Polish intelligentsia, dominated social anthropology at the London

School of Economics from 1924 (when he took up a position as Reader at the School, shortly after completing his first great Trobriand monograph) to 1939. The LSE was associated with new ideas of social improvement, and was committed to the application of the social sciences. Still somewhat marginal, not yet entirely respectable, it offered an ideal environment for an ambitious and creative outsider, and was more hospitable than the ancient universities to the aspirations of women. Malinowski had developed new ideas of intensive ethnographic fieldwork, and was propagating a theory he called 'functionalism'. He 'had no doubt about his greatness', according to Edmund Leach, also one of his students, and saw himself as 'a missionary, a revolutionary innovator in the field of anthropological method and ideas'.[9] Volatile and charismatic, 'a man whose expressions became more extreme with opposition', as Audrey Richards noted,[10] he gathered around him a brilliant group of mature students, often graduates in other fields, and always including a large proportion of women.[11]

Malinowski demanded what he called loyalty, but he engaged his students in debate and challenged them to apply his theory of culture to ethnographic materials, in particular his own Trobriand data. 'The idea', as Audrey Richards has explained, was 'that rites, beliefs and customs, however extraordinary they appear to an observer, actually fill "needs", biological, psychological, and social'. Seminar discussions had 'the fascination of a game for which the *chose donnée* was the necessity of the custom or institution under discussion to the individual, the group or the society. If the Trobriand islanders did it, or had it, it must be assumed to be a necessary thing for them to do or have.' In consequence, 'discussions of the function of aspects or institutions of tribal life led directly into field-work material . . . and we began actually to visualise ourselves "in the field"'.[12] But before going into the field students were required to write library theses, based on the ethnographic literature. Audrey's background in biology was broadly relevant to the Malinowskian project, which insisted that culture was rooted in biological needs, and she chose a topic in which both biology and culture were implicated: nutrition.

Malinowski had dealt with the domestication of sex in his *Sexual Life of Savages* (1929), but in the very first sentence of her book Audrey Richards pronounced: 'Nutrition as a biological process is more fundamental than sex.'[13] Nutrition was also one of the classic subjects of the social surveys favoured by reformers in Britain, and in the 1920s it had become a subject of rapidly growing interest in academic and government circles. Institutes of Nutrition were set up in Aberdeen and Cambridge, and in 1927 with the assistance of the Dietetics Committee of the Economic Advisory Council, the Aberdeen Institute collaborated with the Kenya Medical Service on studies of Kikuyu and Masai nutrition.

However, the functionalist approach promised a fresh perspective. First, 'nutrition in human society cannot be considered as a biological instinct alone'.[14] Moreover, the study of nutrition could not be restricted to a review of agricultural techniques or an analysis of diets. Drawing on the ethnographic literature on the Southern Bantu peoples, Audrey argued that social institutions are organised essentially to meet this fundamental physiological need, and that a 'whole series of institutions and relationships' constitute 'the *nutritional system*'.[15]

This was an orthodox Malinowskian formula, and Audrey Richards was to remain an orthodox Malinowskian, always passionately loyal to him. It is true that she was sensitive to one of the fundamental difficulties of the approach: that it made comparison very difficult. (Later she experimented with structural methods that facilitated comparison.) However, she never accepted the other conventional criticism of functionalism: 'the charge often made by administrators,' she noted, 'that functional anthropologists were not prepared to allow for any changes in the tribes they were studying'.[16] On the contrary, she was convinced that the type of information and analysis that functionalist ethnography provided would be of great value to policy-makers in the colonies, and that it would indeed illuminate the problems of social change.

AFRICA

Audrey Richards and Lucy Mair (step-daughter of Sir William Beveridge, the director of the LSE), another of Malinowski's most loyal students, were among the first anthropologists to carry out applied research in Africa. With Malinowski's blessing, they hoped to bring the insights of functionalist anthropology to bear on the problems of colonial administration.

Audrey's fieldwork proposal, dated July 1929, begins with a conventional enough Malinowskian statement of intent: 'To make an intensive study of the social institutions, customs and beliefs of the Awemba tribe . . . of NE Rhodesia, with special reference to the part played by women in tribal and economic life, the nature and importance of the family system and the marriage contract, and problems connected with the rearing and education of children.' This should not be read as a precociously feminist proposal. Rather, Malinowski was inclined to think that women ethnographers would find it easier to study women. ('As long ago as 1930,' she recalled in a lecture on feminist anthropology in 1974, 'I was sent to study a matrilineal society because it was thought particularly appropriate for a woman anthropologist to study women. When I got there you will not be surprised to hear I found as many men as women!')[17]

In any case, she immediately turned to the potential application of the study:

I believe such work to be of immediate importance in view of the proposed extensions of the railway system to the Plateau area, and the further development of the copper resources of the district. Both these factors are likely to raise important administrative problems in native government, and to lead almost inevitably to new sources of conflict between the white and black races.[18]

From May 1930 to July 1931, and again from January 1933 to July 1934, Audrey did fieldwork in what was then Northern Rhodesia, among the Bemba, who occupy the north-eastern plateau of modern Zambia. In the 1930s the Bemba numbered between 115,000 and 140,000, but lived in small villages dispersed over a very large territory. Their kinship system was indeed matrilineal, they practised shifting cultivation, and they were organised into numerous chiefdoms under a highly ritualised but not very powerful paramount chief.

Pacified without much resistance in the last years of the nineteenth century, they had accepted the imposition of British colonial government. In return, they had been allowed to retain their system of chieftainship. Nevertheless, taxation in cash became general from 1905, and from 1914 large numbers of men were engaged in migrant labour in the mines of Katanga and Southern Rhodesia, and from 1920 in the Copperbelt. By 1914 between 20 and 30 per cent of the men were away from their villages as labour migrants, and food production at home began to suffer in consequence. In 1929 the Native Authority and Native Courts Ordinance introduced Indirect Rule.[19] Audrey was intrigued by the rapid social changes, even if she was perhaps unaware that they had been in train for a generation before her arrival. 'I really think they are an interesting people,' she wrote to Malinowski from Chilonga in September 1930, 'the queer mix up of a conquering people who had only been installed for 50 years in this country when the first white people came, who are now being transformed by the mining industry 500 miles off.'[20]

Malinowski's students were expected to learn the vernacular and to live in close association with the people they were studying. Audrey made long forays into the villages, but she used the estate of the colonial grandee, Stewart Gore-Browne, as her base, and never pretended that she had 'gone native': 'in an area where the only white people consist of three main classes – Government officials, missionaries, and traders – and where the tribe itself is organized on an autocratic basis . . . the anthropologist will find it impossible to be treated as an equal by the natives.' She was accorded the status of Chieftainess, and learnt to use the appropriate Bemba royal speech conventions: 'This position of prestige prevented my attaining any real position of equality with the people but was an advantage in carrying out village censuses when it was helpful to be able to exert a certain amount of authority.'[21]

She lived in a tent, spending between three and six weeks in each village. On the move, she must have made a striking impression:

Off the main road you must travel from village to village by footpaths, the white man or woman ahead on a bicycle or on foot, and the most motley procession of carriers behind. A native can carry a 60 or 70 lb load on his head, and seems to have an infinite capacity for hanging incongruous objects together with strands of bark . . . Behind this will follow your tent, and a clatter of cooking equipment, while the kitchen boy brings up the rear with a live chicken strung by its feet round the barrel of your rifle, and a couple of flat-irons in a basin on his head.[22]

Lorna Gore-Browne, who accompanied her on some expeditions, reported in a letter in 1933, 'Audrey never fusses . . . and is able to laugh and laugh when things go just a little wrong.'[23] She was one of the outstanding ethnographers of her generation, her gregariousness, her stamina, her acuteness of social observation and above all her ability to laugh and make people laugh with her carrying her triumphantly through the inevitable crises and periods of fatigue and discouragement. The difficulties were always reported as farce:

There is the difficulty of taking photographs and simultaneously writing notes during rites that take place in bush and village and on the road between the two. There is also the factor of exhaustion. Songs and dances often went on until two and three in the morning. On such occasions the company is usually elated by beer and accustomed to the heat of a small hut about eight feet in diameter filled with twenty or thirty people and an enormous fire. The observer is dead sober, nearly stifled, with eyes running from the smoke, and straining all the time to catch the words from the songs screeched around her, and to transcribe them by the firelight that penetrates occasionally through the mass of human limbs.[24]

A sober Bemba testimonial is available from an occasional field-assistant, the evangelist Paul Bwembya Mushindo.

I was very much impressed by the character of Dr A. I. Richards who was a European and purely English lady, who treated me, who was a pure African and her servant, very kindly. She had very good will to all African people. She was like a sister to me . . . Dr Richards thought I was helping her in her duties . . . I felt I was in a university for study. In this way Dr Richards learned less, but I felt I had learned much more without my teacher, Dr Richards, realising it.[25]

The first generation of Malinowski's students were encouraged to make a rounded study of a culture, rather than to concentrate on a particular facet of social life. It was only on her return to London that Audrey Richards decided that the focus of her first Bemba monograph should be, once again, nutrition. This had not been her original plan, and she had not organised her fieldwork systematically to collect material on the production and use of foods. Rather, very characteristically, the topic emerged as part of an interdisciplinary project, with a strong 'applied' cast, to which Audrey decided to subordinate her choice of subject-matter.

In 1935 she had taken the chair of the Diet Committee of the International Institute of African Languages and Cultures, a 'small group of anthropologists, medical and nutritional experts', and she persuaded them that social and cultural information should be included in the nutritional surveys being planned. 'It was therefore suggested that it would be instructive if I wrote a short book describing, in the case of one particular tribe . . . the variety of different factors, whether economic, political, legal, or religious which actually affected the people's diet. The result is in effect a description of the whole economic life of the tribe.'[26] It is more, being virtually a complete ethnography of the Bemba with an emphasis on the economy.

In her first book she had 'tried to prove that hunger was the chief determinant of human relationships'. Her aim in the second was rather 'to show how the biological facts of appetite and diet are themselves shaped by the . . . cultural mechanisms for producing, preparing and dividing food'.[27] This is an intriguing shift of emphasis, but the book was still a characteristic Malinowskian ethnography. Its specific model was the first volume of Malinowski's masterpiece, *Coral Gardens and their Magic*, his account of Trobriand husbandry that had appeared in 1935. There was, however, one major difference: unlike Malinowski, she situated her ethnography firmly in the current, colonial context.

In 1940 Audrey Richards published another monograph that was aimed primarily at a readership of colonial administrators: *Bemba Marriage and Present Economic Conditions*, which was published by the Rhodes–Livingstone Institute in Northern Rhodesia. Because of the time and place of the publication it never became widely known, yet it is one of the most sociologically sophisticated accounts of the effects of migrant labour on African family life, illustrating and probing the thesis that while industrial change created similar problems in many parts of the continent, 'the reactions of the different Native tribes . . . are not identical'.[28]

Her first major theoretical article dates from the same period, appearing in 1940 in a famous collection, *African Political Systems*, edited by Meyer Fortes and E. E. Evans-Pritchard. She tried to place the Bemba political system in a more general framework of African government, drawing out the universal features and indicating what was particular about the Bemba; but what is perhaps most remarkable about this essay, in contrast to her contemporary 'applied' publications, is that the influence of British colonial government, and economic and religious change, are noted only in a concluding section, while the Bemba are presented for the most part in a timeless, 'traditional' mode.[29] It is as if she felt that academic anthropology need not address the

231

impact of colonial overrule, while 'applied' anthropology dealt with the realities of social and cultural change. Similarly, her contribution to *African Systems of Kinship and Marriage*, in 1950, ignored the urgent problems of family change with which she had been concerned in her essay on Bemba marriage. This essay is, however, of far greater intrinsic interest than her earlier paper on political systems, presenting as it does a comparative (and notably structural) account of the problems common to matrilineal systems in Central Africa. It greatly influenced thinking about matrilineal kinship.[30]

While she was writing up, Audrey Richards taught at the LSE: and now her personal relationship with Malinowski reached a crisis. She had become an intimate friend both of Malinowski himself and of his chronically ill wife, Elsie. After Elsie's death, in 1935, 'Audrey and Bronio came very close to marrying', according to Malinowski's daughter, Helena. However:

their temperaments were perhaps too much alike; Audrey could not, as my mother had been able to, stand back as it were from his volcanic nature. Audrey tried to intervene for us three children, to see that Bronio fulfilled his fatherly duties, but what he demanded from his friends, especially in the unhappy times right after Elsie's death, was total, uncritical support of all his actions . . . So their marriage plans came – alas – to nothing. His daughters have always wished that they had married.[31]

It is possible that Audrey would have undertaken the marriage only in the interests of the Malinowski daughters, but Raymond Firth attests in a personal communication that both Audrey and Malinowski had other serious attachments at the time. In the event, Malinowski moved to Yale in 1939 and remarried. He died suddenly in the United States in 1942.

Audrey moved to South Africa, teaching from 1937 to 1940 at the University of Witwatersrand in Johannesburg. Characteristically she both began new fieldwork and forged friendships with interesting and powerful people, among them the Prime Minister Jan Smuts, at whose farm, Irene, near Pretoria, she was a regular guest. Intermittent fieldwork among a Tswana group in the Northern Transvaal yielded only one paper, but it is a brilliant piece, analysing the revival of 'tribalism' in an area in which traditional cultures had been destroyed a generation earlier. She argued that the movement had nothing to do with nostalgia for a golden age, or with traditionalism, but was rather to be explained as a manoeuvre in the competition for land rights.[32] Similarly, in a better-known essay on the spread of anti-witchcraft movements in Central Africa, she had argued that they were a response to cultural dislocation and, above all, the social conflicts and uncertainties generated by industrialisation.[33]

THE COLONIAL OFFICE AND THE EAST AFRICAN INSTITUTE OF SOCIAL RESEARCH

'I mean to come back next Xmas,' she wrote from Johannesburg to Raymond Firth in December 1938, 'and then if nothing else turns up to go back for another two years at least. I don't want to stay here all my life and miss much as you may imagine, but it was good to get away and I want to do one bit of fieldwork and get something done at the university here.'[34] However, the war intervened and she returned to London as a temporary principal at the Colonial Office. Working with Lord Hailey, she participated in the reorientation of research policy in the colonies

She became special lecturer in colonial studies at the LSE from 1944 to 1945, and continued as a Reader from 1946 to 1950, but she also served as a member of the Colonial Social Science Research Council. (The appointment of Raymond Firth as Secretary was largely her initiative.) Various career paths were now open to her, for at long last British African policy-makers had come to appreciate that they could benefit from expert social science advice. This presented a great opportunity, especially to someone of Audrey's tastes. 'It is said that youth is the time of enthusiasm,' she wrote later, reflecting on this time, 'but I believe there is no sense of commitment so great as that of middle-aged men and women who suddenly find themselves in a position to do the good they have been trying to do for many years.'[35]

One of the most important initiatives of the CSSRC was the establishment of research institutes in the African colonies. In 1950 she went out to Makerere University in Uganda, as director of the newly established East African Institute of Social Research. The model for the new institute was the Rhodes–Livingstone Institute in Northern Rhodesia under the direction of Max Gluckman. She later wrote that 'both Gluckman's Institute and mine were really experiments in organising field research'.[36] Both also promoted interdisciplinary research, and both were seriously committed to applied studies of interest to colonial governments. Audrey's gregarious, hospitable style nevertheless gave the Makerere Institute a distinctive tone. 'Talented cuisine, great entertainer on a shoe string, informally without fuss,' notes one of her colleagues, Aidan Southall. 'Shrewd vagueness covering sharp precision . . . Catholic in friendship with Ganda princes, chiefs, clerks, as well as the humble . . . Her close friendship with Sir Andrew Cohen [Governor of Uganda] spilled over on to EAISR and made for a unique period of discourse between high government and intellectuals black and white.'[37]

Audrey divided up the work between anthropologists already in the field (co-opting some who were only notionally, if at all, answerable to her) and members of the Institute staff, almost regardless of their formal specialisms, and drawing in, as equals, her secretary Jean Robin and locally recruited interpreters and field assistants. She would chivvy her collaborators to write up, in the last resort commandeering their notes and writing them up herself. It was in this way that the major studies of her Uganda period were produced, most notably *Economic Development and Tribal Change: a Study of Immigrant Labour in Buganda* (1954) and *East African Chiefs* (1960). Many years after she had left East Africa, she organised a comparable study that resulted in the book,

Enid Welsford, 1892–1981

Audrey Richards, 1899–1984

Honor Fell, 1900–1986

Rosalind Franklin, 1920–1958

Subsistence to Commercial Farming in Present Day Buganda (1973). These studies mobilised all her talents for administration, teaching, fieldwork and synthesis, however much she complained that they took her away from the 'theoretical' work she hoped to complete, especially when she found herself filling in for colleagues who had not delivered their promised chapters.

While at Makerere she did, nevertheless, find the time to complete her most extensive 'theoretical' study, *Chisungu* (1956). This is an account of female initiation among the Bemba, based largely on observations of a single ceremony through which two girls passed. The account is painstaking and detailed, and the analysis has often been praised,[38] but the 'functionalist' analytic framework already seemed dated. The ritual is very largely presented as it appears to the outside observer, the actors' experi-ence and native exegesis being subordinated to the sociological and psychological interpretations of the anthropologist.

Just as the book appeared, Victor Turner was beginning his study of initiation ceremonies and other rituals in another Zambian tribe, the Ndembu. In the early 1960s he began to publish richly documented, phenomenological analyses, which were to transform the study of African ritual behaviour,[39] making Audrey Richards's study – which had, after all, been conceived thirty years earlier – seem old-fashioned and inadequate. Jean La Fontaine points out that Turner seldom cited Richards's study, and reproaches him for not acknowledging her influence,[40] but other Africanists were more impressed by the great differences in the approaches of Turner and Richards. A telling instance is the enormous contrast between Richards's straightforward and one-dimensional account of the symbolism of the *musuku* tree and Turner's famous exegesis of the symbolism of the same tree.

Andrey Richards later suggested that her ethnography was necessarily less specialised, since she was working in the Malinowskian tradition of 'multi-purpose' ethnography, in which the fieldworker was expected to cover all the important social institutions.

I once tried to list the symbolic meanings of the immense variety of trees, bushes and plants used in Bemba magic. I got surface meanings for some thirty-four of these and was beginning to get some of the deeper associations, but I had to give up the attempt since I found it impossible to combine this with the study of the main outlines of the social structure, institutions and beliefs of the people in which I was engaged.[41]

CAMBRIDGE

In 1956 she returned to a Fellowship at Newnham College, Cambridge, where she later served as Vice-Principal. She held the Smuts Readership in Commonwealth Studies in the University from 1961 to 1966, and built up the University's African Studies Centre, lobbying for its formal recognition and becoming its first director. She also supervised ethnographic research, carried out largely by Cambridge students, on the small Essex village, Elmdon, in which she lived for most of this period, introducing aspirant anthropologists to the realities of fieldwork and finally facing up to the fact that if she did not herself arrange for the collation of the material it would never be written up. She also produced a pamphlet for the villagers on the genealogical studies that had been made.[42]

She was, however, a marginal figure in the Social Anthropology Department at the University, perhaps largely because she and the Professor, Meyer Fortes, did not get on. She was, of course, a greatly respected figure, and much loved by most of those who worked with her. Her career had been a distinguished one. Her honours included a CBE for her work in Uganda, election to the British Academy, and the Presidency of the Royal Anthropological Institute. Nevertheless, in these Cambridge years she was not a major intellectual influence in the discipline.

It has been suggested that she was undervalued, even

236

discriminated against, because she was a woman.[43] She herself resisted this suggestion, and any handicap she laboured under as a woman was at least counterbalanced by the advantages of her background and connections. 'Her upper-class background no doubt added to her self-confidence,' wrote her friend Edmund Leach, 'her reputation for modesty was perhaps deceptive. She was quick to make the most of unexpected opportunities but sometimes authoritarian in her treatment of collaborators.'[44] (Not 'upper class', perhaps according to her nephew Dr T. Faber, but rather 'upper-middle class' – 'and certainly privileged in being born into a secure, intelligent and comfortably-off clan'.)[45]

Audrey was also a critic of the feminist movement that developed within anthropology in the 1970s. She argued against the ethnocentricism and special pleading that she discerned in the feminist critique, and insisted on 'the duty of the field-anthropologist to distinguish very clearly when she considers the position of women between what shocks her and what shocks "them"'.[46] Are women generally discriminated against? Societies like the Bemba clearly distinguish between 'the reproductive period of a woman's life and the rest. In a sense it would be true to say that Bemba regarded the individual who was producing and rearing children as a woman and the female persons who were not doing so as men.' A similar distinction might come to be accepted in the West: 'We may see a clearer division between women who want children and those who are willing to give them up for professional or other reasons.'[47] This was the sacrifice she had made herself, but it had freed her to enjoy a rewarding career.

Yet within her chosen career she had made a further choice, which she did believe had a deleterious effect on her reputation. This was her primary commitment to 'applied' as against 'theoretical' research. She was prepared to argue that applied research could yield theoretical dividends. 'I personally learnt more about the political organisation of the Ganda while conducting an immigrant labour survey which could be described as "applied anthropology", than I might have done by a "theoretical" study of the political system because I attended local council meetings at all levels to discuss the project.'[48] A specialist in Central African ethnography, Richard Werbner (1979), agrees that her practical knowledge of local politics gives some of her political descriptions unusual interest. However, she felt that her applied work was not properly appreciated by her colleagues, and that it had robbed her of the time she wanted to devote to her pure research. *Chisungu* was finally completed, but not the promised study of Bemba royal ritual, on which she published only a few papers rather than the major monograph she had in mind.

Her theoretical essays were sometimes influential, most notably the classic paper, 'Some Types of Family Structure among the Central Bantu' (1950). Nevertheless, the theoretical framework which she generally retained, rooted in Malinowski's functionalism, was not favoured by the next generation of anthropologists, and she did not sympathise with the very general move from the study of 'function' to the explication of 'meaning'. As Edmund Leach has remarked, 'She showed little sympathy for post-functionalist developments in social anthropology.'[49] This was perhaps surprising, since she increasingly came to concern herself with the study of ritual; but if Victor Turner neglected her work, so did she his, and that of other younger theorists in the field, like Lévi-Strauss and Geertz (although in general she followed closely debates within British social anthropology).

Moreover, while her 'applied' studies were distinguished by their ethnographic realism, and their acute attention to processes of social change, the theoretical papers seemed to shut out the colonial realities. Perhaps it was the legacy of functionalism, or the example of the Trobriand monographs, but when she wrote what she called 'theoretical' studies Audrey Richards adopted the pastoral idiom of the 'ethnographic present'. The richly nuanced accounts of social change in her 'applied' studies were informed by shrewd, pragmatic, if often *ad hoc* sociological analysis, yet they too lacked a crucial dimension, for criticism of the colonial governments could not be risked, at least in print.

Audrey Richards was nothing if not a realist, and she had an intuitive understanding of the official mind. She was well aware that African colonial administrators might accept expert advice on matters of practical policy, but that they were not open to criticisms of fundamentals. She thought it obvious that the anthropologist was not in the business of criticising colonial governments: 'I tried very hard to follow the precepts then taught by Malinowski as to the complete neutrality that was desirable for a fieldworker. I made it my business not to criticize European or African officials or to express strong views on policy.'[50] In any case, however successful in their own terms, the interest of the applied studies was ultimately both short-term and local. They were addressed to 'social problems' defined by the preoccupations of government officials, and they were largely forgotten with the end of the British Empire in Central and East Africa in the early 1960s. The new universities and research institutions, and the international aid agencies, put their faith, for a while, in five-year plans, built around large-scale capital projects: exercises in 'planification' that had little room for anthropologists.

Moreover, in the new African states, anthropologists were discredited precisely on account of their association with colonial regimes. This disconcerted Audrey, and she defended the record of applied anthropology and of the colonial welfare programmes more generally: 'We were all "do gooders",' she wrote, 'trying to organize research which we felt to be helpful for "welfare and development", the term used in the Colonial Development and Welfare Act. Many would deny the validity of our belief . . . especially those who feel that cultural and structural differences between the peoples inhabiting the ex-colonies should be obliterated as soon as possible.'[51]

This suggests that she had limited sympathy with African

nationalism and with the African intellectuals' critique of 'tribalism' and of colonial motives. There is little in her writings, or even her correspondence, to suggest that she appreciated the significance of the post-war nationalist movement. Her main political study of this period, *East African Chiefs* (1960), was formulated in classic colonial terms:

One of the most intractable problems facing East African Governments is the business of selecting and training the officials who make up the core of their local administrations . . . Why is the selection of these chiefs described as a problem? Because British administrators have considered themselves to be committed to a policy of raising the standards of living of the people under their rule and of introducing something like Western types of social service.[52]

There is little in the book about the colonial administration as a whole, which her American colleague and friend Tom Fallers had described so acutely in one Uganda region, Busoga.[53] Two years after the book appeared, Uganda was independent. I taught anthropology at Makerere in the late 1960s, and my students thought that *East African Chiefs* was irrelevant to the political problems of their country.

Ironic, self-mocking, a hilarious companion, famous in Uganda for her party trick of lighting matches with her toes, Audrey was nevertheless a most serious and moral person. 'I have spent most of my life sucked into "do-good" things,' she once wrote to a friend.[54] In her last years, her health fragile, Audrey willingly accepted responsibility for an old friend who was suffering from alcoholism. One evening she tried to carry her upstairs, fell and cracked a bone in her leg. But when I visited her she was buoyant. She knew she was needed, she said, and that if she thought she could no longer be of use to others, then she would rather die. Only a few days before her death, she told a close friend that she was ready to die because 'there is no one any longer for whom I can do anything'. She lived until 1984.

NOTES

I am very grateful to Professor Sir Raymond Firth and to Dr T. E. Faber, for allowing me to consult and cite Audrey Richards's letters in the collection of the London School of Economics, and to Dr Angela Raspin, the Keeper of Manuscripts, for her kind help. Professor Firth and Dr Faber also wrote very helpful comments on an earlier draft, as did Professor Jean La Fontaine and Professor Andrew Roberts. Professor Roberts also directed me to valuable historical sources on the Bemba and corrected some key passages in the original draft. Walker Elkan and Aidan Southall, former colleagues of Audrey Richards in East Africa, answered a number of my questions.

NB A full bibliography of Audrey Richards's publications has been published by T. M. Luhrmann. It appears in *Persons and Powers of Women in Diverse Cultures*, ed. Shirley Ardener (New York and Oxford: Berg 1992), pp. 51–7. This bibliography is also published in a special commemoration number of *Cambridge Anthropology* 10 (1) (1985), which carries memoirs of Audrey Richards by Helena Wayne, Raymond and Rosemary Firth, Sir Richard Faber, and several of her former students and associates.

1 N. G. Annan, 'The Intellectual Aristocracy', in *Studies in Social History*, ed. J. H. Plumb (London: Longmans 1955), p. 244.
2 Ibid., p. 247.
3 Ibid., p. 250.
4 Ibid., pp. 269–73.
5 The citations are from a memoir of her mother written by Audrey Richards and kindly put at my disposal by Dr T. Faber.
6 Cited in Duncan Wilson, *Gilbert Murray O.M., 1866–1957* (Oxford: Clarendon Press 1987), p. 350.
7 Letter to Adam Kuper, 13 June 1978.
8 Letter (in the LSE collection) from Graham Wallas to Malinowski, dated 13 November 1926.
9 E. R. Leach, 'The Epistemological Background to Malinowski's Empiricism', *Man and Culture: an Evaluation of the Work of Bronislaw Malinowski*, ed. Raymond Firth (London: Routledge and Kegan Paul 1957), p. 124.
10 Audrey Richards, 'The Concept of Culture in Malinowski's Work', *Man and Culture: an Evaluation of the Work of Bronislaw Malinowski*, ed. R. Firth (London: Routledge and Kegan Paul 1957), p. 20.
11 Adam Kuper, *Anthropology and Anthropologists: the Modern British School* (London: Routledge 1983), chapter 1.
12 Richards, 'The Concept of Culture', pp. 18–19.

13 Audrey I. Richards, *Hunger and Work in a Savage Tribe: a Functional Study of Nutrition among the Southern Bantu* (London: Routledge and Kegan Paul 1932), p. 1.

14 Ibid., p. 211.

15 Ibid., p. 213.

16 Richards, 'The Concept of Culture', p. 19.

17 Audrey Richards, 'The "Position" of Women – an Anthropological View', *Cambridge Anthropology* 1 (3) (1974): 3–10. Quotation from p. 7.

18 The fieldwork proposal is in Audrey Richards's student file in the LSE archive.

19 On the history of the Bemba, see Andrew Roberts, *A History of the Bemba* (London: Longmans 1923). He comments:

> Audrey, of course may have been unaware of this background when she arrived in 1930. I don't think, indeed, she acknowledges it anywhere; and she doesn't seem to refer at all to the extended study of the N. Rhodesian economy (including labour migration) made in 1932 by Austin Robinson, who was already a Cambridge lecturer in economics (and a member of the Intellectual Aristocracy – his father was Dean of Winchester . . .) I do wonder whether Audrey – at least in the 1930's – regarded even contemporary scholarship of this sort as 'knowledge' – let alone the testimony of 19th century travellers!

20 Letter in LSE collection.

21 Audrey Richards, *Land, Labour and Diet in Northern Rhodesia: an Economic Study of the Bemba Tribe* (London: Oxford University Press for International Institute of African Languages and Cultures 1939), pp. 12–13.

22 Audrey Richards, 'Colonial Future: the Need for Facts', *Spectator*, 4 February 1949, pp. 143–4. Quotation from p. 143.

23 Cited in Rotberg, who gives a good account of the expeditions the two women made together: Robert I. Rotberg, *Black Heart: Gore-Browne and the Politics of Multiracial Zambia* (Berkeley: California University Press 1977).

24 Audrey Richards, *Chisungu: a Girl's Initiation Ceremony among the Bemba of Northern Rhodesia* (London: Faber and Faber 1956), p. 62.

25 Paul Bwembya Mushindo, *The Life of a Zambian Evangelist* (Lusaka: University of Zambia Institute of African Studies, Communication no. 9, 1973), p. 28.

26 Richards, *Land, Labour and Diet*, Preface; see Jo Gladstone for an appreciation of Audrey Richards's contributions in the field of nutrition: 'Significant Sister: Autonomy and Obligation in Audrey Richards' Early Fieldwork', *American Ethnologist* 13 (1986), 338–62;

'Venturing on the Borderline: Audrey Richards' Contribution to the Hungry Thirties Debate in Africa', *Bulletin for the Social History of Medicine*, no. 40 (1987).

27 Richards, *Land, Labour and Diet*, Preface.

28 Audrey Richards, *Bemba Marriage and Present Economic Conditions* (Livingstone: Rhodes–Livingstone Institute, Rhodes–Livingstone Papers no. 4, 1940), p. 7.

29 Later essays on Bemba royal politics offered a more historical perspective, and presented interesting accounts of political functionalism. See especially Richards 1961.

30 Schneider and Gough's important book, *Matrilineal Kinship* (1961), which was dedicated to Audrey Richards, was essentially a working-out and application of ideas she had put forward in that essay.

31 Helena Wayne, 'Bronislaw Malinowski: the Influence of Various Women on His Life and Works', *American Ethnologist* 12 (3) (1985), p. 538.

32 Audrey Richards, 'Some Causes of a Revival of Tribalism in South African Native Reserves', *Man*, no. 41 (1942): 89–90.

33 Audrey Richards, 'A Modern Movement of Witchfinders', *Africa* 8 (1935): 448–61.

34 Letter in Firth papers, LSE collection.

35 Audrey Richards, 'The Colonial Office and the Organisation of Social Research', *Anthropological Forum* 4 (2) (1977): 168–89. Quotation from p. 173.

36 Letter to Firth, 27 May 1984, in Firth Papers, LSE collection.

37 Letter to Adam Kuper, 12 April 1994.

38 See, e.g., Jean La Fontaine's introduction to the reissue of *Chisungu* in 1982: Jean La Fontaine, 'Preface' to second edition of Audrey Richards, *Chisungu* (London: Tavistock 1982).

39 For some of Turner's initial statements, soon after the publication of *Chisungu*, see V. W. Turner, *Ndembu Divination: its Symbolism and Techniques* (Manchester: Manchester University Press for the Rhodes–Livingstone Institute 1961); 'Three Symbols of *Passage* in Ndembu Circumcision Ritual', in *Essays on the Ritual of Social Relations*, ed. M. Gluckman (Manchester: Manchester University Press 1962); 'Symbols in Ndembu Ritual', in *Closed Systems and Open Minds*, ed. M. Gluckman (Edinburgh: Oliver and Boyd 1963).

40 Jean La Fontaine, 'Audrey I. Richards, Obituary', *Africa* 55 (1) (1985), p. 204.

41 Audrey Richards, 'African Systems of Thought: an Anglo-French Dialogue', *Man* 2 (2) (1967): 286–98. She is making a distinction

between what she terms 'British' and 'French' approaches to fieldwork, but is in fact describing the Malinowskian tradition. At a later point in the same paper (p. 296) she distances herself from Turner's approach.

42 Marilyn Strathern, 'Audrey Isabel Richards, 1899–1984', *Proceedings of the British Academy* 82 (1993): 439–53.

43 See, e.g., Jo Gladstone, 'Audrey I. Richards: Africanist and Humanist', in *Persons and Powers of Women in Diverse Cultures*, ed. Shirley Ardener (New York and Oxford: Berg 1992).

44 E. R. Leach, 'Richards, Audrey Isabel (1899–1984)', in *Dictionary of National Biography, 1981–5* (Oxford: Oxford University Press 1990), p. 338.

45 In his comments to me (letter dated 5 May 1994), Dr Faber continued: 'But all the Butlers were made to feel that they had to work, and my grandmother and my mother were both, by training and inclination, economical women in a typically bourgeois way.' He also emphasises, however (letter dated 9 May 1994), that 'a lifetime spent in universities' was more important to Audrey than the particular circumstances of her childhood.

46 Richards, 'The "Position" of Women', p. 4.

47 Ibid., p. 9.

48 Richards, 'The Colonial Office', p. 183.

49 Leach, 'Richards', p. 338.

50 Richards, 'The Colonial Office', p. 169.

51 Ibid., p. 174.

52 Audrey Richards (ed.), *East African Chiefs: a Study of Political Development in Some Uganda and Tanganyika Tribes* (London: Faber and Faber 1960), pp. 13–14.

53 Lloyd A. Fallers, *Bantu Bureaucracy: a Study of Integration and Conflict in the Political Institutions of an East African People* (Chicago: University of Chicago Press 1965).

54 Letter to Jean La Fontaine, quoted in La Fontaine, 'Audrey I. Richards', p. 64.

Chapter 11

HONOR FELL

1900–1986

Joan Mason

Honor Fell's scientific achievement, like Marjory Stephenson's, was celebrated in a rhyme in *Brighter Biochemistry*, comic journal of the Dunn Institute.[1]

> Honour befell
> Miss Honor B. Fell.
> She managed to culture a bone.
> She tried it on muscle
> And after a tussle
> She found that the muscle had grown.
>
> ABC

Barbara Callow's limerick appeared in January 1930, after Honor Fell had been made director of a small research laboratory, the Strangeways, at the age of 29. Her life resembled Marjory Stephenson's in some respects. She was 'almost an only child', she was encouraged in science in early life, and her colleagues in the laboratory were her 'family'. She had kindly gatekeepers, in Thomas Strangeways (1866–1926), and Walter Fletcher of the Medical Research Council (MRC). The honours due to her, for the insights gained by her skills in tissue and organ culture, and for building up the Strangeways Laboratory to achieve an international reputation, took some time to materialise. She was 52 before she was elected to Fellowship of the Royal Society, and 63 when she became Dame Honor Fell. While the institutions discriminated against women, she succeeded in science by the singular feat of building up her own institution, on the strong but small foundation that she inherited from Thomas Strangeways, who died when she was 26.

Honor Bridget Fell[2] was the youngest of a family of nine children, learning self-reliance as a child eight years younger than the next sibling. Her mother, Alice Pickersgill-Cunliffe, was proficient as carpenter and architect, designing the family house at Fowthorpe, in Yorkshire. Her father, Colonel William Fell, a minor landowner, was in the United States when she was small, buying horses for the British Army during the Boer War. He was keenly interested in animals and in nature, and her family thought that her devotion to biology came from him. There was artistic ability in the family, and she was an accomplished artist, as shown by her scientific drawings, before photography became available.

Ferrets are conspicuous in the accounts of Honor's earlier life. At the age of 13 she brought her ferret Janie to her sister Barbara's wedding, as reported in the quarterly journal that the extended family published. Her ferrets lived in the garden at Wychwood School in Oxford, chosen for her because of its bias towards science, biology in particular. She moved to Madras College, St Andrews, at 16, and at 18 to Edinburgh University to read zoology.

She began research at Edinburgh in 1921 with Frank Crew, a geneticist, in charge of the Department of Animal Breeding. They were studying developmental processes in the ovaries and testes of fowls by the methods of histology, the microscopic examination of sections of tissue. Crew heard that Tom Strangeways in Cambridge was able to study living cells, on the warm stage of the microscope, and sent her to spend a few months with him to learn the art of tissue culture. There she recorded her excitement at being one of the first people ever to see the process of cell division, of mitosis, under the microscope. This is a remarkable sight, as each rod-shaped chromosome, the genetic material in the cell nucleus, divides lengthways to form a pair, which then separates, the individuals regrouping, marvellously, to form a set of chromosomes for each daughter nucleus.

Strangeways said she could work with him if there were no openings in Edinburgh, and she returned in 1923 to spend her life in research in Cambridge, funded at first by the MRC, then by Beit Fellowships 1924–31, and then by the Royal Society. She had worked for only three years with Strangeways when the laboratory suffered a great shock in his sudden death, just before his sixtieth birthday.

FROM RESEARCH HOSPITAL TO STRANGEWAYS
RESEARCH LABORATORY

At the time of Strangeways's death his little Cambridge Research Hospital had a growing reputation but substantial debt, amounting to one-third of its cost. He was a remarkable man.[3] He started out in business, then achieved his ambition to study medicine at St Bartholomew's Medical School, known as Barts. There Alfred Kanthack, Professor of Pathology, who was only a year older than Strangeways, appointed him to his staff as clinical pathologist. In 1897 they both moved to Cambridge, where Strangeways became lecturer in Pathology, then Reader, keeping in touch with his Barts friends and colleagues, Ronald Canti and Malcolm Donaldson.

Strangeways was born Thomas Strangeways Pigg, and changed his name when he married Dorothy Beck in 1902. She was sister to one of his students, and eldest daughter of the Master of Trinity Hall. He told her of his scheme to set up a hospital and laboratory to study chronic diseases, such as rheumatoid arthritis, which were poorly understood, using the patients as guinea-pigs. Dorothy Strangeways joined in this with great enthusiasm, as later did the patients.

When the scheme became a struggle, Tom Strangeways offered to abandon it and give more time to medical practice, but Dorothy refused. She later recalled: 'to launch the Scheme we were spending one-third of our income of £150 per annum upon it, and we had two children. He approached his Class and asked if they would back the project to the extent of £5 each; this they all agreed to do, but I am thankful to say they were never called upon.'[4] The 1962 *History of the Strangeways Laboratory* was dedicated 'To E. Dorothy Strangeways, in recognition'. She was described as 'still a guiding spirit of the laboratory',[5] and their first benefactor, 'without whose courage and unselfishness the little Research Hospital would not have lived to grow into the Strangeways Research Laboratory'.

Strangeways was severely deaf and worked with few people, but his enthusiasm was infectious.[6] He raised funds, and in 1905 set up a six-bed hospital in Hartington Grove, with a laboratory made from the coal-shed, and a retired matron and a nurse who worked unpaid. In 1912 they build a larger hospital on the present site on Worts Causeway, near where Addenbrooke's Hospital now stands, the architect, solicitor and landscape gardener working for nothing.[7] During the 1914–18 War his friend Otto Beit, the South African philanthropist, protected him from the demands of the War Office by financing the hospital as a Red Cross Hospital for officers.

Strangeways saw that in order to understand arthritis he needed to study the processes of the living cells of the joints. He learned the basic technique of growing tissues in culture from a Cambridge man who had worked as technician in Alexis Carrel's laboratory in the Rockefeller Institute. By 1923 his clinical research was becoming too successful, and he moved this to Barts. Honor Fell joined him just as he was turning his wards into laboratories, and F. Gordon Spear came the next year to work on radiobiology, as a member of the MRC's external staff.

Malcolm Donaldson told Honor Fell, in a letter in 1967, of a conversation that he had with Strangeways in the 1920s: 'I congratulate you on your team. Many years ago I said to

Strangeways "You should have about 30 people working with you." He replied "No, Miss Fell is sufficient."'

When Strangeways died the Research Hospital faced sudden extinction, in Gordon Spear's words.[8] The Trustees opened a memorial fund to take care of the family, for the five boys were still being educated.[9] Two Trustees wanted to close the Hospital, but the third, Malcolm Donaldson, fought for its survival. The next part of the story has been told by Harold Himsworth, Secretary of the MRC 1949–68:

Honor Fell did a remarkable job, not only by her personal contributions to biological knowledge but also by building up an internationally renowned research organisation, the Strangeways Research Laboratory

On Strangeways' death in 1926, she, then only 26 years old, literally kept the quite small organisation he had founded in being, despite the misgivings of the Trustees who wished to close it down. She realised that what was uppermost in the Trustees' mind was money to support the laboratory. So she came up to London, on her own initiative, to see my predecessor but one at the MRC, Walter Fletcher. He was so impressed by her and her views about the future that he went to the Council and persuaded them to throw their weight behind her. Thereafter, under her direction, the Strangeways never looked back.[10]

Honor Fell was elected to a Senior Beit Fellowship in 1928, and at the age of 29 was appointed by the Trustees to the post of Scientific Director, which she held until she was 70. The Hospital was renamed the Strangeways Research Laboratory, in honour of its founder. 'It seemed to us so silly to close the laboratory when we were perfectly capable of running it,' she wrote. She and Gordon Spear could claim that this was the only institution in the country devoted to the study of cell biology.[11] She was funded by the Royal Society from 1931, as Messel and then Foulerton Research Fellow, and appointed Royal Society Research Professor in 1963. Spear was made assistant Director, then deputy Director, 1931–58.

Their outstanding qualification, she remarked, was that neither of them needed a salary. The Trustees reported in 1934 that they knew of no other laboratory in which so much work was done at so small a cost. No member of the research or technical staff was ever paid out of the Laboratory's own funds. Technicians, some of whom served the Laboratory for over fifty years, were expert in tissue culture, photography, draughtsmanship, and the construction and maintenance of laboratory apparatus, often with imaginative improvisation.

An advisory council was set up with members drawn from Cambridge and London Universities, and the MRC was constant in its support. The Rockefeller Foundation, the Wellcome Trust and the Nuffield Foundation financed building programmes. The British Empire Cancer Campaign, the Halley Stewart Trust, the 1851 Commissioners, the Royal Society, the Fleming Memorial Trust, the Arthritis and Rheumatism Council, and many others responded to appeals for funds for staff and equipment.

Janet Vaughan wrote in her *Memoir*:

Though little is said in the *Annual Reports* about the administration involved in obtaining the grants, the gifts, the new buildings, the expensive equipment needed as techniques evolved, the steady build up of an internationally famous research laboratory must be recognized as part of Honor Fell's achievement.

When she retired as Director in 1970 the laboratory staff were 121 in all, including 62 scientists and 29 technical assistants.[12] Looking through the names of the men and women who have worked at the Strangeways for long or short periods there is hardly a name now famous in the international bone world[13] as a chemist, an orthopaedic surgeon, a rheumatologist, a radiobiologist, a histologist or bone biologist that is missing. They came from every country in the world. Thirty-two countries are mentioned in the *History* published in 1962.[14] They came to learn the art and technique of organ culture. For some Honor Fell obtained grants, some brought their own finance.[15]

Honor Fell's comment on her administrative duties was: 'Throughout my 41 years of office, I found the financial situation something of a nightmare; we could only make ends meet by stringent and often unpopular economies. However we managed somehow and we were never in debt.'[16] The Laboratory continued to run, surviving from grant to grant, on a shoestring if necessary, with mainstays such as the MRC only so long as clear merit could be demonstrated. The most difficult period financially was the 1930s, of which Janet Vaughan wrote:

In the late 1930s Honor Fell had been particularly concerned as a member of the Society for the Protection of Science and Learning with refugees from Hitler's Europe. She would meet them at European conferences, arrange for them to come to England and meet them at Cambridge railway station and offer them employment at the laboratory. Many of them worked for short periods and then moved elsewhere, others . . . stayed on . . . making significant contributions to the work and reputation of the Strangeways, both as scientists and administrators.[17]

ORGAN CULTURE AT THE STRANGEWAYS LABORATORY[18]

Strangeways showed Honor Fell in 1923 a tiny fragment of cartilage from a joint and a little explant of small intestine that he was growing in culture. He had noticed that joint cavities sometimes contained 'loose bodies', small pieces of tissue, usually cartilage, precursor of bone, and found that he could maintain them in glass tubes for study under the microscope. She suggested the use of the method to observe development in the embryo. Embryonic tissue, being small, is suitable for this technique, since the nutrients have to diffuse in from outside. But this was an ambitious project, for embryonic development was little understood. Sixty years later Medawar remarked that embryology was 'the most fiendishly difficult subject in the whole of biology'.[19]

Using early chick embryos, three days after fertilisation of the egg, they explanted leg-buds in which there was no sign of cartilage. To their delight they could see, under the microscope, the cartilage form and then develop as in the chick. When they cultivated the rudimentary eye from a three-day embryo, they watched with excitement as the simple membrane developed to form a normal retina, with typical layers of nerve cells, rods and cones, pigment epithelium (outer layer) and lens fibres. Later in the 1920s Honor Fell observed embryonic cartilage calcifying to form bone, noting changes in calcium and phosphate in the medium.

In contrast to ordinary cell cultures, many of these explants could continue to function, develop and differentiate for up to two to three weeks. The nutrient medium, which was renewed every two days or so, typically contained plasma, salts and embryonic extract ('embryo juice'), providing vitamins and hormones necessary for growth and differentiation. Larger explants were grown on a watchglass inside a large pot containing water to maintain the humidity.

Progressive development was observed at the Strangeways in very small rudiments of the ear, hair, teeth, ovary, and various glands (mammary, salivary, pancreas) as well as bones and joints. This development, in culture, showed that differentiation of the cells could occur in the absence of a blood supply, nervous system, or other association with adjacent structure. These culture techniques thus greatly extend the knowledge gained from animal experiments, and can replace them to some extent.

CINEMICROSCOPY OF LIVING CELLS[20]

Historic treasures, now at the National Film Archive, are the Strangeways Collection of time-lapse films, in which the development of cell tissue can be seen speeded up. The films, which married the superb techniques of the Strangeways with innovations in time-lapse cinemicroscopy, were key sources of information on cellular processes. Films were made in the 1920s by Ronald G. Canti, a clinical pathologist at Barts, using equipment at his home in Hampstead, and later, professionally engineered equipment at Barts. The cultures were prepared at the Strangeways and taken by train to London. After Canti's death in 1936, films were made by Arthur F. W. Hughes, who worked at the Strangeways from 1932 to 1964.

Canti's films were ground-breaking, creating a great stir at the Xth International Congress of Zoology at Budapest in 1927. Sadly, Strangeways did not live to see this. Different films clearly showed the movements of the chromosomes during mitotic division of the nucleus, effects of β and γ rays from radium on tissue cultures of normal cells and on malignant cells, and effects of X-rays on cells, all in tissue culture.

Both Canti and Hughes made substantial contributions to the technique of cinemicroscopy. Little internal structure of living cells could be seen under the microscope by traditional methods. A cell had to be 'fixed' and stained for the internal components to show up. Canti developed 'dark field illumination' in which the internal structure of the living cell shows white against a dark ground. For the first time, mitochondria could be seen moving independently inside the cell, and changing their shape.

A famous film, which Canti and Honor Fell made in 1929, was the Knee-joint Film, in which the characteristic shape of the knee joint in birds could be seen to emerge, in the embryo.

In the later 1940s Hughes pioneered the use of phase contrast microscopy in time-lapse films. Differences in phase of the transmitted light are translated into differences of intensity, so as to give contrast to the image, without staining. The films were used in teaching and research, including biochemical studies of the tissues. They had voice commentaries, and among Honor Fell's unpublished material is a 1966 item entitled 'Prattle for film "Effects of . . . sucrose on Chinese hamster fibroblasts"' (connective tissue).

PHYSICAL TECHNIQUES PIONEERED AT THE STRANGEWAYS

Radiobiology, the study of the effects of radiation on living tissue, was pioneered at the Strangeways. In 1922, Strangeways's friends

Ronald Canti and Malcolm Donaldson came to consult him on effects of β and γ rays from radium on cervical cancer, and found him treating tissue cultures with X-rays. F. Gordon Spear from MRC joined this work in 1924. The work of distinction that was cited by Keilin in Honor Fell's Certificate for the Royal Society in 1948 includes radiobiology, and the study in cultures of Jensen's rat sarcoma, a tumour that appears in muscle, ligament or tendon. Different aspects of cancer research were studied across the years, including effects of condensed tobacco smoke on cultures of human foetal lung and bronchus, by Ilse Lasnitzki.

Audrey Glauert, a physicist, joined the staff of Strangeways in 1950 to try out the new technique of electron microscopy, using the instrument at the Cavendish Laboratory. Honor Fell took to this with great enthusiasm, obtaining an electron microscope for the Strangeways in due course, and encouraging collaborative work within the laboratory, and with other institutions. Electron microscopy at the Strangeways gained an international reputation, with fundamental work on the ultrastructure of connective tissues, and on the fine structure of micro-organisms, in host–parasite relationships for example, as in leprosy. Audrey Glauert spent forty years at the Strangeways, becoming the first woman President of the Royal Microscopical Society in 1970.

SOME COLLABORATORS

Part of Honor Fell's genius in research was her ability to spark off ideas with other people, particularly people from different branches of science. Much of her work was done in collaboration with scientists in Cambridge and beyond, bringing together a wide range of physical, biological, biochemical and medical techniques.

Conrad (Hal) Waddington, who turned from geology to evolution and to genetics, was one of the mavericks who flourished in their association with Honor Fell. At the age of 25, in 1930, he was excited by reading that a transplanted section of an amphibian (newt) embryo could 'induce' embryonic changes in its new neighbour cells, in a historic experiment by Hans Spemann and Hilde Mangold. Honor Fell described how Waddington became a biologist, with her help:[21]

one of my colleagues told me that she had met a young palaeontologist (with a scholarship in moral philosophy) who . . . wondered whether it would be possible to adapt our organ culture technique to the study of induction in warm-blooded animals. I thought it would be a long shot, but marvellous if it worked, so I said he could come along and try.

Elsewhere she remarked that she was 'much impressed with the idea . . . So he came and stayed in a quite unplanned way without any references merely because I was interested in his project.'[22] Waddington was the first to observe embryonic induction in a warm-blooded animal.

During the Second World War there was pressure to do 'war work', and effects of chemical warfare agents such as lewisite and mustard gas were studied at the Strangeways. Honor Fell was glad to get away from this and return to developmental biology. This was made possible by the arrival of Ernest Brieger, who managed to escape from Nazi Germany during the war, and was studying tuberculosis, which was a problem in the armed forces. They worked on the interaction of tubercle bacilli with macrophages, large cells that defend the body by ingesting foreign materials. From the war, also, stemmed work on wound healing, scar tissue, grafts, and effects of vitamin C.

The marrying of physics with biology, which has been responsible for some of the greatest advances in science, is not always painless, as in the solving of the DNA structure, and an earlier experience of Francis Crick. As a physicist whose interests turned to biology at the end of the war, he was sent first to the Strangeways by the MRC in 1947. There he worked for two years with Arthur Hughes in experiments designed to probe physical properties of the cytoplasm, the cell material, with small magnetic particles, which could be twisted, dragged or prodded, by external magnets. Their account of this work criticised existing theories of cytoplasmic structure, in particular, a 'brushheap' theory and a 'frame work' theory, and continued: 'If we were compelled to suggest a model we would propose Mother's Work Basket – a jumble of beads and buttons of all shapes and sizes, with pins and threads for good measure, all jostling about and held together by "colloidal forces".'[23] The results were inconclusive, and Crick said later on that this work put him off experimentation for the rest of his life.[24] But his time at the Strangeways gave him first-hand experience of biological material, and of how biologists think, and time to develop his own ideas, before moving to the MRC's new X-ray Crystallography Unit in the Cavendish, and to work on DNA.

When the MRC set up John Randall's Biophysics Unit at King's College London, they appointed Honor Fell as the Senior Biological Adviser, and she visited once a week from 1947 to 1968. With Jean Hanson (later FRS), who worked on muscle, she advised on their work, on muscle, DNA and collagen, a tough fibrous protein, which gives strength to connective tissue, tendons and membranes.

Honor Fell's observation in the 1920s of the chemical changes in the medium, as cartilage developed into bone, was an early application of biochemistry to cell biology. As time went on, studies at the molecular level increased.[25] The starvation resulting from the war prompted work on nutrition and vitamins. Edward Mellanby decided to work at the Strangeways with Honor Fell on vitamin A when he retired from his post as Secretary of the MRC in 1949. During the First World War Mellanby had shown that Gowland Hopkins's extract of 'vitamin A' contained a second component, vitamin D, which was essential for bone growth. After the war he moved to King's College for Women, and then to the MRC in 1933, continuing his research in collaboration with his wife May.[26]

Deficiency of vitamin A impairs night vision, and can harm the eye, skin or nerves. Excess of the vitamin is also harmful, causing severe damage to the skeleton in children and young animals. Among the more dramatic results of the work with Mellanby was the effect of excess vitamin A on the bones of embryo chickens or mice.[27] Over-stimulation by the vitamin affected the cell membrane, making the cells leaky. The cartilage crumbled and the bone shrank and disintegrated, leaving a sheet of actively growing cells. Later work linked this finding with biochemical mechanisms of joint damage in arthritis, returning to an original purpose of the Strangeways. Edward Mellanby and Honor Fell also studied the formation of bone and cartilage under the influence of hormones such as thyroxine (thyroid hormone), and cortisone, a steroid hormone, as steroids began to be used in the treatment of inflammation.

ELECTION TO THE ROYAL SOCIETY

Honor Fell's election to the Fellowship at the age of 52 in 1952 was late, in comparison, for example, with Waddington's at 42 in 1947, or Abercrombie's at 46 in 1958, as also was Marjory Stephenson's at 60 in 1945. The long process culminating in the election in 1945 of the first two women Fellows, Marjory Stephenson and Kathleen Lonsdale, has been described.[28]

Honor Fell's name appeared early on in the Fellows' discussion of likely women candidates, when this topic first surfaced in 1943.[29] A. V. Hill wrote to J. B. S. Haldane immediately on reading his article in the *Daily Worker* which raised the question of sex discrimination in the Fellowship:

Personally, I should be very glad to see a woman elected, provided, of course, that she was elected purely on merit and not as a consolation prize for being a woman. To do the latter would be a great pity.

You say that there are certainly half a dozen women worthy of the FRS; in that case, they ought to be proposed. I can't think of them myself, although Honor Fell would have a fair chance, I think . . .

Anyhow, it is up to you . . . since you believe there are six women worthy to be elected, to see that they are proposed as candidates. Otherwise you are neglecting your duty!

Yours ever, A. V. Hill

P.S. [handwritten] Don't pick out six people who have already been Fellows for some time, and say that you can find now six women who are cleverer than those. Of course you can. But you can also find 6 men who are cleverer than those. The question is whether the 6 women are better than the 6 men you haven't yet got in.

This year year ought A—— or B—— to be displaced by Honor Fell? Perhaps so. If so, which? or C—— by Dorothy Wrinch? A.V.H.[30]

A. V. Hill was Biological Secretary and went on to become Foreign Secretary, so was unable to propose candidates. Haldane was busy with war work. Charles Harington raised support for Marjory Stephenson, and Lawrence Bragg for Kathleen Lonsdale. Henry Dale, the President, took an active part in the 'Highly Confidential' correspondence, pressing Marjory Stephenson's claim, and also Honor Fell's. He wrote to Adrian, who was a fellow trustee of the Strangeways, on 15 November:

I am writing to let you know, in strict confidence, that I have information of the possibility that a woman candidate will be put forward on the Physical side for the FRS this year . . . I have heard it suggested, behind the scenes, that if and when women candidates come up for consideration, the name of Honor Fell ought to be among them . . . If you have any views as to Miss Fell's claim, there might still be time to act before November 30th; although I realise that the time is short.[31]

In the event only Marjory Stephenson and Kathleen Lonsdale were proposed in 1943, and their election was delayed until 1945 as a postal ballot was held on amendments to the Statutes. Ten per cent of the Fellows voting objected to the admission of women, even though the Sex Disqualification (Removal) Act of 1919 required that certificates presented in favour of women must be accepted.

Agnes Arber, botanist, was elected to the Fellowship in 1946.

Three women, Mary Cartwright, mathematician, Dorothy Hodgkin, crystallographer, and Muriel Robertson, proto-zoologist, were elected in 1947. Sidnie Manton, zoologist and Dorothy Needham, biochemist, were elected in 1948, and Honor Fell was the next woman, in 1952.

Honor Fell was proposed in 1948 by David Keilin, biochemist and Director of the Molteno Institute of Parasitology in Cambridge, seconded by James Gray, cytologist and Professor of Zoology. The seventeen signatories to her Certificate spanned the sciences from genetics to physics. Keilin wrote that she was 'distinguished for her research on the development and differentiation of tissues and rudiments of organs in vitro . . . This work is of outstanding merit and is now recognised as one of the fundamental contributions to the knowledge of skeletogenesis.'

THE SUCCESSION AT THE STRANGEWAYS

Michael Abercrombie described his first job in research, in embryology in tissue culture, as being 'under the serene direction' of Honor Fell. Her description of him was:

In October, 1938, a shy quiet young man from Oxford joined the Laboratory to work for a year under the late C. H. Waddington. His name was Michael Abercrombie. When I retired in 1970, Michael had become one of the world's leading cell biologists, and by great good fortune we were able to persuade him to accept the directorship of the Laboratory.[32]

He moved into the study of regeneration and wound healing. Of his successor she wrote:

In 1955 an enormous, immensely energetic young man from Bath [the Rheumatic Diseases Hospital] arrived, compressed into a minute scarlet car with only 3 wheels; he had come for a short time to learn how to grow limb-bone rudiments in connection with his work on rheumatoid arthritis. His name was John Dingle. He returned to the Laboratory in 1959 as a member of the staff and in 1979 was appointed Director; he took up his post under sad circumstances occasioned by Michael Abercrombie's untimely death.[33]

She had begun to investigate the role played by auto-allergic or auto-immune reactions in rheumatoid arthritis, in collaboration with Robin Coombs, and when she retired from the Directorship she moved into new work in his Immunology Laboratory, in the University Department of Pathology. Here she began a new study of effects of blood serum containing antibodies produced by the immune system, showing damage to cartilage, in complicated processes that involved damage to the soft tissue. As time went on her work on cellular interactions, which was more closely associated with the Strangeways, increased relative to the immunology work. In 1979 she accepted John Dingle's invitation to return to the Strangeways, and worked there until she died, of cancer.

WOMEN IN SCIENCE

Many institutions have made it difficult for women to practise science, and the climate tends to be chillier for women in the more elite establishments. In Cambridge the men's colleges did not admit women until 1972, and the small number of women's colleges restricted the places available to women as under-graduates or as Fellows. Now, in the mid-1990s, women are less than 10 per cent of Fellows of the former men's colleges, and few women reach positions of any seniority even in biological science, in which women outnumber men among the students. Honor Fell relished the independence of the Strangeways Laboratory from the University and its departments, as also from the National Health Service. The relationship with many of the University departments was, however, one of mutual enrichment, and there were usually one or two research students working for a Cambridge Ph.D.

Most of the women who went into science dropped out when they married or had young children, and most were unable to get back into a scientific career when their children needed less attention. Lawrence Raisz, who came from Connecticut to learn organ culture techniques from Honor Fell, said that when he wanted to talk to her he would go in on a Sunday morning, to find her cutting sections on the old Cambridge Rocking Microtome. As he was trying to finish his experiments before going on holiday with his sizeable family, she remarked, 'he travels fastest who travels alone'.[34] She was known to advise women scientists against getting married, and said that her mother warned her that marriage could be a trap to a woman who wanted a career. She lived near the Laboratory, 'looked after for some years by her old nanny, then by a succession of devoted daily ladies. She did her own domestic shopping before walking to the Strangeways with a corned beef sandwich and a banana for her lunch.'[35]

Honor Fell encouraged girls and women in science, responding to invitations to lecture to schoolgirls, and serving on the Research Fellowships Board at Girton College, where she was a Life Fellow. She welcomed women equally with men at the Strangeways. The funding organisations, not least the Beit Fellowship, the Royal Society and the MRC, have a good record in supporting women.

HER JOY IN HER WORK

Honor Fell's close associates[36] describe her as married to biology, which was her first and continuing love. Maurice Wilkins recalls Honor Fell's close relationship with her experimental material, calling the cells she grew 'the little dears'.

Comments in her letters to Edward Mellanby show her delight in her work: 'I had a lovely Saturday afternoon, with the whole lab to myself', 'On Sunday I shall have an orgy of staining slides', and 'this is a small cry of joy'.[37]

Keilin's certificate mentioned her skills in micro-manipulation. Lawrence Raisz wrote:

Dame Honor also liked to show off her skill at microdissection. One day . . .
I came to her with some tiny mouse fetuses . . . and said that these look like
the right bones . . . but that I just could not handle the dissection. She
proceeded to dissect the radius, ulna, humerus and for an encore took out the
clavicles [collarbones] and scapulae [shoulder blades] and lined them up
beautifully for my edification and astonishment. She was careful to point out
to me that I must distinguish between the bones themselves and the . . .
'mucky bits'.[38]

In addressing the Symposium to celebrate her eightieth birthday,
she said: 'Few people can have enjoyed their working life more
than I have, both in the Strangeways and during the happy
interlude in Robin Coombs's laboratory, and at 80 I am still
having fun in quite a big way.'[39]

Her nephew's wife described her evident glee, as an old lady in
her eighties, at being awarded yet another 2-year research grant,
and recorded that she 'danced away with the best of us' at a party
for her eightieth birthday.[40]

HONOR FELL, THE PERSON

Honor Fell and Thomas and Dorothy Strangeways were well
matched. Tribute was paid to Dorothy's courage, and also to
Honor's. In New York, she fought off a mugger with her
umbrella, even though he slashed her wrist.

Dorothy wrote of Tom: 'He worked his students very hard, but
they became as keen as he was, and lecturer and class would even
return to the Laboratory after [dinner in] Hall and continue
work.'[41] Honor inspired devotion with her scientific curiosity,
imaginative faculty and sense of fun. At the same time, she could
be formidable in her professional dealing, because of the high
standards she set.

Honor Fell was fashion conscious, and liked to be well dressed,
with matching shoes, gloves, handbag and hat.[42] Her presidential
address to the International Society for Cell Biology, in Paris in

1960, was on 'Fashion in Cell Biology'. She explained her choice of topic:

I published my first paper in 1922 . . . To an astronomer or a geologist this might not seem a very long period, but to a cell biologist of 1960, 1922 is prehistory, and the customs official at New York was perfectly right. He asked me what I did for a living; I replied that I was a biologist and studied cells. 'Gee, doctor', he said, 'I guess you've seen plenty of protoplasm in your time' . . . [C]asting my mind back over my long protoplasmic past . . . it suddenly struck me what an important part fashion had played in the development of our science during the past 40 years, and it occurred to me that this would make a rather suitable subject for a female president at a Paris congress.[43]

She made fun of some less estimable habits of researchers, salesmanship, for example, reinventing the wheel, jumping on bandwaggons, and snobbery: expensive instruments were the 'mink coats' of research. She remarked on fluctuating fashion in tissue culture, now that single cells could be studied in culture:

by 1939 [tissue culture] had sunk to a low ebb in public esteem. The sheer beauty of the technique was partly its undoing. The very idea of growing cells outside the body was so romantic and exciting, and the living cells in culture were such lovely objects under the microscope, that far too much was expected, and the expectations were not fulfilled. In a sense, tissue culture was born before its time, because the optical and biochemical methods necessary for its proper exploitation were not yet available. But after World War II, the development of phase contrast microscopy and of micro-chemistry enormously enlarged the possibilities . . . and the technique underwent a striking renaissance. Even organ culture is now enjoying a modest vogue.

She received a large number of honours, including honorary degrees, but would not include them in her curriculum vitae, saying she had not earned them. She was one of the few people whose entries in *Who's Who* shrank as the years went on. She would never put her name to a paper unless she had contributed to the benchwork. She considered it dishonourable not to publish work that had been funded by public or charitable money. Review papers didn't count: these were 'blah papers', which you wrote in your spare time. She considered it a privilege to make discoveries in biology. She was committed to the training of young scientists, and took part in courses as well as conferences around the world. In *Who's Who*, she gave her recreation as 'Travel'.

Honor Fell achieved distinction in science by building up the Strangeways Laboratory from a hand-to-mouth existence to one which attracted scientists of distinction from all over the world. They were attracted as much by her enthusiasm and sense of adventure, as by the multidisciplinary approach, and the special skills. The 1962 count of past and present members and visiting workers was 334 from 32 countries.[44]

The Times obituarist described her as 'one of the most remarkable biologists of this century'. Janet Vaughan, working on her biography, wrote: 'the more I read it the more superb the work is', and 'I just became bewitched by Honor herself'.

Three and a half weeks before she died, aged 86, she was working at the bench in the Strangeways, calling out, 'It's worked, isn't it exciting, come and see'.

NOTES

I thank Audrey Glauert for her invaluable help, and Lesley Hall, archivist, for information about Honor Fell's papers in the Contemporary Medical Archives Centre (CMAC) at the Wellcome Institute for the History of Medicine.

1 *BB* 7 (1929–30), 53. Anne Barbara Callow was a biochemist who doubled as librarian. Haldane wrote of her in his 'Report to the Sir William Dunn Trustees for the Year 1924–1925', *BB* 3 (1925), 14, reproduced in *Hopkins and Biochemistry*, ed. J. Needham and E. Baldwin (Cambridge: Heffer 1949), p. 322:

> I should be worse than a barbarian
> If I omitted the Librarian;
> The ways impartially she probes
> Of publishers and anaerobes.

2 Audrey Glauert, *Dictionary of National Biography*, forthcoming (1996), and personal communication; Janet Vaughan, *Biographical Memoirs of Fellows of the Royal Society* 33 (1987), 237. The papers of Honor Fell, as Director of the Strangeways Research Laboratory, are housed in the Contemporary Medical Archives Centre (CMAC) at the Wellcome Institute for the History of Medicine. A handlist, compiled by Lesley A. Hall, is available. Her 'Illustrations from the Wellcome Institute Library: the Strangeways Research Laboratory' is forthcoming in *Medical History*.

3 E. D. Strangeways, F. G Spear and H. B. Fell, *History of the Strangeways Research Laboratory (Formerly Cambridge Research Hospital) 1912–1962* (Cambridge: Heffer 1962).

4 Honor B. Fell, 'Fiftieth Anniversary of the Strangeways Research Laboratory, Cambridge, 1912–1962', *Nature* 196 (1962), 316–18.

5 *Nature*, 27 October 1962, p. 320.

6 H. B. Fell, 'The Strangeways Research Laboratory and Cellular Interactions', in *Cellular Interactions*, ed. J. T. Dingle and J. L. Gordon (North-Holland Biomedical Press: Elsevier 1981), pp. 1–14.

7 An acre of land was bought for them by the marine biologist George Parker Bidder.

8 Papers of Honor Fell.

9 The two daughters read science at Newnham, and the five sons went to Trinity Hall.

10 I thank Sir Harold Himsworth for these comments, in a letter to me dated 4 April 1992.

11 Strangeways *et al.*, *History of the Strangeways*.

12 J. T. Dingle, 'Dame Honor Fell, Eightieth Birthday Congratulations', *Biochemical Society Bulletin* 2 (1980), 8.

13 Many other worlds were represented as well. Bones were a particular interest of Janet Vaughan's.

14 Strangeways *et al.*, *History of the Strangeways*.

15 Vaughan, *Biographical Memoirs*.

16 Fell, 'The Strangeways Research Laboratory'.

17 Vaughan, *Biographical Memoirs*.

18 Papers of Honor Fell; Strangeways *et al.*, *History of the Strangeways*; Fell, 'The Strangeways Research Laboratory'.

19 Peter Medawar, 'Michael Abercrombie', *Biographical Memoirs* 26 (1980), 1.

20 G. E. H. Foxon, 'The Strangeways Collection', National Film Archive, British Film Institute (1976).

21 Quoted by Alan Robertson, 'Conrad Hal Waddington', *Biographical Memoirs* 23 (1977), 575–622.

22 Quoted by Edward Yoxen, 'Career of C. H. Waddington', in *A History of Embryology*, ed. T. J. Horder, J. A. Witkowski and C. C. Wylie (Cambridge: Cambridge University Press 1986).

23 F. H. C. Crick and A. F. W. Hughes, 'The Physical Properties of the Cytoplasm: a Study by Means of the Magnetic Particle Method', *Experimental Cell Research* 1 (1950), 37.

24 In conversation with Audrey Glauert.

25 Honor B. Fell, *Nature*, 26 March 1960, p. 882.

26 May (Tweedy) Mellanby worked independently on nutritional influences on dental development, as described in *Women Physiologists*, ed. Lynn Bindman, Alison Brading and Tilli Tansey (London: Portland Press 1993), pp. 197ff.

27 H. H. Dale, 'Edward Mellanby', *Biographical Memoirs* 1 (1955), 193.

28 See pp. 121–6.

29 Joan Mason, 'The Admission of the First Women to the Royal Society of London', *Notes and Records of the Royal Society of London* 46 (2) (1992), 279.

30 Haldane papers (Burdon Sanderson Archive), University College London. Personal references in A. V. Hill's postscript have been removed.

31 RS, 93HD, 5 March 1948. Adrian was the Society's Foreign Secretary 1946–50, and President 1950–5.

32 Fell, 'The Strangeways Research Laboratory'.

33 Fell, 'Fiftieth Anniversary'.

34 Vaughan, *Biographical Memoirs*.

35 Ibid.

36 Audrey Glauert, personal communication.

37 Papers of Honor Fell; Lesley Hall, contribution to *This Working-Day World: Women's Lives and Culture(s) in Britain 1914–1945*, ed. Sybil Oldfield (London: Taylor and Francis 1994), p. 199.

38 Vaughan, *Biographical Memoirs*.

39 Fell, 'The Strangeways Research Laboratory'.

40 Vaughan, *Biographical Memoirs*.

41 Strangeways *et al.*, *History of the Strangeways*.

42 Audrey Glauert, personal communication.

43 Honor B. Fell, *Science* 132 (1960), 1625.

44 Strangeways *et al.*, *History of the Strangeways*

Chapter 12

ROSALIND FRANKLIN
1920–1958

Jenifer Glynn

When Rosalind Franklin died aged 37 in 1958, she was the head of a small group working on virus structure at Birkbeck College. Her laboratory was on the fifth floor of a rickety old house; the roof leaked, the X-ray equipment was in the cellar and there was no lift. The group was funded by the US Department of Health because the British Agricultural Research Council had withdrawn their support; indeed the Secretary of the ARC had refused in 1955 to give Rosalind the grade of Principal Scientific Officer on the grounds that at her age it would be 'only for the exceptionally distinguished'.[1] This was two years after the publication of her paper on the X-ray crystallography of DNA, which had appeared in *Nature*, together with one from Maurice Wilkins, alongside the paper in which Crick and Watson described their model.[2] The DNA story – and certainly her part in it – was not yet famous outside scientific circles. She had no prizes and was never a Fellow of the Royal Society – even Francis Crick did not get his Fellowship until the year after her death, six years after the discovery, and the Nobel prizes were to follow three years later.

Since then there has been an overwhelming change, and publicity has grown in a way that would have appalled her, for she was a private person. In 1968 – fifteen years after the *Nature* papers – came the cruel and absurd caricature in Watson's *Double Helix*[3] which led to defences and counter-attacks, to a full-length biography and a *Horizon* feature film (*Life Story*) as well as many shorter articles. To put the record straight, her Birkbeck colleague Aaron Klug, by patiently searching through her scientific notebooks, has traced the development of her DNA work and explained her thinking and her contribution, writing authoritative articles in *Nature*[4] and in the recent *Missing Persons* volume of the *Dictionary of National Biography*. I should like to try here, with the help of family letters[5] and memories, to put her scientific work into the context of her life.

I hope she would have been pleased to find herself in the Cambridge company of this book, though I am sure she would have preferred her companions not to be all female. While expecting to be accepted as a scientist, regardless of gender, she was in no way a feminist. Certainly she did not, as has sometimes been suggested, reject for the sake of her career any idea of marriage. I believe that she had simply not met anyone that she wanted to marry.

Rosalind was born in 1920, fifteen months after her brother David, and there were to be two more brothers, Colin and Roland, before I was born, nine years her junior. My rather appropriate first memory of her is her attempt to explain to me that the sky appears to come down to meet the ground; at the age of 4 or so I did not believe her, and went on leaving a proper gap in my drawings. But her explanation, as always when dealing with someone who genuinely had difficulty in understanding, was careful and patient.

Our parents, Ellis and Muriel, belonged to Jewish families who had come to England in the eighteenth century. The Franklins were merchant bankers; Muriel's family, the Waleys, included lawyers, civil servants and academics. There was a tradition of social work in both families, partly but by no means entirely for Jewish causes – the Working Men's College played a large part in our lives. In earlier Franklin generations, girls might be educated – our grandmother had been to Bedford College – and they might run endless charitable institutions and sit on endless committees, but they were not expected to have professional careers; one of Ellis's sisters worked for the Townswomen's Guilds and the Fawcett Society, and the other became Chairman of the London County Council – all this being unpaid and commendable. Ellis, unlike the rest of his family, failed to realise that times were changing. He hoped that his daughters would follow the old pattern – that after Cambridge, since he could provide for them and they would not have to provide for families, they might devote themselves to voluntary work. But by the time Rosalind graduated there was no question of her not pursuing her career. He accepted defeat without protest and, his own planned scientific studies having been prevented by the 1914 War, became proud of Rosalind's achievements.

Politically, too, Ellis was the most conservative member of the family. Since his LCC sister was an active member of the Labour Party, and his other sister and one brother had been much involved with the suffragette movement, there was plenty of scope for amiable family disagreement. Rosalind became a Labour Party supporter, to the extent of helping with occasional chores at election times.

As a small child Rosalind was highly intelligent and articulate, early showing herself to be logical, determined and perfectionist, enjoying making things or drawing, and despising dolls. Later it was Rosalind, rather than my brothers, who made use of the well-equipped workshop our parents set up for us. Between the ages of 9 and 11 she was sent to a boarding school by the sea, because of a parental belief that she was 'delicate'. She herself always considered this to have been nonsense and remembered the time with resentment, but it had the advantage of leaving us with letters. These give a picture of a competitive little schoolgirl, somewhere in the top four of her class, enthusiastic about games, dutiful about music lessons, counting the days to the end of term. Letters from her family were important to her then and throughout her life – at Cambridge she expected two letters a week (one from each parent), and at least one a week when she was working in Paris in her twenties.

St Paul's, the academic day-school half an hour's bus journey from our home at Notting Hill, was the obvious next stage – an aunt had been there, and Rosalind joined a scattering of cousins of various degrees of remoteness. She made lasting friends there, worked well, played a lot of tennis and hockey, but abandoned the music. Gustav Holst, the music director, was baffled by her untrainable ear.

'We spent the whole arithmetic lesson to-day with a lovely discussion about gravity and all that sort of stuff,' Rosalind wrote happily when she was 13. There was never a doubt that she would specialise in science; nor, at that stage, was there any family opposition. The only conflict was in 1939 after her first year at Newnham when Ellis, looking to the pattern of previous gener-ations, thought she should do conventional war work such as joining the Land Army as his sisters had done in 1914, rather than indulge in the luxury of a university. It was not easy for Rosalind to persuade him that it was in no way a luxury, that she would be far more useful as a trained scientist. She was not trying to retreat from the problems of the world; when she went up to Cambridge in 1938 she had already spent some time helping her parents in their work for Jewish refugees, she fitted in as much volunteer war work as she could during the vacations, and one of her concerns when she graduated in 1941 was that her research should relate to the war.

At Newnham Rosalind was at first overwhelmed by the work – the ever-accumulating mass of reading, the problems of tackling unfamiliar practicals, the difficulties of getting the best courses. After managing to change from unsatisfactory chemistry lectures:

I am in the middle of a struggle over maths lectures, but I'm very much afraid I'm on the losing side. The ones I want to go to (I have been to two of them) are on analysis . . . The lecturer is very good, though female . . . The tutor wrote me a letter last night which was obviously meant to be final and unanswerable saying that I was 'definitely not in a position to profit by' the best lectures, but I answered it, and am waiting to see what happens.

(She was not so much of a feminist when she wrote that.) As she feared, she lost that round:

Two of us fought from every possible angle, and nearly brought them round, but were finally beaten on the grounds that 'nobody from Newnham has ever been to course B so why should we?' I have now been to two lectures of course A. They are *awful*. He stands in front of what he is writing and says 'square this' 'take away that' without saying what, and then rubs it off. When we do catch a glimpse of his writing it is generally no more than 1/2 inch high. He also has a maddening habit of walking up and down the whole length of the room, so that if you are near the gangway, the effect is something like the fragments of conversation one hears when passing someone in the street.

To me these letters seem to give fragments of Rosalind's conversation – she wrote very much as she talked.

She was immensely conscientious and set herself high standards, so she was for ever worrying that she was not doing well enough, or that her exams were disastrous – though she got her Firsts, until her final year when it was perhaps a mixture of 'flu and lack of sleep that led to an Upper Second. But her letters are full too of the many activities of an energetic, if rather austere, undergraduate life – walks, bicycle rides ('Why were you so surprised about cycling home? I want my bike in London, and it seems the simplest way of getting it there'), tennis, skating on the frozen fens, politics, friends, plans for youth-hostelling holidays.

Rosalind's love for France, which had developed during a summer in Paris before Cambridge, was stirred by contact with French refugees in Newnham, a contact which was to have great influence on her:

Last week I went to a talk (in French) by a Mme Weill on Mme Curie. She is a French physicist – 'eminent', we are told – who came out in response to de Gaulle's appeal for scientific specialists, and has been 'adopted' by

Newnham and is now researching in the Cavendish. She was a pupil of Mme Curie and later researched with her in the lab. I was really thrilled by the lecture . . . She is a delightful person, full of good stories, and most interesting to talk to on any scientific or political subject.

Adrienne Weill, who set up the graduate lodging house at 12 Mill Lane where Rosalind lived at the end of her fourth Cambridge year, helped her to find a job in Paris in 1947, and became a lifelong friend.

Many of Rosalind's Newnham letters are dominated by the war – by accounts of Newnham trenches and fire-watching, or increasingly by political arguments with Ellis, using her logic to attack his and Muriel's rather vague faith and optimism. They were deeply felt arguments, but written with no ill-will, more as a manifestation of her honesty – the next sentence might change back to ideas for a birthday present, or plans for a parental visit.

One letter, written probably in the summer of 1940, gives a remarkable statement of her beliefs. Always consciously a Jew, she rejected religion:

Science, for me, gives a partial explanation of life. In so far as it goes, it is based on fact, experience and experiment. Your theories are those which you and many other people find easiest and pleasantest to believe, but, so far as I can see, they have no foundation other than that they lead to a pleasant view of life (and an exaggerated idea of our own importance) . . . In my view, all that is necessary for faith is the belief that by doing our best we shall come nearer to success and that success in our aims (the improvement of the lot of mankind, present and future) is worth attaining. Anyone able to believe in all that religion implies obviously must have such faith, but I maintain that faith in this world is perfectly possible without faith in another world . . . Your faith rests on the future of yourself and others as individuals, mine on the future and fate of our successors. It seems to me that yours is the more selfish . . . Well, now my normal letter . . .

Bombs fell at the back of the family house in Notting Hill, so we moved temporarily to a rented house in Hertfordshire, taking as many possessions as we could. Rosalind's list of essentials is revealing:

I don't think you mentioned my desk. If it does not go, I would like *everything* out of it, in as little muddle as possible – I know exactly where everything in it is, though it may look confused. Also nearly everything from the drawers of my bookcase, and my climbing boots from the cupboard underneath – I couldn't bear to have them bombed . . . As for books, I don't think there are any I can say I 'specially want', but I would like, naturally, to have as many with me as possible. One cannot live in a house permanently without books . . . in particular, I might mention all French books, my French dictionary, and encyclopaedia – though this does not mean that I don't want any others.

Climbing, and everything French – those were, and remained, the enthusiasms in her life.

Newnham awarded her a fourth-year scholarship, and she started research under the Professor of Physical Chemistry, Ronald Norrish. This turned out to be a frustrating war. Even Norrish's biographers admit that he could be 'obstinate and almost perverse in argument, overbearing and sensitive to criticism',[6] and it is not surprising that Rosalind soon found herself, in a foreshadowing of her relationship with Maurice Wilkins at King's, heading for a misery of non-communication. She was working, without great enthusiasm, on the polymerisation of acetaldehyde and formic acid. The experiments were not progressing well, and she could not persuade Norrish to change his approach. It all seemed a waste of time and a failure.

It was not an unhappy year socially. Her life in Mill Road ('45 shillings per week including 3 meals, but excluding heating') got off to a promising start. She was independent for the first time, and able to have friends and relations to stay: 'I'm thoroughly enjoying living alone at present – of course I haven't had time to get bored with it yet. I've never had so much time for reading – I read at and after every meal, and in the evenings when I'm doing nothing else.' She invited me for a weekend, and took immense care to amuse a 12-year-old. She took me to see the obvious Cambridge sights, but also, memorably, to see the baker in Newnham village mixing his dough, and to her laboratory, where she showed me how she blew and assembled her glassware.

We went, too, to the film *49th Parallel*. There are few other childhood weekends that I can remember so fully.

When life in the laboratory became depressing, Rosalind began to find her lonely digs depressing and irritating too, so in the summer she was glad to join Adrienne Weill's very international lodging-house. She felt unsettled, not wanting to stay in an unsatisfactory job in Cambridge, but worried that, with wartime regulations, she might be drafted into something very uncongenial in industry – 'As long as one stays in a university, even on utilitarian work, it is science for knowledge. I'm so afraid that in industry I should find only science for money.' She was fortunate in the industrial job that did turn up, under Dr D. H. Bangham at the British Coal Utilisation Research Association (CURA). A disadvantage was its position outside London, in Kingston

miles from anything, without even the consolation of a lunch-hour in town – it'll be lunch in the labs, with lab people, all horribly shut off. But the alternatives are probably worse. I did not seriously consider the Ministry of Fuel job. I'm sure I should be very much more efficient in administrative work, but I should lose touch and never be able to go back to lab work, which would be much more exciting if only one could succeed.

Norrish had done nothing for her confidence.

Kingston might be less fun than Cambridge, but the work was more satisfying. CURA gave Rosalind her first experience of independent research, in a field that proved worthwhile and productive and that pointed her in the direction she was to follow – though she later moved from physical to biological problems. From 1942 to 1946 she was studying the microstructures of coals, work which led to her crystallographic work in Paris on carbons, and ultimately to her investigation of the structures of DNA and of tobacco mosaic virus. Her Ph.D. came in 1945 from the CURA work, and so did her first publications, five papers which appeared between 1946 and 1949. There were to be papers on the structure of carbons nearly every year for the rest of her life.

Rosalind lived for a time in digs in Kingston, then shared a house with a cousin and a friend and a kitten in Putney. She would normally come home at weekends (when her duties as an Air Raid Warden allowed), so almost the only letters I have giving clues to her views at that time are from the few weeks she spent at Newnham in the summer of 1945 finishing her Ph.D. These show her still lacking confidence in her work, and in her thesis, and also looking around for her next move.

I change my mind almost hourly about the future, but pottering between Newnham garden and the Philosophical Library convinces me that I can't return to CURA for an indefinite period. I am, of course, terribly tempted to return here . . . *But*, firstly I feel that my present views on Cambridge must be highly coloured by the weather and by the complete freedom and independence of my present condition. And secondly I think that where I have tried and failed once I would stand a greater chance of failing again, and it would be better to break new ground. The other alternative which may be open to me is at Bedford College . . . I have also written after a job in Aberdeen.

It was not until the last year of Rosalind's life that there was beginning to be a serious prospect of returning to Cambridge, when there was talk of her Birkbeck group joining the projected Laboratory of Molecular Biology. She would have returned then with enormous pleasure. It is good to know that Newnham are now bringing her back in name with their new Rosalind Franklin graduate building.

In 1946 Rosalind had her first post-war holiday in France. In no way put off by a letter warning her that French youth hostels 'can only fit very sportive persons who are free from any prejudice', she was totally happy to be back in the mountains and back in France. She was a good traveller, energetic, observant, interested in people and places, enjoying the preliminaries of maps and planning, and she became a formidable walker and climber. There is a letter written to her brother Colin from Savoy in 1947, which first talks of a tough 16-hour hike, and then goes on to describe 'the most heavenly expedition I have ever done – the Peclet-Polset

Aretes and Aiguilles. We started out in cloud at 4.30 a.m. and the cloud lifted suddenly at sunrise, just as we came onto the glacier, revealing pink summits above a "mer de nuages". I cannot describe the effects, I can only tell you that the sheer beauty of it made me weep.'

It was wonderful to holiday in France, but it dawned on Rosalind that she could do more than that. 'I am free to leave as soon as I can find another job,' she wrote to Adrienne Weill in Paris in 1946: 'If ever you hear of anybody anxious for the services of a physical chemist who knows very little about physical chemistry, but quite a lot about the holes in coal, please let me know.' Adrienne responded with advice and introductions, and in February 1947 Rosalind arrived in Paris as a researcher in the Laboratoire Central des Services Chimiques de l'Etat, an old-fashioned building on the quai Henri IV. She stayed in Paris for four years.

Living on an absurdly small salary (starting at about £5 a week) in a large shabby room in a widow's flat, Rosalind shared the difficulties of post-war France, and was happy. She reacted with sympathy, not irritation, to shortages, electricity cuts, transport strikes. No one could have been less bothered about money, as long as she had enough for food and for travel (third class, sitting up all night). Food was helped by rather basic requests to English visitors – dried potatoes, bovril, nescafé, jam, powdered milk, drinking chocolate. One visiting cousin, she wrote, was 'rather shocked by my somewhat Bohemian existence, and particularly by the absence of a bath. I tried to console him by reminding him that I could have a bath in May, but that seemed to make matters worse.'

She would walk or cycle along the Seine to the laboratory, where she joined a lively and international group who would argue energetically about work and politics, lunch together, and go off into the countryside at weekends. Although all her life she tended to retreat into a disconcerting silence or obvious disapproval if she felt out of tune with her surroundings, here she felt stimulated and at ease. At such times she was animated, witty, very good company. She always worked seriously and hard, demanding much both of herself and her colleagues, but she also saw the need to enjoy what she did – 'What is the point of doing all this work', she once said to Aaron Klug, 'if you don't get some fun out of it?' In Paris her work was to learn X-ray diffraction techniques, and to use those techniques, in the words of J. D. Bernal, to discover 'in a series of beautifully executed researches the fundamental distinction between carbons that turned on heating into graphite and those that did not. Further she related this difference to the chemical constitution of the molecules from which carbon was made'.[7] This work helped form the basis for the development of carbon fibres.

If life was so good and work was going so well, why did Rosalind come back to London? From the evidence of her letters, the reasons were personal, a feeling that after four years it was time to decide whether her future lay permanently in France. It was not easy, and she was full of last-minute doubts. 'If I had succeeded in creating for myself a wider circle I shouldn't hesitate to stay on indefinitely,' she wrote. The problem was that 'while liking the mass of people around me very much my intimate circle remains small . . . My one and only reason for returning to London is that the family and perhaps the greater part of my friends are there.' But in another letter she added, 'I'm not a bit reconciled to leaving, and still look round vaguely hoping for a way out. To change the banks of the Seine for a cellar in the Strand seems to me quite insane.'

The cellar in the Strand was the laboratory at King's College where, funded by a Turner-Newall Fellowship, she was to do X-ray diffraction studies on the structure of DNA. A letter[8] from the Professor of Physics, John Randall, makes it clear both that the project involved a change of plan (from work on the structure of proteins in solution, to 'the structure of certain biological fibres'), and also that 'as far as the experimental X-ray effort is concerned there will be at the moment only yourself and Gosling' (a research student) and a temporary American assistant. The letter goes on to say that Raymond Gosling, working with Wilkins, had already got good fibre diagrams from fibres of DNA and that 'it would be very valuable if this could be followed up in detail . . . I am not in this way suggesting that we should give up all thought of work on solutions, but we do feel that the work on fibres would be more immediately profitable and, perhaps, fundamental.'

The *Radio Times*, in their *Life Story* blurb,[9] saw things more dramatically:

It's 1951. There's a race on and two of the brightest and brashest young men in Cambridge are determined to win it. The prize is glittering. Eternal fame, glory, almost certainly a Nobel prize, await whoever is first past the post – for the goal is nothing less than the secret of life itself. So begins the extraordinary story of the race to the double helix of DNA, one of the greatest true detective stories of the 20th century. Watson and Crick have the bright ideas and the will to win. But there's one little problem; Rosalind Franklin has the crucial data . . . and she plays the game by very different rules.

It is a pity that, under the influence of the *Double Helix*, the DNA story is still told in those terms. For Rosalind there was no race and no game. She was working with immense patience and skill, designing new equipment and experiments, and taking and interpreting the X-ray photographs which did indeed provide the crucial data Crick and Watson needed for their brilliant model. But she was not aware – and perhaps was never aware – of how much her data helped them because, as a result of the disastrous personal situation that developed at King's, the information had been given behind her back.[10]

There were two problems combining to produce that situation. One was King's itself, where Rosalind was shocked to find that, although there was a surprisingly high number of women scientists, they were not allowed in the men's common room where there was lunch and coffee, the normal place for contact and discussion with colleagues; this came as even more of a blow after the freedom and liveliness of quai Henri IV. The second problem was the unfortunate hostility that grew between her and Maurice Wilkins, nurtured by this exclusiveness and by misunderstanding of their respective roles in the DNA research. Rosalind understood from Randall that the DNA X-ray studies had been handed over to her and that Wilkins would not be continuing with the work, but Wilkins had no intention of leaving DNA and studying cells as Randall had planned; unfortunately Randall, as Wilkins wrote later, 'was not specially skilful at dealing with differences and tensions between staff'.[11] Other laboratories have seen clashes of personalities, but this clash has had undue publicity because Watson exploited it in his book to produce a dramatic story. And it was important at the time because it obstructed progress and led to Rosalind's working in virtual isolation at King's, able to discuss the work only with Gosling, while Wilkins privately repeated her experiments and showed Watson her results,[12] waiting in the wings to reclaim the problem as soon as she left the laboratory.[13]

So the two years 1951–3, the period of the DNA work, were scarred by unhappiness. Briefly Rosalind even considered returning to Paris. There is no place here to describe her achievement in detail; she showed that the DNA molecule could exist in two forms, and she made a thorough crystallographic analysis of both. It is easy, but unfair, to portray her as the plodding experimenter, all the inspiration lying with Crick and Watson. Crick has said that she lacked intuition, was too concerned with the evidence, but he also said in the same interview that 'Rosalind would have solved it . . . with Rosalind it was only a matter of time'[14] – and Rosalind was not racing. The essentials of the paper which appeared in *Nature* together with Crick and Watson's were, as Aaron Klug has shown, already in typescript before news of the model had reached King's:

She had deduced that the phosphate groups of the backbone lay on the outside, and the bases on the inside, of the double helix; and her notebooks show that she had already formed the notion of base interchangeability. The step from this to the specific base pairing postulated by Crick and Watson is a large one, but there is little doubt that she was poised to make it.[15]

There are again no family letters, because she was living in London,[16] but I do not remember her feeling that she had lost a competition, only that something exciting had been discovered, and that she longed now to work somewhere more congenial. A month before the *Nature* papers appeared, and with a year of her Fellowship still to run, Rosalind shook off the dust of King's and moved to Birkbeck, to work in Bernal's department on virus structures. I am delighted – and Rosalind would be amazed – that King's too are naming a new student building after her. Forty years ago they were less gracious, with Randall writing that now she had left she should 'stop thinking' about the work she had been doing, 'clear up or write up' what she had done, and stop supervising Gosling because she must not remain 'in an intellectual sense, a member of the laboratory'.[17] But time does its best to heal, and the laboratory has commemorated her, together with the four other authors of the King's DNA papers, on a plaque which was unveiled in September 1993.

In March 1953 Rosalind moved from her cellar in the Strand to her fifth-floor attic in Torrington Square. She was to work there very productively for the last five years of her life, happy in the group that she was building up, stimulated by increasing contacts with colleagues overseas, especially in America. It was a distinguished group – she was joined by Aaron Klug, who was to win a Nobel prize in 1982, and her two research students were Kenneth Holmes and John Finch, both now Fellows of the Royal Society.

The connection of the tobacco mosaic virus to her previous work, and its importance, is made clear in a report Rosalind wrote on her research group in 1956:

The work is concerned with what is probably the most fundamental of all questions concerning the mechanism of living processes, namely the relationship between protein and nucleic acid in the living cell . . . The plant viruses consist of ribonucleic acid and protein, and provide the ideal system for the study of the in vivo structure of both ribonucleic acid and protein and of the structural relationship of the one to the other . . . there is no doubt that a large part of the results obtained will also be relevant to the problems of animal viruses.[18]

The work went wonderfully well. Having confirmed Watson's hypothesis of the helical structure of tobacco mosaic virus, she showed that the infective element, the ribonucleic acid, formed a long single chain embedded in the protein framework.

There were frustrations – worries about the ARC grant (one extraordinary reason for its withdrawal was that the Secretary disapproved of 'work on second-hand material' – a reference to Rosalind's highly successful collaboration with colleagues at Berkeley and at Tübingen),[19] and worries about the future of the group.[20] But the greatest frustration was that she was not to be given time. She was full of plans for the future, including a major investigation of the polio virus – I remember her alarming my mother by putting a thermos flask containing polio in our fridge – but her illness first struck in the summer of 1956. She worked on to the end, through the traumas of operations and treatments and renewals of hope. She believed that her work might one day help in the fight against cancer, though she came to realise it would be too late for her. In those last months, as throughout her life, she was following her undergraduate aim to do her best 'to improve the lot of mankind, present and future'.

NOTES

1 REF's notes of a meeting with Sir William Slater, 29 September 1955.
2 The papers in *Nature* (25 April 1953) were: J. D. Watson and F. H. C. Crick, 'A Structure for Deoxyribose Nucleic Acid'; M. H. F. Wilkins, A. R. Stokes and H. R. Wilson, 'Molecular Structure of Deoxypentose

Nucleic Acids'; Rosalind E. Franklin and R. G. Gosling, 'Molecular Configuration in Sodium Thymonucleate'.

3 James Watson, *The Double Helix* (London: Weidenfeld and Nicolson 1968).

4 A. Klug, 'Rosalind Franklin and the Discovery of the Structure of DNA', *Nature*, 24 August 1968; 'Rosalind Franklin and the Double Helix', *Nature*, 26 April 1974.

5 All letters quoted are to her parents unless stated otherwise.

6 Frederick Dainton and B. A. Thrush, in *Biographical Memoirs of Fellows of the Royal Society* (1981), p. 406.

7 Obituary of REF in *The Times*, 19 April 1958.

8 Letter dated 4 December 1950.

9 *Radio Times*, 25 April 1987.

10 See Anne Sayre, *Rosalind Franklin and DNA* (New York: W. W. Norton 1975), pp. 167 and 172; Watson, *The Double Helix*, pp. 167 and 181.

11 M. H. F. Wilkins, 'John Turton Randall', in *Biographical Memoirs of Fellows of the Royal Society* (1987), p. 520.

12 Sayre, *Rosalind Franklin*, p. 151; Watson, *Double Helix*, p. 167.

13 Sayre, *Rosalind Franklin*, pp. 144 and 170; Watson, *Double Helix*, p. 158.

14 Sayre, *Rosalind Franklin*, p. 213.

15 *Nature*, 24 August 1968. A brief summary is given in the article on REF in *Dictionary of National Biography Missing Persons*, from which the quotation is taken.

16 In Donovan Court, Drayton Gardens, where in 1992 a British Heritage plaque was placed in her memory.

17 Letter dated 17 April 1953.

18 REF, 'Note on the Future of the ARC Research Group in Birkbeck Crystallography Laboratory', 9 March 1956.

19 REF's notes of a meeting with Sir William Slater, 29 September 1955.

20 Eventually the group was to move to the MRC Molecular Biology Laboratory in Cambridge, and REF would certainly have moved with them.

INDEX

Index

Index

Index

Evans, Arthur, 45
Evans-Pritchard, E. E., 231
Eyre of London, 111

Faber, T., 237
Fabian Society, 139
Fairbank, John K., 176
Fallers, Tom, 240
Faroese ballads, 189
Fawcett, Millicent, 162
Fay, C. R., 83
Fell, Honor, xvii
female initiation, among the Bemba, 235
Female Radical Reformers of Manchester, 124
Fildes, Mary, 124
Fildes, Paul, 120, 124
Finch, John, 280
First World War, 97, 142
Firth, Raymond, 232, 233
Fleming, Alexander, 114
Fletcher, Walter, 130, 245
'Folklore Method', the, 37
Fool, The, x;vi, 204, 205, 208, 210, 212, 214, 217
Forbes, Mary, 209
Fortes, Meyer, 231, 236
Four Hymns and an Epithalamion, 218
Four Stages of Greek Religion, 53
Fowler, Helen, xiv, xvi, 7, 137, 216
Franklin, Ellis, 268, 269, 270, 272
Franklin, Muriel, 268
Franklin, Rosalind, xvii
Frazer, J. G., 37, 40, 60, 193
Frazer, Lady, 40
Freud, Sigmund, 50, 58
Freund, Ida, 115
Fry, Roger, 37, 155
'functionalism', xvii, 155, 225, 226, 238

Gaitskell, Hugh, 175
Gale, Ernest, 119–21, 128
Gandhi, Mahatma, 171, 210
Gardner, Alice, 79
Gardner, E. A., 38
Gargoyle Club, 175
Garrett, Margery, 162, 164, 167, 169, 170
Garrod, Dorothy, 4

Gaster, Theodore, 60
Gaudy Night, 212
Geertz, Clifford, 238
George, Dorothy, 173
George, Henry, 84
Gernet, Louis, 54, 60, 61
ghosts, 43
Giggleswick Grammar School, 73
Gill, Eric, 145, 154
Girton College, xi, xv, 8, 13, 14, 93, 94, 97, 98, 110, 160, 161, 165, 169, 197, 261
Gladstone, Helen, 12, 24, 32
Gladstone, Mary, 9, 10, 12
Gluckman, Max, 234
Glynn, Jenifer, xvii, 267
Goddess, goddesses, 44, 45, 90
Golden Bough, The, 37, 193
Goodman of Paris, The, 172
Gore-Browne, Lorna, 229
Gore-Browne, Stewart, 228
Gorgons, 43
Goschens, the, 85
Gosling, Raymond, 278, 279, 280
Graduates' Association, University of London, 96
Graiai, 43
Grantchester, 143
Graves, Robert, 149
Gray, James, 259
Greece, 34, 37
Greek myths, 38
Greek religion, 38
Grier, Lynda, 24
Grimshaw, Margaret, 209
Growth of Literature, The, xvi, 192, 193, 194, 195, 199, 217
Gurney, Edmund, 15, 17, 18, 39

Hades, 45
Hailey, Lord, 233
Haileybury School, 222
Haldane, J. B. S., 116, 118, 122–4, 129, 257, 258
Hall, Hubert, 98, 164
Hanson, Jean, 256
Harington, Charles, 123, 124, 258
Harrison, Charles, 29, 30
Harrison, Jane, xv, 1, 18, 23, 24, 29, 79, 138–40, 204, 216

286

Index

Harrow School, 222
Hastings's *Encyclopaedia of Religion and Ethics*, 207
Haviland, Maud, 207
Hebrew literature, 193
Heinrichs, Albert, 45, 51, 55
Henderson, Isobel, 199
Hera, 44, 45
Herakles, 46
Heroic Age, The, 191
Hesiod, 43, 50
Heyne, Christian Gottlob, 35, 41
Hieatt, Professor, 218
Hill, A. V., 122, 123, 124, 257, 258
Hill, Polly, 222
Hillcroft College, 105, 110
Hillside, 10–17
Himsworth, Harold, 126, 249
Hoare, Dorothy, 212
Hodgkin, Dorothy, 121, 259
Hodgson, Ralph, 168
Hogarth Press, 59
Hogben, Lancelot, 123
Holmes, Kenneth, 280
Holst, Gustav, 270
Homer, 43, 54, 209
Homeric poems, 191
Hooke, S. H., 60
Hope-Taylor, Brian, 199
Hopkins, Frederick Gowland, 113, 117, 119, 125, 128–30, 131, 256
Horai (Seasons), 44
Howard, Lady Mary, 40
Hubert, H., 61
Hughes, Arthur F. W., 253, 255
Hundred Rolls of Cambridgeshire and Suffolk, xv, 97–9
Huxley, J., 62
Huxleys, the, 85

Icelandic sagas, 189
India, 171
Indian literature, 193
Indian Vice-Regal Council, 222
Industry and Trade, 88
Institut Curie, 121
Intellectuals and their Powers, xviii
International Society for Cell Biology, 262
Introductory Studies in Greek Art, 34

Irish Clairvoyant fool, 217
Isabella of France, 163

Jackson, Kenneth, 186, 193, 194, 198
James, Henry, 32, 211
Jeanmaire, Henri, 60
Jebb, Lady, 15, 22, 87, 88
Jebb, Richard, 38
Jenkins, Elizabeth, 210
Jenkinson, Hilary, 98
Jensen's rat sarcoma, 254
Jex-Blake, Katherine, 162, 169
John, Augustus, 49
Johnson, Dr, 210, 212
Johnston, Reginald, 170
Joliot-Curie, Irène, 121
Jones, Emily E. C., 161
Jones, M. G. (Gwladys), 98, 100, 159, 162, 176
Jourdain, E. F., 23
Journal of Hellenic Studies, 40
Jowett, Benjamin, 25, 84, 85
Joyce, James, 50
Jung, C. G., 58

Kahn Travelling Fellowship, 170
Kantharck, Alfred, 247
Karström, Henning, 119
Keilin, David, 259, 261
Kennedy, Dr, 78
Kennedy, Mary, 77
Kennedy, the Misses, 78
Ker, W. P., 207
'Keres', 43
Keynes, Ada, 4
Keynes, Geoffrey, 138
Keynes, John Maynard, xv, 73, 221
King's College for Women, 256
King's College London, 256, 277, 278, 280
Kingsley, Charles, 109
Kipling, Rudyard, 105
Kirk, G. S., 32, 42
Klein, Wilhelm, 33
Klug, Aaron, xvii, 268, 277, 279, 280
Knight, B. C. G., 120
Knowles, David, 108
Knowles, Lilian, 161, 165, 173
Kore, 44
Kouretes, 58

287

Index

Index

Mistress of Animals, 45
Moberley, C. A. E., 23
Moirai (Fates), 44
Molteno Institute of Parasitology, 259
Morier, Robert, 85
Müller, Karl Otfried, 35, 36, 41
Müller, Max, 35, 84
Murray, Gilbert, xv, 29, 32, 39, 40, 48, 50, 53–8, 60, 62, 223
Muses, 44
Mushindo, Paul Bwemba, 230
Myers, F. W. H., 15, 18, 39
Mythology and Monuments of Ancient Athens: Being a Translation of a Portion of the 'Attica' of Pausanias, 35
Myths of the Odyssey in Art and Literature, 34

Narasimhan, Sita, 209, 210, 219
Nathan, Sir Mathew, 175
National Health Service, 260
National University of Ireland, 198
Nature, 126, 267, 268, 279, 280
nature myth theory, 36
Ndembu, 235
Needham, Dorothy, 4, 121, 127, 130, 131, 259
Needham, Joseph, 116
Neil, R. A., 39
Nelson, Elizabeth Hawksley, 29
Nesbitt, Kathleen, 143
Nettleship, Lewis, 84
Newnham College, xi, xiii, xiv, 7, 8, 11, 13, 14, 21, 25, 26, 31, 33, 38, 49, 74, 77, 78, 83, 115, 130, 163, 183, 197, 198, 204, 212, 223, 236, 270–5
Newton, Charles, 33
Nichols, Robert, 147
Nietzsche, F. W., 30, 46
Nilsson, Martin, 43, 60, 61
Nobel prize, 13, 280
Norrish, Ronald, 273, 274
Norse literature, 191
Norse studies, 205
nutrition, 226, 230

Odin, 185, 189
Old English, 207
Old Irish, 192, 193
Old Norse, 183, 189, 190, 192

Old Welsh, 192
Olivier, Noel, 141
Olympians, 45, 53, 58
Olympic Games, 52
Oral Epics of Central Asia, 195
organ culture, 251
Origin of Species, 30
Orpheus, 46–8, 59
Oshinsky, Dorothy, 175
Otto, Walter F., 55
Owen, Morfydd, 200
Oxford, 215
Oxford Book of Modern Verse, 149
Oxford Book of Victorian Verse, 149
Oxford Companion to English Literature, 150
Oxford High School for Girls, 160

Paladino, Eusapia, 16
Palaikastro, 50, 52
Palermo, 81
'Paley's Evidences', 73
Paley, Mary, 31; *see also* Marshall, Mary Paley
Paley, William, 73
Pall Mall Gazette, 19
Parthenon, 54
Partridge, Frances, 26
Pasteur, Louis, 119, 128
Paues, Anna, 24
Pausanias, 35, 36, 37
Paycockes of Coggeshall, 170
Peile, Mrs, 77
Pembroke College Cambridge, 222
Perham, Margery, 222
Period Piece, 138
Perry, Sir Cooper, 170
Perry, Kate, 112
Persephone, 44
Persian language, 32, 57
Peterhouse, 159, 176
Pfeiffer, 18
Phantasms of the Living, 16
Pickard-Cambridge, A., 56
Pinchbeck, Ivy, 173
Pirie, Tony, 121
Pius XI, 59
Plato, 54
Plimmer, R. H. A., 115
Pluto, 42

Index

Plymouth Brethren, 87
Poetry and Letters of Early Christian Gaul,
    197
Poetry and Prophecy, 194
Political Economy, 86
Polynesian literature, 191, 193
Poole, R. S., 38
Poseidon, 44
Postan, M. M. (Munia), 159, 174–6
Potnia Theron, 45
Powell, York, 84
Power, Beryl, 164
Power, Eileen, xvi, 1, 2, 93
Power, Rhoda, 164, 165
*Primitive Athens as Described by
    Thucydides*, 38
Primitive Culture, 36
Progress and Poverty, 84
Prolegomena to the Study of Greek Religion,
    35, 39, 40, 48, 49, 52, 54
*Prolegomena zu einer wissenschaftlichen
    Mythologie*, 35
Prothero, Mrs, 88
Psyche, 35, 46
psychical research, 39
Psychical Research circle, 18
Psychology of the Unconscious, 58
Pybus, Josie, 212
Pythagoras, 47

Quastel, Juda, 118
Queen Elizabeth the Queen Mother, xiv
Queen's College, Oxford, 161
Quo Warranto Pleas, 99

Radcliffe-Brown, A. R., 50
Raisz, Lawrence, 261
Raleigh Lecture, 107
Randall, John, 256, 277, 279, 280
Rapp, A., 46
Raverat, Gwen, 138, 141, 144, 153, 154
Ray, Ryle, 91
Rayleigh, Lady, 12, 13, 22
Rayleigh, Lord, 10, 12, 13, 15, 21
Reeve, James, 149
Reeves, Amber, 24
Reeves, James, 212
Reinach, Adolphe, 54
Religion of the Semites, 36
religion, origin of, 55

Remembering the University of Chicago, 3
'resting cells', 117
Richard, Gwynedd, 224
Richard, Henry Erle (Sir Erle), 222
Richards, Audrey, xvii, 1
Richards, I. A., 209
Ridgeway, William, 38
Robertson, Dennis, 91
Robertson, Muriel, 259
Robertson Smith, William, 36, 37
Robeson, Paul, 175
Robin, Jean, 234
Robinson, Austin, xv
Robinson, Margaret Hayes, 000
Rogers, 'Dam Theology', 85
Rohde, Erwin, 36, 41, 43, 46
Rose, H. J., 60
Rosebery, Lady, 85
Rossetti, D. G., 31
Rothenstein, William, 91, 139
Royal Anthropological Institute, 236
Royal Holloway College, 95, 96, 97
Royal Society, xv, xvii, 13, 114, 121–6,
    131, 245, 247, 249, 267, 280
Ruddock, Alwyn, 175
runners, for the Tripos, 78
Ruskin, John, 32, 41, 85
Russell, Alys, 162, 163
Russell, Bertrand, 38
Russell, Dora, 162, 168, 169
Russia, 56, 183, 217
Russophilia, 57

St Andrews, 188
St Bartholomew's Medical School, 247
St Benet's Church, 213
St Paul's School for Girls, 270
Salaman, Esther, 154, 155
Salisbury Plain, 218
Sayers, Dorothy, 212
Schlesier, Renate, 48
Sea Dyaks of Borneo, 183, 193
Second World War, 147, 255
Selden Society, 111
Senate House, 20
Sex Disqualification (Removal) Act, xv,
    121, 125, 258
Shakespeare, William, 210
shamanism, among the Tatars, 195
Shils, Edward, xviii, 1

Index

Ship of Fools, 209
Siam, Prince of, 85
Sidgwick, Arthur, 84, 85
Sidgwick Avenue, 18
Sidgwick, Eleanor or Nora, xi, xiii, 7, 8, 27, 31, 206, 207
Sidgwick, Henry, xi, xiv, 7, 15, 18, 27, 77, 79, 206, 207
Simeonite sect, 74, 75
Simpson, Percy, 215
Sirens, 43
Skipton Grammar School, 8
Smith, Eleanor, 85
Smith, Henry, 84
Smith, Stevie, 150
Smuts, Field Marshal, 107, 232
Smuts Readership in Commonwealth Studies, 236
snake, in representation, 42
Society for Psychical Research, xiv, 15, 18, 21, 24, 26
Soloviov, Vladimir, 59
Somerville College, 95, 110
Sommer, Frau, 212
Sondheimer, Janet, xv, 93
Sorabji, Cornelia, 85
soul, beliefs about, 36
Souls, the, 9
Southall, Aidan, 234
Southern Bantu peoples, 226
Spanish Civil War, 147
Spear, F. Gordon, 248, 249, 254
Spemann, Hans, 255
Spender, Stephen, 154, 155
Sphinx, 43
Sraffa, Piero, 91
Stephenson, Elizabeth, 115
Stephenson, Marjory, xv, 257, 258
Stephenson, Robert, 115
Stevenson, J. J., 86
Stewart, Jessie, 57
Stocks, Mary Brinton, 170
Strachey, Miss J. Pernel, 213, 214
Strachey, Lytton, 23, 219
Strangeways Research Laboratory, xvii, 245, 248–57, 260–4
Strangeways, Dorothy, 247, 248, 262
Strangeways, Thomas, 245–7, 253, 262
Strauss, D. F., 31
Street, Fanny, 105

Strickland, Leonard, 119
Stuart, Professor, 80
Stubbs, Bishop, 102
Study of Anglo-Saxon, The, 196
suffrage work, 166, 167
suffragette movement, 269
Swinburne, Algernon, 31
Symonds, J. A., 10

Tatar peoples, 183, 193
Tatars, shamanism among, 195
Taussig, Professor and Mrs, 87
Tawney, R. H., 1, 172, 173, 175
Tennyson, Alfred Lord, 32, 94
Terling, 10, 21
Themis, 50–61
Thespis, 60
Thrupp, Sylvia, 175
Titans, 47
Totem and Taboo, 50
totemic animal, 52
totemism, 55
Toynbee Hall, 85
Toynbee, Arnold, 83
Toynbee, Jocelyn, 4, 212
Tradition, Center, and Periphery, xviii
Trevelyan, G. M., 221
Trevelyan, G. O., 221
'tribalism', 233, 240
Trim, A. R., 120
trinities of goddesses, 44
Trinity College, Cambridge, 7, 8, 11, 21, 145, 146, 222
Trinity College, Dublin, 19
Trobriand Islands, 225, 231, 238
Tungus female shaman, 195
Turgenev, Ivan, 32
Turkish, 193
Turner, Victor, 235, 238
Tylor, Edward, 36

Ulysses, 50
University Assistants' Association, 3
University College, Bristol, 81
University College London, 174, 207
University Library, Cambridge, 205
Universities
    London, 95
    St Andrews, 183, 198
    Wales, 198

Index